TWO FAITHS,
ONE BANNER

TWO FAITHS, ONE BANNER

When Muslims Marched with Christians
across Europe's Battlegrounds

IAN ALMOND

Harvard University Press
Cambridge, Massachusetts
2009

Printed by the MPG Books Group in the UK

First published by I.B.Tauris & Co Ltd
in the United Kingdom

Library of Congress Cataloging-in-Publication Data

Almond, Ian, 1969-Two faiths, One Banner:
When Muslims marched with Christians
across Europe's Battlegrounds / Ian Almond.
p. cm. ISBN 978-0-674-03397-9 (alk. paper)
1. Military history. 2. Christianity and other religions.
3. Islam--Relations--Christianity. I. Title.
D25.5.A46 2009
355.02088'297094--dc22
2008042978

CONTENTS

LIST OF ILLUSTRATIONS

All efforts have been made to contact the relevant permissions' holders for the right to reproduce the illustrations in this book. Future editions of this book will rectify any omissions in this regard.

ACKNOWLEDGEMENTS

Many parties have been involved in the writing of this book.

First of all, I thank the K. Blundell Trust, as well as the Society of Authors, for their tremendous financial support. Particular thanks go to the secretary Paula Johnson, as well as the judges Ali Smith and Sir Michael Holroyd.

There were academics who did not hesitate to provide me with help and information: G. Ágoston, Isa Blumi, Brian A. Catlos, Cemal Kafadar and Julie Taylor. I would like to thank, in particular, the historian Candan Badem for allowing me access to his unpublished doctoral thesis, a text which gave me some extremely valuable perspectives. Flyss Macgilchrist and Boris Michalik helped a great deal with the proofreading of some early drafts, as well as my editor at I.B.Tauris, Alex Wright. Suzanne Berger displayed tireless energy tracking down unfamiliar and anonymous sources, often into the small hours of the morning – her efforts are much appreciated. A number of the seminars I attended at the Wissenschaftskolleg zu Berlin were also invaluable for giving me ideas and inspiration.

Many thanks in particular to Philip Mansel, author of *Constantinople: City of the World's Desire*, for permission to reproduce his photograph.

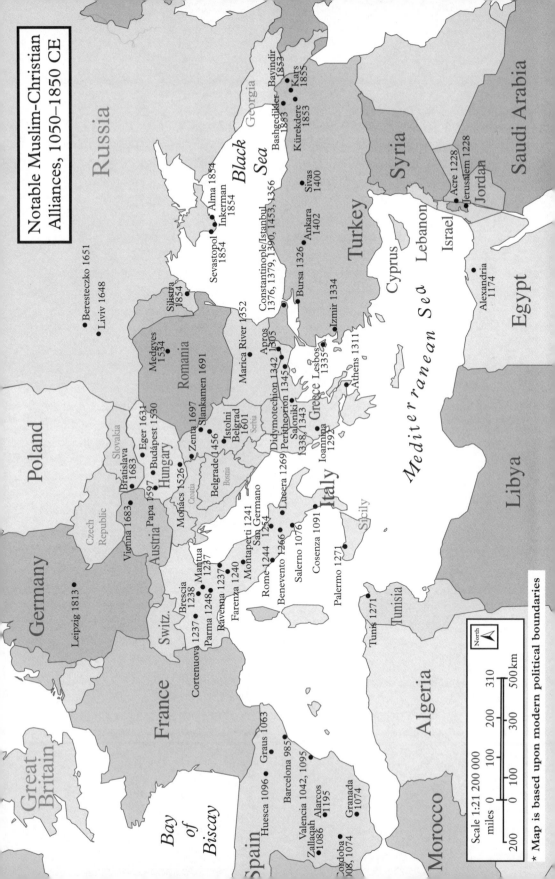

Notable Muslim-Christian Alliances, 1050–1850 CE

Russia

Great Britain

Germany
- Leipzig 1813

Poland

France

Switz.

Czech Republic

Slovakia
- Bratislava 1683

Austria
- Vienna 1683
- Papa 1597

Hungary
- Eger 1631
- Budapest 1530
- Mohács 1526

Croatia

Bosnia
- Belgrade 1456

Serbia
- Istolni Belgrad 1601
- Zenta 1697
- Slankamen 1691

Romania
- Medgyes 1534

Georgia

Black Sea
- Alma 1854
- Inkerman 1854
- Sevastopol 1854
- Silistra 1854
- Marica River 1352

Turkey
- Constantinople/Istanbul 1376, 1379, 1390, 1453, 1356
- Apros 1305
- Didymoteichon 1342
- Peritheorion 1345
- Bursa 1326
- Ankara 1402
- Izmir 1334
- Sivas 1400
- Bavindir 1853
- Bashgediker 1853
- Kürekdere 1853
- Kars 1855

Syria
- Acre 1228

Jordan
- Jerusalem 1228

Saudi Arabia

Lebanon

Cyprus

Israel

Egypt
- Alexandria 1174

Greece
- Saloniki 1338, 1343
- Ioannina 1292
- Lesbos 1335
- Athens 1311

Italy
- Mantua 1237
- Brescia 1238
- Cortenuova 1237
- Parma 1248
- Ravenna 1237
- Farenza 1240
- Montaperti 1260
- Rome 1244
- San Germano 1254
- Benevento 1266
- Lucera 1269
- Salerno 1076
- Cosenza 1091
- Palermo 1271

Sicily

Mediterranean Sea

Tunisia
- Tunis 1271

Algeria

Libya

Morocco

Spain
- Huesca 1096
- Graus 1063
- Barcelona 1063
- Valencia 1042, 1095
- Zallaqah 1086
- Alarcos 1195
- Granada 1074
- Córdoba 1008, 1074

Bay of Biscay

- Beresteczko 1651
- Lviv 1648

Scale 1:21 200 000

miles 0   100   200   310

0   100   200   300   500km

North

* Map is based upon modern political boundaries

INTRODUCTION

This book is a somewhat primitive book. It has a very straightforward purpose: to relate a selection of moments in European history when, in the very heart of countries such as Spain, Italy, Greece and Hungary, Muslims and Christians collaborated and co-operated with one another to fight against a common enemy – often an enemy also composed of Muslims and Christians. The book does not really do much more than this. It is not some vast overview of Muslim-Christian relations since 1100, nor an in-depth analysis of inter-cultural exchange between Islam and Christianity. It does not offer profound gems of philosophical insight into how human beings can learn to love one another, nor moving moments of idealism concerning the common humanity which can overcome all political/social/religious divisions, etc., etc. The book's very modest aim, on the contrary, is to show how Muslims do not belong to an 'other' civilisation, but rather to the essence of a 'Europe' we are quickly in the process of forgetting.

As we airbrush Muslims and Jews out of our European heritage – the seven hundred years of Muslim presence in Spain, Sicily and the Balkans is barely recollected in public discourse today outside the occasional tourist poster from Granada – this book attempts to show how the history of Islam and the history of Europe belong to one another. It is an aim which explains the slightly obsessive thread which stitches the book, and the eight hundred years it spans, together: in a media age obsessed with Muslim-Christian conflict, I have simply decided to flip the model inside-out and concentrate on unity and collaboration instead of friction and division. Time and time again, we will return to the widespread yet woefully under-reported phenomenon of Muslim-Christian military alliances: the thousands of Arabs who fought for medieval Christian emperors outside the walls of Milan and Bologna, the Castilians and Catalans who regularly allied themselves with Muslims to fight their Christian neighbours, the extraordinary level of Greek-

Turkish co-operation in the last century of the Byzantine empire, the equally extraordinary number of Christian soldiers in the Ottoman armies which occupied the Balkans, and the tens of thousands of Hungarian Protestants, not to mention disaffected Hungarian peasants, who marched with the armies of the Turk on Vienna.

The Fantasy of Europe

Today, words such as 'Islam' and 'Europe' appear to have all the consistency of oil and water. As good Europeans, we walk around the centres of our cities, filled with church spires and cathedral faces; in museums and galleries, we admire endless images of the same mothers and babes, reproduced through the centuries by the same hundred or so artists of genius; our classical music tradition springs from the adoration of these same figures, even in its rebellion against it; the names of our children, our public holidays, the suburbs and quarters of our towns are determined after the followers and disciples of the first-century Palestinian carpenter whose memory and teachings have dominated the trajectory of our small, northern continent. In other words, the Christian tradition swims about us, its values inform our world-view even in our most secular moments – for the Enlightenment, we now understand, was just as much a consequence of Christianity as a reaction to it. Whether it is a Bach concerto or a fresco by Michelangelo, a Baroque church or a spire-dotted skyline, the history of Europe as a Christian place seems to be the most normal of assumptions. Within the same logic, Islam seems to be the essence of everything we are not. The very word 'Muslim' brings a whole host of connotations to the fore – fanaticism, rigidity, devotion to tradition. Once we add to this words such as 'Arab' or 'Turk', a whole explosion of nuances takes place – an exotic Orient, wild, unruly, ungovernable, not having 'European values' and, more importantly, not wanting to have them. In other words, Arabs, Turks, along with Muslims in general, belong to that fascinating place called 'non-Europe'. They come from those strange, nebulous edges on the map of Europe, a ferry ticket from Gibraltar, a boat ride from Sicily, a bus trip from Greece. This map of Europe is so firmly set in our minds, so clearly set off from Asia and Africa, so unconsciously cemented together with a whole range of Christian images, that we can barely recall a time when

'Europe' did not exist – even though it is a relatively recent invention. Its borders are clear and distinct for us. Its Christian essence is uncontested.

If, on the other hand, we decide to employ a little historical energy and look more carefully at the map of Europe, a different picture gradually begins to emerge. It starts with some academic ironies: one of the suggested etymologies for 'Europe' links it to the same root as the word 'Arab' – ereb, a Semitic root meaning west, darkness or descent (the terms Maghrib and the name of the Portugese coast Algarve both come from this term for 'west' – the Arabs, in this sense, would have been the first 'West Asians'). A little more concretely, if we persist with our curiosity, we begin to realise that some of our most European phenomenon actually have strong Muslim influences: several centuries of medieval philosophy in the West relied not only on Arabic translations of classical philosophers, but also on their commentators – Averroes, Avicenna, Ghazali. Oriental influences, coming up through Spain and Sicily, had a central part to play in the development of the courtly love tradition which flowered in medieval French poetry;European literature such as Boccaccio and Chaucer find the origins of their multiple-narratives in the various Latin/vernacular versions of the Arabian Nights which were circulating in Europe throughout the Middle Ages. Some scholars even suggest the cosmology of Dante's *Divine Comedy* was partly inspired by a medieval Islamic mystic. Continuing on this thought-train, we remember, sooner or later, that our own Christianity is actually a Middle Eastern faith. The world-view of a Palestinian Jew who spoke a language (Aramaic) somewhere between Hebrew and Arabic. We begin to recall that one of the founding fathers of the Western Christian tradition, St Augustine, was an African, the Bishop of Hippo; that the formative years of the early church took place in the areas which today go by the name of central and western Turkey. And if we stretch our historical imaginations further, we will begin to realise that most of Europe has only been Christian for about a thousand years – some countries, such as Spain, were Muslim before they were Catholic. We may even wish to reflect on the irony that the Arabs were Christians a good six hundred years before the English ever adopted the faith.

And if we keep on looking – if we don't give up and allow ourselves to slide back into lazy abstractions such as 'Europe' and 'the West' – what emerges is no clear-cut realm of pure, untouched Christianity, but rather a continent whose southern half would have been in constant interaction with Jewish and Muslim populations. A Europe where, by the tenth century, the first meetings had already taken place between Arab travellers and Vikings; where Muslim merchants had reached Prague as early as 965; where Anglo-Saxon coins bore the marks of the Caliphate, and north African armies reached the town of Poitiers, south west of Paris. A Mediterranean Europe which would have been criss-crossed with trade routes, and filled with Spanish, Italian and Greek cities where Muslims and Christians lived together side by side. For many centuries, the concept of the 'Europe' we know today simply did not exist – the Orthodox world formed part of the Orient for many Latins, and the cities of Venice, Genoa, Brindisi and Saloniki shared a common space with Constantinople, Beirut and Alexandria.

This borderless 'Europe', this poly-cultured, multi-faith Mediterranean space which for centuries was home to peoples of all three religions, has only recently begun to be transformed into a 'Fortress Europe', sealed off and designated exclusively 'Christian' (as late as the 1960s, Greek was still widely spoken on the streets of Istanbul and Alexandria). What we will see, as we move through this book, are a number of figures who in their time and context were quite typical, but today seem strange and incredible: medieval Holy Roman emperors and Norman kings with a knowledge of Arabic, Byzantine rulers who speak Turkish, Spanish imams who can barely speak a word of their grandparents' tongue, Macedonian Christians so intimately familiar with their Muslim neighbours' culture that they could successfully imitate a local mullah in front of their friends. We will encounter Arab Muslim poets in Granada and Seville who fell in love with Christian boys and dedicated homosexual verse to them; Ottoman Italians who, being fluent in both Greek and Turkish, worked as envoys for the Sultan; Polish Ukrainians who dedicated themselves to the Turkish cause and tried to organise Polish regiments for the Padishah's army; Muslims from the Spanish town of Zaragoza whose culture was so close to their Christian neighbours they were able, as spies, to walk undetected into the enemy's camp and kill the king (at the behest of his brother).

For the unfamiliar reader, the military alliances in this book will also come as a surprise. Muslim-Christian coalitions throughout the ages (and the selection we will read about in the following chapters is only a small portion of them) were not simply the temporary, suspicious alliances of two hostile communities against a common foe – the Muslim soldiers skulking in one corner of the field, the Christians in another.

In the Ottoman army registers of the Balkan campaigns in the sixteenth century, for example, we find mixed Muslim and Christian soldiers serving together in extremely small companies – Tomas next to Abdullah, Dimitri next to Ali, Stefan alongside "Davud, son of Mustafa". The same can be said of the Byzantine armies which employed Turkish mercenaries – we find soldiers of both faiths intermingled in the order of the cavalry and infantry. In other words, when Christians decided to fight alongside Muslims in a common cause, it was not necessarily with some strange, alien tribe of exotic creatures, but often with other human beings who spoke the same language (even with the same accent), or ate the same food, or danced to the same kind of music. In a nineteenth century Ottoman town such as Sivas, we find Armenians living next to mosques, and Turks next to churches – and both of them using the same *bakkal* or grocer; in nineteenth century Kosovo, we learn that Serbs would deliberately leave pork out of the food preparations on feast-days, so that their Muslim neighbours could join them; in cities such as Budapest or Lucera, the medieval Muslim town established a hundred and fifty miles south-east of Rome, we find streets of shops with Muslim and Christian tradesmen packed next to one another. For all the rants and diatribes about how Muslims have "different values" and belong to "another culture", the fact remains that in the history of Europe, for hundreds of years, Muslims and Christians shared common cultures, spoke common languages, and did not necessarily see one another as 'strange' or 'other'.

It is remarkable to see how quickly this past has been deleted. For many people today, Islam comes from the planet Mars. Most media discussions concerning anything to do with Islam remain on the intellectual level of a twelve year-old: public debates on whether women should be allowed to wear full burkhas border on the hysterical (how do we know they won't be hiding explosives beneath them? asked one paper). The columnists of many British newspapers pump out a poisonous mixture of wife-beaters, anti-Semites, terrorists and fanatics under the name of 'Muslim'; in Germany, immigrant Turkish children with toy pistols in their hands are splashed out on the leading pages of a major newspaper (the *Tagesspiegel*), whilst even the liberal *Süddeutsche Zeitung* features, in a magazine supplement, a section on Islam with swords and guns melting into Arabic letters as a background. In Austria, the contemporary debate concerning Turkey's entry into the EU is still influenced by the memory of the Ottoman siege of Vienna, three centuries earlier.

If the selective amnesia of Europe is remarkable, then the level of hypocrisy involved in this demonization and alienation of what is dubiously termed 'the Muslim world' is equally striking. The case of Turkey, a Muslim country trying to join the EU, provides a number of examples. Whilst Turkey is (quite rightly) exhorted to acknowledge and fully examine the systematic ethnic cleansing of its Armenian populations in 1915, the largest genocide in the world to date – that of the Belgian Congo, twenty years earlier, where an estimated 10 to 15 million Africans are said to have died between 1877 and 1908 – is wholly unacknowledged by any of the European countries involved. Turkey's human rights record against the Kurds is certainly deplorable; and yet in the Nineties (the time of the very worst atrocities), a country such as Germany could reprimand the Turkish state for its torture and human rights abuses, whilst remaining the second largest supplier of arms to Turkey after the United States. Even the allegations of corruption which are levelled at Muslim countries – and which are certainly not without justification – begin to acquire a faint irony, when they emanate from a European Union where Swedish prime ministers go on to become corporate lobbyists, German chancellors acquire lucrative jobs in the very Russian pipeline companies they negotiated with when in office, and UK government ministers authorise the payment of hundreds of millions of dollars in what are effectively bribes to the Saudi government.

The fantasy of Europe, therefore, relies on an idea of non-Europe to exist. It relies on the habit of convincing ourselves we are somehow different from the uncivilised, backward regions outside the Union. The Christianising of our history – and the subsequent airbrushing-out of the Muslim from the European tapestry we are all learning to love – goes hand in hand with this gesture of self-affirmation and demarcation. In this sense, it feeds into a much more general belief in an alleged 'clash of civilisations' – the idea that Islam and Islamic cultures are not only fundamentally different from 'Western' ones, but that they are embarked upon a collision course with one another.

Of course, pushing the 'Islam' button is always useful. Societies with unequal distributions of wealth and power have always used bogeymen and foreigners to draw attention from their own schemes of control, and in this sense the overwhelmingly capital-friendly European media is no exception. Talking endlessly about immigrants stealing jobs and claiming welfare provides a pleasant distraction from the pay-rises of company executives or the enormous profits and ruthless job cuts of banks and mobile phone companies; the catch-phrases of 'security' and 'Islamic terror' allows airlines such as British Airways to prohibit protests by environmental groups, and 80-year old peace activists to be thrown out of British Labour Party meetings on the basis of 'anti-terror' legislation; endless debates about whether a certain mosque should be built in Cologne or East London draws attention away from the wholesale destruction of historical buildings in Britain, Germany and Italy by an alliance of finance companies and real estate developers. It is no surprise that, in Britain, the most right-wing, business-friendly, anti-trade union newspapers also happen to be the most xenophobic: in the case of morally conservative papers such as The Daily Mail and the Express, we have the truly bizarre spectacle of columnists such as Melanie Philips, Peter Hitchens and Simon Caldwell ranting and railing against homosexuality, abortions, feminism, blasphemy and promiscuity, whilst simultaneously claiming Muslims (amongst whom the most conservative will undoubtedly share the same prejudices)do not share "British majority values".

Pushing the 'Islamist/Jihad/Terror' button for explanations also does the trick when justifying the dubious wisdom of foreign policy. In countries such as Pakistan and Afghanistan, growing support for Islamic opposition has more to do with a profound dissatisfaction with the corrupt, Western-supported plutocracies of these countries than any theological notion of jihad. When the current president of Afghanistan is a senior consultant for a Californian pipeline company (and when a line drawn through American bases in Afghanistan, as one Israeli newspaper pointed out, follows the same route as the pipeline), it becomes easier to understand why we prefer to talk about the Islamic fervour of the Taliban rather than any benefit Western countries might draw from our continued presence there. In describing Palestinian suicide bombers, 'Islam' also comes in handy to 'explain' why economically-oppressed, half-starved human beings, many of whom have had at least one family member or relative shot dead by Israeli defense forces, choose to take their own lives in a final act of desperation. The question of Iran is also a case in point: no-one should have much sympathy for the mullocracy of Ahmadinejad, although one might suggest Iran's resistance to foreign investment and unwillingness to comply with the demands of the world's wealthiest countries is what earns the Islamic state's complete demonization in our media; the Islamic code of a country such as Saudi Arabia, in many respects much more conservative than Iran (women are not even allowed to drive), recieves much less attention – principally because Saudi Arabia is wide open to foreign capital, and more or less co-operative on larger, geo-political questions. Were it not so, we would be hearing much more about how 'Islamic' the Saudis are. In this respect, the term 'Muslim moderate' is usually mediaspeak for a Western-friendly businessman – Mahmoud Abbas, Jelal Talabani, Recep Tayyip Erdoğan, Ahmed Kharzai, as well as the now reformed Gadafi and his entrepreneurial son. Muslims who object to Western structures of finance and energy control, particularly those who take real steps to appropriate local resources for themselves, are usually called 'Islamists' or 'extremists' in the media.

To point out this process is not to idealise or exonerate real Muslim extremists, nor to portray Islam as a faith any freer from the dilemmas a modern liberal might find in Judaism or Christianity. It is not to argue that hate-filled homophobic clerics are deep down 'nice' human beings, or that figures such as Bin Laden are really misunderstood victims. The point, rather, is to emphasise that the selective repetition of such images from the Muslim world in the Western media serves a variety of particular functions – to preserve a status quo, distract attention from genuine political issues and provide a justification for an increasing obsession with 'security measures'. Moreover, the aim of this brief history is certainly not to show that Muslims and Muslim authorities were somehow 'better' than their Christian equivalents – they were not. Strategically choosing when to talk about religious differences and when to keep quiet is the oldest trick in history, and one which Muslims employed just as much as Christians. When the classical Ottomans were up against a Christian enemy, they constantly referred to his 'infidel' (gavur) status, and to themselves as the true army of Islam. The Christian faith of their allies, however, they simply didn't mention at all.

The subject of the book: Muslim-Christian alliances

Muslim-Christian alliances are as old as Islam itself. Unfamiliar readers will probably be surprised to learn that there is a chapter of the Koran entitled 'The Greeks' (al-Rūm), in which the Prophet Mohammed laments the defeat of the Christian Byzantine armies by the Persians in 615. The idea of a surah in the Koran, praying for a Greek victory over an Iranian army, is not as surreal as it sounds. The Persians, of course, were neither Muslim nor Christian at this time but Sasanid Zoroastrians (fire-worshippers, to put it crudely). It was only natural that Mohammed, himself heavily influenced by Jewish and Christian teachings, hoped and prayed for a Byzantine victory against what he perceived to be pagan, idol-serving Persians.

The alliances we will be examining in this book fall into a number of categories. Firstly there are what we may term purely political alliances – collaborations which spring exclusively out of opportunity, and which do not indicate any level of cultural or ideological sympathy between the leaders or the soldiers themselves. Although the seventeenth-century correspondence between Louis XIV and the Ottoman Sultan Mehmet IV expressed itself in cordial terms, it is clear that a common hatred of Vienna was bringing the two sovereigns together. Such alliances also remained strategic, rather like Charles V's negotiations with the Persian enemies of the Turks in Barcelona – the armies of the two partners would never have fought together on the same battlefield, but merely supported one another on different fronts with their parallel hostility.

A second category of Muslim-Christian alliance, however, is what could tentatively be called 'warm' alliances: those based not merely on political necessity, but also on a sense of genuine friendship. The most obvious example here is the decade-long relationship between the Byzantine emperor Kantakouzenos and Umur Pasha, the Muslim Prince of Aydin. Reliable documentary sources from both sides seem to suggest the two men admired and respected one another – Kantakouzenos even offered the hand of his daughter to the Turkish emir, who allegedly refused it because Kantakouzenos was too much like his 'brother'. Such alliances, although born of political needs, would not merely be the result of cold, ruthless calculations, but also be facilitated by a much more psychological bond between the two parties. This psychological bond would be assisted by a knowledge of the other party's culture – Kantakouzenos, in this case, could speak Turkish quite well. The medieval emperor Frederick II's knowledge of Islam and ability to speak Arabic certainly helped him to communicate and negotiate with the Muslim world more successfully than his Christian contemporaries.

This brings us closer to the third category of Muslim-Christian alliance – one in which the Muslims and Christians involved would have shared a common level of culture and language. The Sicilian Arabs who defended their city of Lucera against the French alongside their Italian neighbours would have spoken the same language, as would the Muslim Zaragozans who helped the Castilians in their eleventh-century struggle against the

Aragonese. In 1541, the number of southern Slavs in the Ottoman garrisons on the Danube, as we shall see, appears to have been so high that Greek and Bosnian were heard more often than Turkish. In all of these cases, the terms 'Muslim' and 'Christian' are simply not enough to address the identities of the soldiers concerned, particularly in the case of Anatolia, Andalusia and the Balkans. More than any sense of realpolitik, a common set of cultural practices – language, food, landscape, dress – accounts for two faiths existing under one banner.

Three further categories of Muslim-Christian military collaboration need to be mentioned: vassal states, mercenaries and serfs. A vassal state is usually a state which has been provisionally conquered by a more powerful sovereign, and whose ruler has to comply with the requests of that sovereign. It is not the happiest of marriages. Byzantine emperors were occasionally forced to assist the more powerful Ottomans in a variety of battles, sometimes quite far away (Manuel II and his Greek army found themselves in the depths of eastern Turkey, fighting Turkmens on behalf of Sultan Bayezid I). The thousands of Serb soldiers who helped the Turks capture Constantinople were also there against their will. Friendship and good will, however, was not impossible in a vassal relationship; Alfonso VI and his vassal al-Mu'tamid of Seville were hardly filled with enmity for one another, for all the storminess of their relationship, and the bravery with which a Serb prince could save the Turkish sultan's son at the doomed Battle of Ankara suggests there were a variety of dimensions to the obligation of vassaldom.

Being a mercenary must constitute, to distort an adage, one of the world's oldest military professions. Mercenaries are among the most widespread and significant sources of examples of Christians fighting in Muslim armies (and vice versa). The phenomenon took place everywhere (in the Mediterranean, on the North African coast, in the Crimea), in all kinds of cities (at the sieges of Vienna, Valencia, Constantinople, Tunis), at all times (during Crusades as well as between them), on both sides (the Pope had Muslims in his armies, just as the Ottomans employed Westerners in their fight against the infidel) and at all levels (from footsoldiers and gunners to admirals and engineers). By 1307 The Grand Catalan Company, one of the largest mercenary enterprises, had over 3,000 Turks on its side (ironically the very Turks the Catalans had originally been employed to fight). The promise of payment – gold, booty, land, food – in return for service probably accounts for more cross-faith collaboration than any other factor in this book.

A final category of alliance is probably the hardest to analyse, partly because it was so unwillingly reported, and partly because it concerned a section of society whose illiteracy renders them historically transparent: peasants. A serf who has been beaten, whipped and starved by his 'Christian' landlords for the first twenty years of his short life may well be forgiven for wondering whether the Arab or Turk would bring anything worse (or as Bob Dylan said, 'When you ain't got nothing, you got nothing to lose'). In Ottoman-controlled Hungary, the Turks made full use of the atrocious conditions of the country's serfs by offering them all kinds of incentives to change sides – as we shall see, with some success.

In other words, this book is an attempt to dissolve the idea of a Christian, 'enlightened' Europe – and implicitly, that of a Muslim, 'backward' non-Europe which conveniently begins with ink-like clarity at the borders of Kosovo, Cyprus and Gibraltar. In many ways, the millennium-old presence of Christians and Jews along the North African and Eastern Mediterranean coasts (the Catholic and Orthodox of Beirut, the once-enormous Jewish communities of Algiers, Cairo and Alexandria) constitutes one of the unspoken subtexts of this book. The birthplace of one of the founding fathers of the Western Christian tradition, St Augustine, in a town on the Tunisian coast – or the formative years spent by Aristotle in a town now located in Western Turkey – is ironic only if we continue to cling to the synonymy of Christianity and 'Europe'.

However, in trying to 'de-Christianise' Europe and remind the reader of its interaction with the Muslim world, the aim of this book is not to erase religious belief from the history of Europe, or to anachronistically reduce the history of religions to a series of economic factors or realpolitical strategies. The belief in a transcendent God was a profoundly influential factor in the social and political realities of both Muslims and Christians. It could move people to violent anger, to sadness, to feelings of compassion and genuine solidarity. Such religious identities did lie, however, alongside a number of other identities – cultural, linguistic, ethnic, even economic; identities which sometimes became more important than being simply 'Christian' or 'Muslim'. The European princes who chided the Hungarian Protestants for siding with the Turk against their fellow Christians did not live in Hungary, anymore than the North African mullahs who criticised the alliances of Spanish Muslims with the infidel lived in Spain. In the following chapters we will see, again and again, how people's own immediate situations gave them ways of seeing themselves that were much more convincing than any notion of crusade or jihad.

Hopefully, one of the consequences of reading this book will be that an alternative history of Europe will gradually begin to emerge – a landscape which does not merely involve Gothic cathedrals, Beethoven symphonies and Renaissance frescoes, but which brings Muslim architecture, Jewish thinkers, Arab poetry and Turkish music into the very heart of our continent's history. Today, a whole variety of TV channels and newspapers will deliver a certain kind of 'Muslim' to the consumer: usually a bearded, frowning zealot, screaming into a camera lens or jumping up and down on a burning effigy or flag, a violent, unapproachable figure whose image is endlessly relayed to us, day in day out, so that by now the images have fossilised into an unerasable reality. Selected stories – of Muslims banning pictures of pigs, slandering homosexuals or being led away as terrorist suspects – do their predictable rounds, emphasising how different Islam is from everything 'we Europeans' cherish and hold dear. The whole thrust of this book goes in the opposite direction: to try to show how Muslims have always been involved in the history of Europe, from the very beginning. For the tale of the formation of Europe is still worth the telling; it is a compelling narrative, and no amount of political correctness should make us abandon it. However, if the tale is to be told properly, its Islamic and Jewish elements have to be included. These 'elements' are no separate chapters, but veins of influence and power which run throughout the history of Europe. To remind ourselves of the presence of Muslims among the Castilians, the Hohenstaufen, the Hungarians and the Greeks is to begin to arrive at a richer, stranger and more authentic European heritage than the one we have at present. The five moments of Muslim-Christian alliance you are about to read constitute one step in this direction.

Chapter One

THE ELEVENTH-CENTURY SPAIN OF ALFONSO VI: EMPEROR OF THE TWO RELIGIONS

Our first chapter will begin with an examination of Muslim-Christian co-operation in eleventh-century Spain, ultimately centring on the Christian king Alfonso VI and the kind of alliances both he and his Christian rivals made with other Muslim kingdoms in the region. The period is a turbulent one, and two things should be kept in mind if we are to understand the complexity of what follows. First of all, the rivalry and tensions between the various Christian kingdoms in the north of Spain – Castile, Aragon and Catalania; secondly, the break-up of Muslim Spain into a carpet of smaller states and fiefdoms, producing a patchwork of struggles and quarrels just as divisive as those among the Christians. It is only when one king on the Christian side, Alfonso VI, begins to grow in power and dominate his Christian neighbours, that the Castilians can slowly begin to move southwards, annexing one Muslim kingdom after another. Alfonso VI, as we shall see, took full advantage of the Muslim disunity in Spain to play one prince against another.

The eleventh century was not the time of the *reconquista* – the 'taking back' as it were – of the Spanish peninsula from the Muslims who had conquered it almost four hundred years earlier. This process was only really to begin a century later at the battle of Las Navas de Tolosa (1212). King Alfonso's temporary expansion into Muslim Spain was merely a foreshadowing of the defeat the Muslim kings would one day suffer in a much more permanent fashion. What this chapter will try to show, however, is the extent to which Muslims and Christians were involved *on both sides* with these struggles. Far from being a straightforward religious war (if indeed there is ever anything such as a 'straightforward religious war'), the alliances of Catalans and Aragonese with Muslims against their hated Castilian neighbours – and the alliances of Castile with Muslim Seville against the Catalans – reflect the contours of a conflict which was just as much regional as it was religious.

To tell the story of the Spanish eleventh century properly, with its alliances and quarrels, its assassinations and *putschen*, its break-up of the Caliphate into a carpet of tiny kingdoms, its outside invaders, admonitory massacres, patient sieges, careful murders, one would need a wall of television screens, each telling a different story of the same period from a different place, all of them running at the same time. One camera would focus on Castile, on the gradual evolution of a king's armies as they spread slowly across the mainland; another camera would focus on Roderigo of Vivar (better known as El Cid) as he defends one Muslim kingdom against the Aragonese, and then conquers another Muslim town (Valencia) in the name of Christendom. The developing stories of Seville and Toledo would also have to be related simultaneously, of the various deals and manoeuvres their Muslim rulers had to make with the Christian armies in order to protect their own interests; the melancholy figure of Abd' Allah, the sensitive, intellectual yet politically inept ruler of Granada, would have to feature as its plot wove in and out of the general history of eleventh-century Spain. A separate camera would have to be turned to North Africa, and the gradual build-up of the Muslim forces which, led by a brilliant conservative radical, would sweep across the Spanish mainland towards the end of the century, saving the Muslim kingdoms temporarily from the looming threat of a Christian re-conquest. The fate of the kingdom of Badajoz (now roughly covering modern Portugal), the independence of Murcia, the ambitions of Aragon, the interest of Rome from the very beginning in the re-conquering of 'Christian' Spain from the 'heathen' Moors, all of these plots would weave in and out of one another in a completely unnarratable way, reminding us of the impossible task of the medieval historian.

And what moments to include in a single chapter, which ones to leave out? The morning the North African Almoravids arrive in Spain, cheered by Muslim locals as their saviours; the moment Roderigo of Vivar forces his king, before a crowd of nobles, to swear he had no part in his brother's killing; the burning alive of the Muslim governor of Valencia, before his wife and children, for conspiring to re-take the city from El Cid; the debacle of the uprising of Seville, where the Muslim ruler had to leave disguised as a woman after allying himself with a Christian king ... the whirlwind of events and forces which make up the history of eleventh-century Spain – from Al-Mansur's sacking of Compostela in 997 to the death of Alfonso VI in 1109 – is truly unrepresentable. The non-sectarian subtleties of its Muslim-Christian alliances, moreover, will elude the sensibilities of a careless modern reader. Christian soldiers fighting alongside Muslim infantry on behalf of an al-Muqtadir or a Mu'tamid; Arab military engineers operating siege machinery for Castilian armies in order to take Muslim towns; even moments such as Al-Mansur's sacrilegious destruction of the shrine of St James reveal, very probably, the presence of Christian mercenaries in the army which destroyed the church and carried the bells back to be hung in the mosque of Cordoba.[1] The Cid who was a hero for the Muslims of Zaragoza, vanquishing the forces of Aragon in the battle of Graus (1063), was most certainly a devil for the inhabitants of Islamic Valencia, the city he ruled with an iron fist after 1095. Christian or Muslim, Spanish or Arab, one king after another in this period ignored calls to crusade or jihad, putting their own regional interests and agendas above their religious identity. To understand the criss-cross pattern of Muslim, Christian and Jewish alliances in the endless wars of the Spanish eleventh century requires background, attention and context.

The Muslim conquest of Spain

It is ironic, for the purposes of a book on Muslim-Christian alliances, to note that the Muslim invasion of the Spanish mainland first took place at the request of another group of Christians. When the Visigoths, the Germanic tribespeople who had already been living in the Iberian mainland for three hundred years, invited the North African representatives of the Caliphate of Damascus (the Umayyads) to assist them in defeating a rival king, no one could have imagined the eight-hundred-year consequences of such a request. The Umayyads sent a general called Tariq ibn Zayd across the straits which now bear his name (Gibr-al-Tar) in 711, leading an expedition into Southern Spain. Within twenty years, the Muslim armies would reach northwestern France, and their advance further into northern Europe was only turned back with difficulty at the battle of Poitiers (732).

From an Arab perspective, the conquest of Spain was initially the conquest of a strange, alien land. Writing almost a hundred years later after Tariq's initial expedition, the historian Ibn Habib describes what the first Muslim conquerors would have seen as they moved further into the land of 'Andalusia' – a surreal landscape of earthquakes, frozen seas, copper fortresses, strange idols and frightening devils. If Ibn Habib's history more closely resembles science fiction than reliable geography, it reflects how 'Andalusia' was understood – a strange, barbaric terrain on the edges of civilisation and the Arab world, in much the same way Western cartographers would draw sea-monsters and dragons on the outer limits of their own maps. When we read a later Arab account, an anonymous tenth-century history, we see how two centuries of Muslim settlement in Spain has rendered Andalusia a more familiar place. Gone are tales of metal castles, strange devils, unreal landscapes; the later account talks familiarly of a country with cities, governments, crops, and even refers to the country's pre-Islamic (Visigothic) past. Spain has become a settled, civilised part of the Maghrib or Muslim West, and continues to be so until the last Muslim king of Granada leaves Spanish soil to return to North African shores in 1492. That the discovery of the 'New' world coincides with the ejection of Islam from the 'Old' one remains one of the many ironies of Spanish history.[2]

Up to now I have used the phrase 'Muslim conquest', although this is quite a simplistic term. Certainly, when the Arab forces agreed to invade the Spanish mainland and help the Visigoths who called them, it was with the agreement of Count Julian, the Christian ruler of another North African town (Ceuta). However synonymous for Western readers the term 'Arab' may be with the inhabitants of today's Algeria, Tunisia and Morocco, we should remember that in 711 the Arabs were recent arrivals in North Africa. Based in Damascus, a city as far away from Morocco as Stockholm, they had swept along the south Mediterranean coast within fifty years, bringing Islam and the cultural fruits of their own Arab civilisation to the indigenous Berbers living there. This Arab Islamification of the Berber tribes was largely successful; among the Almoravids, some of the most conservative Sunni Muslims were of Berber origin. There were, however, also Christian Berbers, and some historians have even suggested the Zanata tribe to be of Jewish origin.[3] More importantly, there were tensions between the two racial groups, despite their largely common faith. It is certainly true that some Arabs looked down on Berbers as being culturally backward and historically insignificant – the renowned Arab historian Ibn Khaldun (d. 1406) suggested Berbers were stupid because of their diet, and the writer al-Shaqundi (d. 1231) famously claimed that if it had not been for Andalusia, no one would ever have heard of the Berbers at all. Another reason for the uneasy relationship between Arab and Berber Muslims was a racial proximity to the Prophet Mohammed and his descendants, something which Arabs at times saw as a sign of their superiority over their African fellow Muslims, and which sometimes prompted Berbers to change their family names or invent genealogies for themselves leading their origins back more clearly to the Arabian peninsula. On the other hand, North African Berbers did practise a more conservative and austere form of Islam than their Andalusian Arab counterparts (even if this difference has been exaggerated by later historians), and sometimes looked across the water with some disdain at the worldly cities of Cordoba and Seville and the lax lifestyles of their extravagant rulers, contributing to a more general, conservative, North African disapproval of liberal Andalusia, where the faithful openly mixed with swine-eaters and *yahudi* (Jews). These tensions between Arabs and Berbers, exaggerated or not, could express themselves in rebellion. Berber revolts against their Arab rulers and co-religionists were by no means an uncommon phenomenon, and when they took place in Spain neighbouring Christian kingdoms were more than willing to exploit them for their own ends. When, in Andalusia, the Berber revolt of 1008–10 resulted in the sacking of Cordoba, both sides received help from different parts of the Christian North. The Andalusian Arabs were supported by the Christians of Barcelona, while soldiers from Castile came to the aid of the rebellious Berbers.[4] For the eleventh century, as we shall see, such cross-faith alliances were norms, not exceptions.

In short, having been invited into Spain by a Christian faction of Visigoths in 711, and assisted by another Christian governor, the Arab conquest of Spain took a remarkable three years before the larger part of the Iberian peninsula was under Muslim domination. For three hundred years it would remain so, a good three-quarters of the Spanish mainland controlled by a succession of Arab caliphates, with the Christian kingdoms of the north pushed into the upper fringes of the country. These kingdoms, at least until the start of the eleventh century, were very much the poor relatives of Spain. Andalusi Muslim writers, if they spoke of them at all, regarded them as backward and impoverished.[5] There were no cities the size of Cordoba or Toledo there, no magnificent palaces or great works of art, no real centres of culture and learning such as Seville or Granada. Nor did Muslims, in this period, feel any particular fear concerning the Christian armies; the last real threat had been the ill-fated advance into Northern Spain of the emperor Charlemagne (778), turned back not by Arabs but by the Basques (mistakenly described in subsequent legend as 'Saracens' or 'Moors'). On the contrary, rulers such as Al-Mansur regularly made punitive raids into the Christian north to keep them in check, sack their cities and generally remind them who was in charge on the Iberian peninsula. For three centuries, Spain was a Muslim kingdom, with a fringe of oppressed Christian principalities trying to survive on its borders.

Before describing how this situation was to change, some mention should be made of two further sub-groups in 'Muslim Spain' which makes the term itself slightly more problematic – the Mozarabs and the Slavs. Mozarabs (from the Arabic *must'arib* or 'would-be Arab') were 'Arabised' Christians who resisted conversion to Islam under Muslim rule, but who adopted many of the practices and customs of the Arab culture the Muslims brought with them. They preserved the Visigothic version of Christianity they had practised before the invasion, but culturally formed an integral part of Muslim society, gradually acquiring Arabic as a second and possibly mother tongue. Mozarabs (along with, as we shall see, many Jews) often occupied posts of authority in Muslim Spain – in 1064 the Muslim ruler of Zaragoza sent a Mozarab bishop as an envoy to Fernando I, and also employed the Christian Abu Umar as his prime minister. Probably one of the most important Mozarabs was the tenth-century bishop of Elvira, Recemund, who represented the Caliphate at the German and Byzantine courts.[6] Mozarabs often followed converted Spanish Muslims in changing their names to Arabic forms – just as a noble Christian family such as Cassius changed its name to 'Banu Qasi' after becoming Muslims, Mozarabic Christians called 'Lope' or 'Fortun' frequently wrote their names as 'al-Lubb' or 'al-Fortūn'. Sometimes they translated the meaning of their names into Arabic, so a Felix (meaning 'happy' in Latin) would become a 'Sa'ad' (the same word in Arabic).[7] Their ambiguous status, rather like Palestinian Christians living in today's West Bank, sometimes made them an object of suspicion for both sides. Pope Gregory VII certainly tried hard enough to have them substitute the Roman liturgy for the Mozarabic one. The fervour of some of the Mozarabs' faith – in the ninth century, dozens of them had been put to death by the Muslim authorities for consciously and provocatively blaspheming the Prophet Mohammed in public – was clearly not enough to merit the term 'Christian' for the Catholic church. When the Crusaders captured the city of Lisbon in 1147, they took the aged Mozarabic bishop of the city out of the cathedral and slit his throat.

Among the mixture of North African Berbers and Iraqi/Syrian Arabs who came to settle in Muslim Spain alongside either Spanish converts to Islam (in Arabic *muwalladun*) or 'Arabised' Christians, the final significant minority group were the Slavs or *Saqalibah*. Originally these were East European slaves, usually young boys and often from the Crimea and the Balkans, who were bought and raised by Muslim rulers to serve as soldiers, servants and administrators in their kingdoms (in some ways an Arab version of the Turkish janissaries). By the end of the eighth century, thousands of them were working for the caliph, some in considerable positions of power. The Slav general Najda commanded the entire Muslim army against the forces of Leon in 939; when the Caliphate finally broke up in the 1030s, Slavs took control of many of the independent states on the eastern coast – Valencia, Denia, Tortosa. The Slavs, as a gene pool, were doubtless responsible for many fair heads and blue eyes in Muslim Spain. The famous Ibn Hazm (d. 1064), who himself confessed to a fondness for blondes, explained the fair hair and blue eyes of the Andalusian caliphs as a result of their inter-marriage with Slavs – certainly, the families of the caliphs were not averse to marrying non-Arabs ('Abd al-Rahman III was the grandson of a Christian Basque princess, and his son Hakem II also married a girl from the Basque region).[8] Needless to say, irrespective of any nominal Christianity the first *Saqalibah* may have had, the Slavs as a group were wholly Muslim.

When people today speak in a general way of the 'conquest' and 're-conquest' of 'Muslim Spain', the impression is of a football match, two sets of ideologically opposite teams playing in perfect unity against one another. The image of a whole swarm of turbaned 'Moors' rushing into Christian Spain with their scimitars poised high above their heads has had a strong effect on the European mind, despite it being a complete and utter illusion. What any serious and sober look at the Muslim conquest of the Iberian peninsula in the 700s reveals is a much more complicated picture: the rapid (though not instantaneous) settlement of Berbers and Syrian/Iraqi Arabs, the gradual conversion of many indigenous Spaniards to Islam, the influx of non-Spanish

Slavs, Berbers and Jews into the mainland and the effective Arabisation of other, more religious local Christian communities. This mixture of different groups under one Caliphate concealed a whole variety of tensions and strained relationships – between Berbers and Arabs, between different Arab groups among themselves, and between those who had arrived earliest and those Arab/Berber immigrants who came later to the Spanish mainland from abroad. The tensions between these groups, unsurprisingly, were every bit as volatile as the tensions between Christian Castilians and Aragonese, or between Catalans and 'outsiders' such as Franks or Normans – and yet these tensions were kept in check. In the three centuries following the conquest of Spain, Muslim Andalusia was more or less centrally governed either by a single emirate or caliphate. This continuity of rule meant that, for all its internal differences and ethnic diversity, Muslim Spain managed to avoid petty squabbles or regional infighting between groups, united as it was under the rule of an Al-Mansur or an 'Abd er-Rahman. Its unity gave it strength to bully and exact tributes from the tinpot, backward Christian states which were its neighbours. At the beginning of the eleventh century, however, all this was to change, and the map of Spain was to be completely re-drawn.

The break-up of the Caliphate

As I have said, in 997 Al-Mansur sacks the far northern city of Compostela, razes the holy shrine to the ground and takes the bells of the church back with him to Cordoba. Muslim hegemony over the northern Christian kingdoms is complete. Within twenty years, the very same city is desperately trying to find Christian allies to assist its own internal faction-fighting – Castilian soldiers are destined to walk the streets of Muslim Cordoba first as support troops, then later as conquerors; within a further couple of decades, Muslim states such as Zaragoza and Granada will almost go broke paying Christian armies to protect them from their neighbours (and, of course, from their 'protectors'). In 1083, barely eighty years after Al-Mansur's sacking of one of Spain's holiest and most northern cities, we find the figure of King Alfonso VI riding his horse into the sea off the very southernmost tip of Spain, crying triumphantly: 'I have trampled Andalusia beneath my feet!'[9] What caused such a reversal of events?

To begin with, Alfonso VI's cry was both arrogant and premature. Three years later, he would be badly defeated at the battle of Zallaqah (1086). Muslim reinforcements from North Africa, in the form of the Almoravids and then later the Almohads, would roll back his gains as quickly as he had made them, turning the temporary expansion of the kingdom of Castile into the mere premonition of a Christian 're-conquest' which would really only begin a hundred years later. Nevertheless, it was in the eleventh century that we begin to see the first cracks in the unity of the Muslim presence which would one day have to leave Spain for good.

Although historians have proposed many reasons for the gradual retreat of the Muslim kingdoms from Spain – growing Italian maritime power, repeated Berber revolts in North Africa – the collapse of the Caliphate of Cordoba after 1013 is seen as the single most decisive factor. Within the space of a dozen years, Andalusia was transformed from a single power into a patchwork quilt of warring factions and mini-states as numerous as the regions of France. These mini-states were known as *taifas*, from an Arabic word for 'faction' originally used, interestingly enough, to describe the successors of Alexander the Great. By 1035 there were over twenty of them. It was a situation which, naturally, delighted the Christian nations to the north, who found they could now play one Muslim mini-kingdom against another in a game of divide-and-conquer. The Caliphate, which in the Muslim world has some similarities to our idea of the Papacy, represented the succession of temporal (and sometimes even spiritual) power handed down from the Prophet himself. There were, naturally, arguments concerning who should inherit the Caliphate as it was passed on from one descendant to another. Indeed, the first caliph of Andalusia in 756 was the sole survivor of his clan, which had been massacred on the Arabian peninsula in a power struggle every bit as vicious and bloody as those which affected the Tudors or Borgias. 'Abd ar-Rahman I had fled to Spain for his life. Although in Muslim Spain there were certainly interruptions in the rule of the Caliphate, as the occasional worldly dictator tried to seize power for himself, the rule of the Umayyad dynasty in Spain was by and large one of continuity until 1013, when the next successor to the title of the Caliphate – a man called Hisham II – disappeared.

It is now generally believed that the unfortunate Hisham II died in the Berber sack of Cordoba in 1013. In the power struggles which followed, supporters of the Caliphate tried to argue that he was still alive, trapped somewhere in hiding for fear of his life. Numerous stories abound about his 're-discovery' and the endless claims to have found him. In 1035, the kingdom of Seville even acknowledged him as caliph. The wily ruler Al-Mu'tadid found a carpet-weaver from Calatrava with an uncanny resemblance to the missing caliph and tried to present him as the long-lost Hisham II, without much success. As late as 1060, claims were still being made to have found the mythical caliph, who by that time would have been well over a hundred years old.[10]

The result of the dissolution of the Caliphate was a sudden profusion of *taifas* and a complete re-drawing of the map of Muslim Spain. Factionism, strife and an increasing number of Muslim-Christian alliances followed as kingdoms such as Zaragoza and Seville declared their willingness to pay Christian armies to attack their Muslim neighbours. Across Andalusia, the once-solid Caliphate of Cordoba broke up into a mosaic of over twenty-three independent kingdoms. Some of them were large and domineering – the most expansive was certainly Seville, which almost immediately entered into war with neighbouring Granada. Other kingdoms, such as Almeria and Denia, were relatively small with local armies and limited manpower. The rulers who came to power in these kingdoms were not always royalty or long-established nobles, but often local warlords, tyrants and small-time mafiosi who tried to enhance their provincial status with grand-sounding titles such as The Magnificent, The All-Conquering or The Invincible (al-Muqtadir, al-Qadir, al-Mu'tamid). Although some of the *taifa* rulers were indeed wise and just (such as al-Muqtadir of Zaragoza), many of them were either incompetent (such as al-Qadir, the short-lived puppet ruler of Valencia) or ruthless, unscrupulous pragmatists (such as al-Musta'in II) dependent on the growing Christian powers to the north of them for their existence. Commenting on the grandiose titles the *taifa* rulers gave themselves, the poet Ibn Rashiq (d. 1064) said they were as ridiculous as the cat who, puffing up its chest, believes itself to be a lion.

The eighty or so years between 1009 and 1090 – between the collapse of the Caliphate and the invasion from North Africa of the Almoravids – is known as the *taifa* period. When the Muslim armies of the North African Berbers finally sweep definitively across Andalusia at the end of the century, one *taifa* ruler after another will be deposed like a tinpot dictator and either executed or sent, almost childlike, into exile to spend their autumn years writing poetry or their memoirs in some distant North African town. Until this takes place, what we have

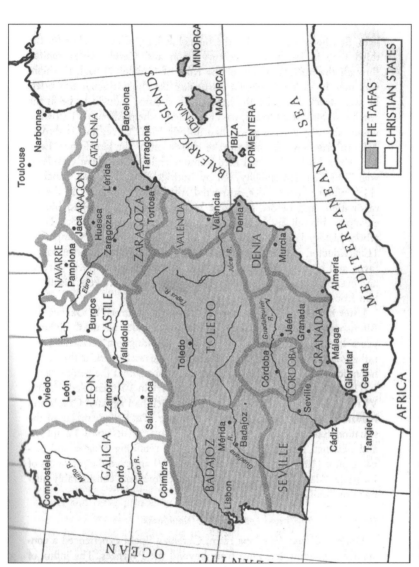

Map of Spain in 1065

between 1009 and 1090 is, paradoxically, a period of utter political instability, intense military activity and absolute creative and artistic energy. Many historians have remarked upon the strange profusion of intellectuals, thinkers and poets in a time of constant war; while cities fell, battles raged and sieges persisted, Muslim Spain produced arguably its finest period of Arabic letters. Poets such as Ibn Rashiq and Ibn Zaydun of Cordoba, writers such as Ibn Shuhayd, brilliant thinkers such as the renowned Ibn Hazm and the historian Ibn Hayyan blossomed amid the endless coups, political assassinations, communal massacres and military campaigns of their day.

The culture of Muslim Spain in the taifa *period*

It is not surprising that, in the midst of such a confused and strife-torn period, a whole number of Muslim-Christian alliances should have sprung up as the kingdoms of both faiths jockeyed and vied for primacy over one another. These alliances are a complex phenomenon to record, as they often shifted and mutated according to the situation of the moment. In 1090, for example, the Muslims of Huesca changed their Christian allies, switching from Aragon to Castile. In the siege of Seville, Mu'tamid turned from his former North African allies and appealed for help from the very Spanish king he had allied against. The local people of a town, sometimes, disagreed with the policies of their rulers and welcomed a regime change, which also resulted in a shifting of alliances – the taxes local Muslims had to pay to their Christian-friendly rulers in order to finance their defence were widely unpopular. Nevertheless, some kings did develop quite a long-standing friendship across the religions. Alfonso VI and al-Ma'mun of Toledo, for example, or al-Muqtadir and Sancho IV of Pamplona, both cultivated famous friendships. Over the second half of the eleventh century, two of the steadiest coalitions in this period arose between, on the one side, the (Christian) kingdom of Leon-Castile and Muslim Zaragoza, and against them, the kingdoms of Aragon, Catalonia and the Muslims of Lerida.

Of course for today's reader, given the familiar enmity between Madrid and Barcelona, a rivalry which expresses itself in everything from football to linguistics, the idea of early medieval Catalans and Castilians choosing to side with Muslims rather than with one another is anachronistically amusing, perhaps even romantic. What has to be stressed is that such Muslim-Christian alliances in the eleventh century are *examples*, not exceptions. Even as early as 1050, both Christian Spain and Andalusia already had a long history of such alliances, beginning in 777 when Yusuf of Zaragoza had tried to forge a coalition with Charlemagne. In 933, the Muslim town of Huesca refused to help the caliph's army at the battle of Simancas. In 1009 the Berbers enlisted the help of King Sancho Garcia in overthrowing the Andalusis of Cordoba. Around the same time, the Dhu an-Nunids of Toledo had made an alliance with the Christian kingdom of Navarre in their border war with Muslim Zaragoza. In 958 Sancho I of Leon (sometimes referred to as Sancho the Fat, because he was reputedly too fat to ride a horse) travelled to the Muslim court at Cordoba to obtain military support to win his kingdom back.[11] This latter episode is only one example of many instances where exiled Christian kings/nobles travelled to Muslim courts to look for help – Alfonso VI, in 1072, spent nine months in Toledo at the court of al-Mamun, while the exiled El Cid famously spent four years serving the Muslim ruler of the court of Zaragoza.

If the *official* Christian-Muslim alliances of the eleventh century, between states, can be described as common and unremarkable, then the *un*official employment of Christian and Muslim soldiers as mercenaries, fighting alongside one another against other Christians and Muslims, was an even more pervasive, widespread and long-established practice. The Emir of Cordoba al-Hakam I (d. 822) was probably the first Muslim ruler to employ Christian mercenaries in his armies. The tenth-century al-Mansur, in the fifty-two expeditions he led against Christian states (sacking, among other places, the city of Barcelona in 985), employed a large number of extremely loyal Christian knights in his ranks.[12] Throughout the 980s and 990s, a number of rebellious Leonese nobles were more than happy to help Muslim attacks on the monarch Vermudo II in exchange for financial reward. The arrival of a 'Crusader' ideology after the eleventh century diminished though by no means extinguished such cross-religious activities. Endless accounts still persist, well into the twelfth, thirteenth and even fourteenth centuries, of Christian mercenaries fighting with great zeal on the side of Muslim armies against a Christian foe. The tale of the famous 'Reverter', a viscount of Barcelona (d. 1144) who led many of the Almoravids' armies with great success, is only one example of this mercenary indifference to religious divides. The fact that Pope Innocent III, in 1214, had to threaten excommunication to

any believer who helped the 'Saracen' in a struggle against the faith
of Rome, suggests not everyone in medieval Europe was responding
to the call for crusade.[13]

There was, of course, also a reverse version of this paradigm – that
is, Muslim soldiers who fought in Christian armies against other
Muslims. We know of such events partly through Muslim anger at
them. In a document written by a certain Ibn Rushd (d. 1126), we
find indignation at a large number of Muslims in the region of Barcelona
who, barely a year after the Christian re-conquest, were helping the
infidel in their raids on Muslim lands.[14] Figures such as Sayf al-Dawla,
a Muslim noble of Zaragoza who died in battle for the cause of Castile
in the south of the country, were by no means uncommon. The
bewildering play of alliances among the ever-shifting map of the *taifa*
and Christian kingdoms, and the changing tensions and variations the
rise and fall of each principality's fortunes introduced into the bigger
picture, meant that a distinctly unorthodox range of combinations
was possible. When a town full of Muslims in the north of Spain
(Barbastro) is massacred by Normans one year, we should not be
surprised to find it re-taken, and the massacre avenged, by a
Muslim/Christian contingent the very next.

How sceptical should we be about such alliances? At first sight the
most obvious thing to say, it would seem, is that they were a mere
consequence of political necessity. The logic of 'my enemy's enemy
is my friend' has always been a consistent one, we could argue. In
desperate military/political/economic situations, completely opposed
parties have often been willing to suppress a mutual animosity, or
even pretend to share a series of common values, in order temporarily
to join forces against the common foe of the moment. The fact that,
in 2003, thousands of Iraqi Kurds initially greeted the arrival of US
troops in their country with joy (the pictures of such jubilation were
endlessly disseminated by CNN and Fox news), and actively
participated in the US/British overthrow of the Ba'athist regime,
reflected no 'discovery' of a common humanity between US soldiers
and Iraqi Kurds. The alliance between the Kurds and US forces was
no permanent expression of cultural/ideological solidarity, but simply
a mutually beneficial exercise: both the Kurds and the US, for very
different reasons, wanted rid of Saddam Hussein. We might be tempted
to say the same of Castilian-Zaragozan alliances or Catalan-Muslim
military units – that they were products of expediency and strategy,
not friendship and cultural like-mindedness. The eleventh-century

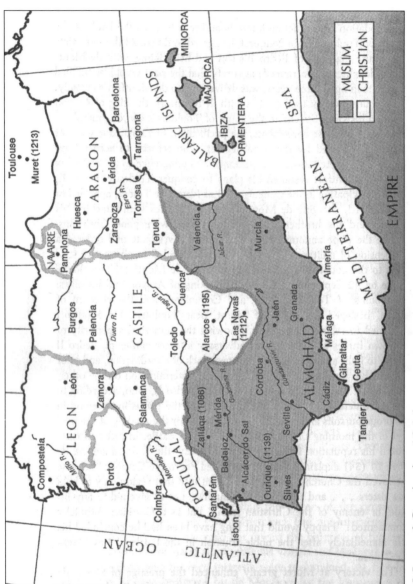

Map of Spain in 1214

Muslims and Christians who fought in the same armies at Graus or Huesca, who laid siege to the same towns at Barbastro or Tudela, we might conclude, simply found themselves fighting alongside one another for reasons of purely political necessity.

There are two reasons why such scepticism, at least in its excessive form, should be rejected. The first lies in the highly personal nature of the interaction between Spanish Christian and Muslim rulers up to this time – Muslim and Christian kings enjoyed one another's friendship, attended and hosted each other's weddings, at times even married one another's relatives. The ruler al-Mundhir of Zaragoza (1010–16), for example, hosted one of the biggest wedding ceremonies in the Pyrenees of his day – that of Sancha of Castile to Ramon Berenguer of Barcelona.[15] Marriages between the offspring of Christian and Muslim rulers, and sometimes involving the rulers themselves, were far from uncommon. The union of King Sancho of Pamplona's daughter with al-Mansur in 992 is certainly not the only example we have – apart from the many Basque princesses who appear to have repeatedly married the Andalusian caliphs, there is also the more famous example of King Alfonso VI's Muslim wife, Zaida, widowed daughter-in-law of al-Mu'tamid of Seville, with whom he got married and sired a child in 1093. In 909, when one Muslim prince of Huesca is overthrown by his subjects, he flees (an Arabic source tells us) to the court of 'Sancho ibn Garcia, to whom he was related by marriage'.[16] If we are to avoid the trap of *reconquista* clichés, these cordial relations between Muslim and Christian rulers, sometimes superficial, sometimes based on genuine affection and even blood ties, have to be taken into account.

A second, much more significant reason why we should not be so cynical about Muslim-Christian alliances in this period has to do with the cultural history of Muslim Spain. To see Catalan/Muslim coalitions as mere exercises in medieval *Realpolitik* is to overlook the centuries-long co-existence of three faiths on the Iberian peninsula. Muslim Spain was a place where, quite simply, Jews, Muslims and Christians shared a wide variety of languages, arts and customs. It was a place where bishops spoke Arabic, imams spoke Ladino and Jewish viziers advised caliphs and gave dinner parties for Muslim poets in their presidential gardens. In order to understand this fully, we need to spend a few moments reviewing what society was like in eleventh-century Andalusia.

Modern historical debates concerning how 'multicultural' Muslim Spain really was – how far cities such as Seville and Cordoba could be considered an 'inter-faith utopia'[17] – run the risk of developing into various versions of an 'Is the glass half-empty or half-full?' debate. By today's standards, some aspects of Andalusian society seem to be a far cry from what we generally understand by the word 'tolerance': sectarian polemics among all three faiths were more than common, often abusive, at times even deliberately provocative. Communal massacres did take place, most often against Jewish populations (in Seville, for example, in 1066). In the most intolerant periods, under the most intolerant rulers, relations between Muslims and non-Muslims could be strictly regulated: Muslim books were forbidden to be sold to Jews and Christians, nor were church bells allowed to be rung, nor could Jewish/Christian doctors treat Muslim patients.[18] In some extreme cases, Christians and Jews even had to wear different clothes from Muslims.

Such realities certainly warn us against romanticising medieval Spain into some blissful lost paradise of tolerance and multiculturalism (as Disraeli was later to do in his arguments for an Anglo-Ottoman alliance). What does emerge, however, from the vast amount of historical research devoted to the many centuries of Muslim Spain is a largely tolerant, polylingual, endlessly faceted collection of cities and small towns. A society where purists from all three faiths repeatedly warned against mixing too much with the cultures of their unbelieving neighbours – and where such warnings were largely ignored (as we can see in the widespread consumption of wine among Andalusian Muslims or the participation of Mozarabs in Muslim festivals). Although anti-Semitism, for example, was a constant feature of eleventh-century Spain, there is almost universal agreement that Muslim Spain possessed an infinitely more tolerant environment towards Jews than any Christian society could offer. Indeed, such tolerance was a reason why outside Jews came to Spain in their thousands during Muslim dominion – and, naturally, why they also left with equal speed when the Christian rulers regained control. This comparison is also true for the other parts of the Maghrib of which Andalusia formed a part. A letter of 1100, written by a Spanish Jewish merchant to his son back home while travelling in Morocco, expresses amazement at the levels of anti-Semitism he finds there – and declares life in his native Almeria to be 'like salvation' in comparison.

Language certainly played a central factor in all of this. It is not that eleventh-century Muslim Spain possessed one transparent, Esperanto-

like idiom in which everyone could express themselves clearly. The
actual situation was one of bi- or multi-lingualism, where a number of
languages (Latin, the medieval Romance version of what we now call
Spanish, Hebrew, Berber dialects) appeared to vie with the dominant
Arabic for pole position in social discourse. The endless complaints of
purists for the preservation of their religion/culture/language is a good
sign that the boundaries between Muslim, Christian and Jew were not
only porous but endlessly shifting. Probably the best-known of these
is the lament of the Bishop of Cordoba, Paulus Alvarus (d. 861), who
famously expressed his alarm that all the young Christians were flocking
to Arabic and forgetting their own culture:

> Who, I ask, is there today among our faithful laymen who studies the
> sacred scriptures and inquiries into the Latin writings of the doctors?
> ... Rather, our Christian young men ... proud of their Arabic
> eloquence, avidly study the books of the Chaldeans [Muslims]. Alas,
> Christians do not know their own language, nor do the Latins study
> their own language, so that in the whole assembly of Christ, one
> would scarcely find one in a thousand who is capable of addressing
> his brother in the correct form ... [19]

The passage is a reminder of how Muslim Spain, alongside the Syrian
monks' transcriptions and translations of Plato and Aristotle, offers
another example of how the world of Arabised Christianity would
later re-introduce the West to its own Greek tradition. Nowadays the
inferiority complex early medieval Christianity had before the Muslim
world is conveniently forgotten – Plato of Tivoli, writing in Barcelona
in the 1130s, complained of Western ignorance, and of how Rome
had been 'for long inferior to Egypt, Greece and Arabia'.[20] Alvarus'
alarm for Christian youth is ironic not only because he makes 'Arabic
eloquence' sound like pop music or the internet, but also because
many Muslim writers were making the same complaints. The
lexicographer Ibn Sida (d. 1066) bemoans the impure state of Arabic
in a country where 'one has to live familiarly with those who speak
Romance'; anecdotes concerning thirteenth-century Muslim
missionaries in Andalusia suggest some Muslims did not speak Arabic
very well at all, while a certain Muslim judge of Toledo was said to
be so well-versed in Romance that he seemed to be a Christian.[21]
Probably the greatest Jewish philosopher of all time, Maimonides of
Cordoba, wrote his *Guide for the Perplexed* (1191) not in Hebrew but

in Arabic. Naturally, it comes as no surprise to find that there were also Jews who were unhappy about such multi-lingualism. Abraham ibn Hasdai of Barcelona, writing in the 1200s, laments how Muslim eloquence and influence has corrupted the Hebrew of the Jews, so that they are unable to compose elegantly in their own language any more.

If anyone were to ask for a single, physical example of the multiply-overlapping cultures of eleventh-century Spain, then the hybrid style of *zajal* would probably suffice. This was an Arabic verse form, usually a love poem, of Andalusian origin, noted for its mixing of languages. An Arabic *zajal* would often end in a Romance couplet, or sometimes even a Hebrew couplet, using any of the three alphabets available at the time. This presence of two or sometimes even three languages on the same page, melting together to form a single, Andalusian expression of creativity, probably does more than a whole phalanx of academic arguments to convey the sophisticated interplay of cultures at this time.

Jews, Muslims and Christians lived together in Muslim Spain, not always harmoniously but with a fairly intimate knowledge of one another – certainly more intimate than the average Berliner has today of the German Turks in his neighbourhood, or than the middle-class British family has of the Syrians living in their London suburb. Arguments and bitter controversies abounded, sometimes flaring up into full-scale violence (such as the murderous public riot against Jews in Granada in 1066). A good example of one such polemicist – and how schizophrenic such polemicists could be – is the brilliant Muslim thinker Ibn Hazm (d. 1064). Ibn Hazm, author of over 400 works including his treatise on love *The Ring of the Dove*, comes across as a man who simply had to have an argument with everyone he met. We find records of a lively theological debate around 1027–30 between Ibn Hazm and a Christian judge of Cordoba, one which was doubtless fuelled by the very same energy which drove his expositions of the inconsistencies of the Gospels, his belief in the essential atheism of the Jewish faith, his charges of heresy at Muslim esotericists and his disagreement with, basically, anyone who was not Ibn Hazm. For all of this, two ironies lie beneath the polemics of such a fervently Islamic thinker: first of all, Ibn Hazm's own diatribes against other religions reveal a remarkable knowledge of, for example, the Rabbinical commentary tradition, one which paradoxically reinforces how closely the intellectual cultures of the three faiths lived next to one another.

Secondly, Ibn Hazm's own biography reflects such a co-existence with Jewish intellectuals – in his youth, he had been friendly with a number of Jews in Cordoba, and had learnt a considerable amount of Hebrew in his conversations with them. Of course, such meetings between different religionists did not have to be argumentative or polemical; the Christians of Toledo would travel to Baeza just to have a meeting with a famous Muslim scholar, 'Abd Allah (d. 1158). Nevertheless the Jewish and Christian thinkers Ibn Hazm debated with, in Cordoba and elsewhere, reflected the level of mutual acknowledgement ('dialogue' would be an anachronism) which took place in the cities of Muslim Spain.

Cross-religious encounters in Andalusia were not always of a purely religious kind. There is certainly a tradition of love poetry, sometimes homosexual, between the members of different faiths. Poets such as Ibn al-Zaqqaq of Valencia (d. 1133) often wrote poems of unrequited love for Christian girls. Tales are told of an eminent Mu'tazilite scholar who became so obsessed with his love for a Christian boy that he wrote a treatise extolling the virtues of the Trinity for him, or of another Muslim poet (al-Ramadi) who 'became so infatuated with a Christian youth' that he started to wear the distinctive belt of a Christian and would pretend to make the sign of the cross on a cup of wine before drinking it. Jewish poets, too, such as Ibrahim ibn Sahl of Seville, would sometimes fall in love with Muslim boys and dedicate their poetry to them.[22] Somewhat less erotically (and probably less sincerely), there was also a tradition of Muslim poets dedicating poems to Jewish viziers and courtiers. The significant position of many Spanish Jews as prime ministers in the *taifa* kingdoms encouraged this mini-genre. Muslim poets would address viziers such as Samuel ibn Naghrila (in many ways the Granadan Disraeli) as the 'son of Joseph' and springing from 'the clan of Moses', a refreshing change from the more common anti-Semitic epithets which both Christian and Muslim writers were capable of delivering against Jews – even if such obsequious praises, undoubtedly, more often than not sought political favours rather than mutual understanding.

The phrase 'clash of civilisations' has been bandied about a great deal in recent years, often to describe some specific disagreement or cultural conflict in pan-global, geopolitical terms. What a careful study of the cultural setting of eleventh-century Muslim Spain reveals, above all else, is the historical ignorance of such a term. In a medieval society where Jewish viziers shared jokes with their Muslim dinner guests, where languages such as Arabic or Romance belonged equally to the church and the mosque, and could be found in a *zajal* or a hymn, even where Muslim and Christian criminals joined together in moving moments of inter-cultural co-operation to loot a village or steal sheep from their co-religionists, what emerges is how easily the inhabitants of Muslim Spain were able to put aside their religious identities when the occasion demanded. The fact that, at the battle of Graus (1063), the Muslim assassin who sneaked into the camp of King Ramiro I to kill him was able to do so undetected, speaking the Christians' language perfectly, tells us a great deal about how culturally similar Muslims and Christians were.[23] It is not ridiculous idealism to suggest that such cultural similarity, in addition to political expediency, would have greatly helped Muslims and Christians to fight alongside each other, and given them fewer grudges to fight against their fellow believers.

The play of events: from the end of the Caliphate to the coronation of Alfonso VI

The story of the beginning of the end of Muslim Spain, which is what the Iberian eleventh century essentially is, can be told not just through the collapse of the Caliphate, but also through the deaths of two kings. There is an ironic symmetry to the demise of Sancho the Great and Fernando I, father and son dying thirty years apart (1035 and 1065) and, in each case, bequeathing a whole kingdom in several parts to several sons, who were to squabble with, imprison and even murder one another to piece the inheritance back together again. Sancho the Great had begun with the tiny kingdom of Navarre in the Pyrenees and, through a well-engineered series of marriages and the occasional assassination of an in-law, managed to bring the other northern kingdoms of Aragon, Leon and Castile into amalgamation with his own. The growing internecine strife within the Muslim Caliphate, as we have seen, changed the entire political situation for the Christian kingdoms of the north. The peripheral, disadvantaged, much put-upon neighbours of powerful, wealthy Andalusia were starting to change into rival centres of power that could ally, intervene and even control some of the factions within the disintegrating Caliphate. The fact that different Christian armies had been able to help opposing sides in the Berber revolt of 1008–10 reflects this striking shift northwards in the balance of power.

By the time of his death in 1035, Sancho the Great had accomplished a number of things for the modest northern ridge of Spain that his cramped kingdoms occupied. He had established the shrine of St James at Compostela as a major pilgrimage site for non-Spanish Christendom, second only to Rome and Jerusalem; while in the south, as the various Slav, Berber and Andalusi factions were fighting with one another for control of the peninsula, he had taken advantage of the respite not only to unify (if momentarily) the Christian kingdoms of the north, but also to integrate Christian Spain better into Western Christendom. Upon his death, Sancho sliced up the cake of his newly unified kingdom into four parts, following Visigothic tradition, one for each of his sons. Fernando I thus inherited the kingdom of Castile at the tender age of seventeen, and promptly went on, in the space of two years, to acquire Leon and Navarre through the deaths of his brother (Garcia) and his brother-in-law (Vermudo III).

Within the thirty years of Fernando I's reign (1035–65), a whole series of processes began to take place and unfold on either side of the Muslim-Christian divide. As Fernando's kingdom of Leon-Castile grew, and as the *taifa* kingdoms quarrelled, split up and multiplied, a wide pattern of different, changing alliances began to emerge between the various northern Christian kings (not just Fernando but also the quarrelling kings of Navarre and Aragon) and the bickering Muslim mini-states. These invariably consisted of the Muslim kings offering gold as 'protection money' or *parias* in exchange for military support from their Christian neighbours when attacked. The manpower of some of the *taifa* kingdoms was astonishingly low – poor 'Abd Allah of Granada had barely a hundred Zanata Berbers in his garrison, while his brother Tamim of Malaga had just over three hundred. Although the estimate of ten thousand men given to Fernando I's army by the commentator Ibn Idhari seems excessive, the disunity of the *taifas* and the simultaneous expansion of Leon-Castile effectively transformed the once-powerful domain of Andalusia into a series of pawns, which the Aragonese and Castilians would increasingly play off against one another for their own profit.

Zaragoza, a Muslim kingdom in the north bordered on almost all sides by Catalonia, Navarre, Aragon and Castile, is a good case in point. Geographically disadvantaged by its borders on not one but *four* Christian kingdoms, it sometimes found itself paying out *parias* to four kings at the same time. Sometimes, however, Muslim kingdoms were happy to pay for extra support against their enemies, Christian or Muslim. In 1055 al-Muqtadir of Zaragoza signed an alliance with 'his friend' (*amicum suum*) Sancho IV of Navarre. In this treaty Sancho promised to attack his Aragonese neighbour if any of their armies attempted to take the Muslim town of Huesca. Such alliances were not by any means 'temporary arrangements' – the co-operation between Muslim Zaragoza and Castile/Navarre had a history, and would continue well into the next century. Forty years later, when the Aragonese finally take back the Muslim city in 1096, local commentators will record the presence of 'some evil Christians' who helped the Muslims try to keep hold of the town – these 'evil Christians' were, of course, Castilians who were fighting for the old Muslim *taifa* ruler against their sworn enemies, the Aragonese.[24] The peculiar history of fratricide and brotherly hatred among the Zaragozan rulers made the kingdom particularly susceptible to cross-religious alliances with convenient Christian neighbours. There was certainly no love lost between al-Muqtadir and his brother, Yusuf of Lerida. As early as 1051 we find Yusuf paying the Catalans (on the *other* side of Zaragoza's border from Navarre) to protect him from his brother's forces in Zaragoza. With good reason, too – in 1058 a failed assassination attempt takes place, as al-Muqtadir pays a Christian knight of Navarre to try to kill his brother Yusuf. This splitting of the Muslim kingdom into two halves, Zaragoza and Lerida, ruled by two brothers who hate one another, will be a source of cross-religious alliances well into the next century – eastern Lerida gaining support from the Christian armies of Barcelona and Aragon, while western Zaragoza seeks the alliance of Castile and Navarre. Indeed, one of the first battles the famous El Cid takes part in, at the age of eighteen, is the Castilian campaign to re-take the Zaragozan town of Graus, in 1063, from the Aragonese with a combined army of Muslims and Christians. The battle, in which the King of Aragon (Ramiro I) loses his life, takes place as a precise consequence of the promise Sancho IV made to al-Muqtadir. The fact that a Christian ruler is willing to kill his Aragonese uncle in order to keep a promise made to a Muslim noble, once again, should make us reflect on the nature of the Muslim-Christian relationship in this epoch.

Within Muslim Spain itself, one of the most expansionist and aggressive kingdoms was the *taifa* of Seville, which after the disarray of the post-Caliphate period almost immediately began swallowing up the smaller Muslim kingdoms such as Ronda and Algeciras. Its seventeen-year war with the kingdom of Granada (1039–56), the other 'big player' in the *taifa* period of Muslim Spain, constrained its rulers to seek the support of Castile. Al-Mu'tamid of Seville, in his increasing dependency on Fernando I's armies, even agreed to send back to the cathedral of Leon the body of the holy Saint Isidore. Throwing a sheet over the coffin, the story goes, he sighed and told the corpse: 'Now you are leaving, revered Isidore; well you know how much your fame was mine!'[25] As we shall see, this relationship eventually gave Seville the status of a vassal, as it was forced to pay crippling annual tributes (up to 10,000 gold dinars a year) to the Christian kings to preserve its independence. Historians have also pointed out, in its long war against Granada, the irony of two Muslim kingdoms going to war against one another with armies led by two Jewish prime ministers. The Granadan armies, in this case, were led by the brilliant general, poet and politician Samuel ibn Naghrila. Such internal Muslim conflicts naturally created ample opportunities for Christian armies, official and mercenary, to intervene out of pure self-interest, and often professional Christian soldiers could be found on either side of a Muslim war. In 1042, for example, on the eastern coast of Spain, we find a large army of Catalan mercenaries assisting soldiers from Denia and Valencia in an attempt to oust the ruler of Valencia on behalf of another Muslim vizier.[26]

And so the growing strength and solidity of Fernando's Castile, crucially coinciding with the growing disunity and instability of the quarrelling Muslim kingdoms, began to foster a series not just of alliances but also vassalships between the Christian north and the Muslim south. If Fernando I initiated this practice of *parias* or 'protection money' (which is basically what it was), it was his son Alfonso VI who would ruthlessly develop and enlarge this system, milking the *taifa* kingdoms for every gold dinar he could get out of them. When Fernando I dies in 1065, he leaves his kingdom (like his father before him) divided equally among his three sons, Garcia, Sancho and Alfonso. And like his father before him, it is Alfonso who moves quickly and ruthlessly, working with his sister Urraca (with whom, it is widely held, he had a long and cultivated incestuous relationship) to imprison and eliminate his two brothers. Within the space of seven years, Alfonso is able to crown himself king of the kingdoms of Leon, Castile, Galicia and Navarre – practically three-quarters of Christian Spain.

The philosopher Walter Benjamin famously said that all great moments of civilisation were based on acts of barbarism. It is certainly true that some great moments of spirituality have been financed by acts of war.

From the chronicle of faction-fighting, military campaigns, siege warfare, fratricide and even incest that eleventh-century Spain presents us with, a flow of money came which would finance one of the great spiritual centres of Western Christendom: Cluny. To a large extent, Muslim gold, obtained as tribute from the kingdoms of Zaragoza, Seville and Granada, went to developing and enlarging the French monastery, which in future years would not only provide a workplace for Peter the Venerable and a refuge for Abelard, but also one of the first Latin translations of the Koran (1164). However, the less spiritual effects of the large sums of gold which King Alfonso VI was able to harvest each year were, in many ways, more significant. They enabled him to keep an enormous standing army ready, one which could bully and threaten any Muslim *taifa* ruler who defaulted on his protection payments. Even more importantly, they forced the Muslim kings themselves constantly to raise the taxes of their own subjects in order to keep up with the payments. In many ways, this gave rulers such as Abd Allah of Granada or al-Mu'tamid of Seville the same kind of unpopularity as Western-friendly governments of Muslim countries suffer from the present-day citizens of Egypt, Saudi Arabia or Pakistan. By the middle of the 1070s local subjects in many cities were revolting against their rulers, deeply resentful of their money being used to pay Christian armies. When the North African Almoravids finally landed as a relief force in Algeciras in 1086, the local Muslims cheered them as saviours.

And so in 1072 a king was crowned (or rather crowned himself – interestingly, given the regicides and imprisonments which had led to Alfonso's coronation, the local bishop did not dare do it) who, through cunning, skill and downright brutality, would turn the fractured, imploding shell of Muslim Spain, and all its quarrelling *taifas*, into a highly profitable series of ventures. If all this seems to set the image of Alfonso VI as a Great Christian Warrior of the Re-conquest, we should remember that many Arab and Spanish commentators referred to Alfonso as the 'Emperor of the Two Religions'. Alfonso's undoubted, if problematic, friendships with al-Mamun and al-Mu'tamid, his siring of a son by the Muslim widow Zaida, his generous treatment of the Muslims in Toledo after he had conquered the city – above all the unpopularity he courted in Christian circles for refusing to convert the city's mosque immediately into a cathedral, and his own threat to behead the bishop who wanted to do this straightaway – remind us of how carefully we have to tread. As Alfonso placed the ring of gold upon his head in the royal city of Leon, he doubtless had many plans for the years which lay ahead of him. What he could not have possibly guessed, however, was that forces were already moving, far outside Spain, which would soon bring an end to whatever dreams of dominion he may have had in mind.

Outside Spain: the interest of Rome and the rise of the Almoravids

Outside interest in the events taking place on the Spanish peninsula – the rise of the Christian north, the various inter-*taifa* rivalries and makeshift cross-religious alliances – came from two directions: Italy and North Africa. The Papacy had already been following developments across the Mediterranean for some time. Reading the history of communiqués between Rome and the Castilian kings, it is not difficult to see the tension between a Spanish monarchy, with its own five-hundred-year-old Mozarabic/Arian version of Christianity and Visigothic heritage, and a Papacy trying to mingle rebuke and accommodation, praise and claim, in its request for a Spanish church more in line with its own. The Pope certainly made it clear that Spain had *always* been a Catholic country – in 1073 Pope Gregory VII told Alfonso how Spain had belonged to St Peter since ancient times.[27] It is perhaps surprising to imagine that, if Rome had not endlessly pressed for the Mozarabic liturgy to be dropped and be replaced with the Catholic version, Spain today would have a completely different Christianity, one in theology perhaps closer to the Unitarians, and with an outward form perhaps more closely resembling that of the Arab orthodox churches.

There was also, of course, the question of Islam. Quite apart from the very different Christianity of pre-Catholic Spain, which the Pope in his most hostile letter considered to be nothing more than a mixture of Arianism, Muslim heresy and the Arab conquest, the co-existence of 'Saracens' with Christians, along with their impious alliances, also made the Catholic Church uneasy. Very often this feeling was mutual: when the Pope authorises a new, French crusade against Muslim Spain in 1073, employing the Aragonese as his main representatives, Sancho of Navarre and al-Muqtadir of Zaragoza immediately form an alliance to protect themselves against it. Rome must have felt tremendously frustrated by this constant willingness of the Christian Spanish to enter into alliance with the 'Mohammedan' enemies of Christ, particularly in opposition against their own armies. The very same Sancho of Aragon who, in 1068, travels all the way to Rome to make himself a vassal of the Pope and declare himself a warrior of Christ, is quite happy to help the Muslims of Lerida fight against El Cid in 1083. For the rest of the century, Rome would constantly try to get the Christian kings to work together in what it saw as a second, Western front in the war on Islam, running parallel to its crusade in the East. However, in the Catholic Church's attempt to turn the whole panoply of power struggles on the Iberian peninsula into a conflict between Islam and Christianity, they were to receive help from an unexpected quarter.

The story of the rise of the Almoravids is exotic, even though popular accounts of their appearance as a Mediterranean power in the eleventh century have more to do with European stereotypes of Muslims as conservative, fanatical and hostile to culture than with any historical reality. The Hollywood version of their leader in the Charlton Heston film *El Cid*, for example (1961, dir. Antony Mann), portrays a rolling-eyed, deranged zealot, perfectly fitting the kind of Muslim invader Christians would like to hear about. The North African collection of Saharan Berbers we call the Almoravids (from the Arabic *al murabitun* or 'those who dwell in fortresses') were certainly much more conservative and cohesive than their Spanish Muslim neighbours, whose luxurious palaces, fraternisation with Jews/Christians and open practices of drinking and boy-love they looked upon with religious disapproval, and yet 'barbarians' or 'fanatics' would be an unjust description for this well-organised and highly effective fighting force. Beginning in the 1030s as a small Islamic sect in a castle on the banks of the river Niger, somewhere between northern modern-day Ghana and southern Morocco, they expanded rapidly under the radical leadership of a lean, clever, devout Berber called Yusuf ibn Tashufin. Yusuf led the Almoravids for almost exactly the same period as Alfonso VI was king of Leon-Castile – from 1061 to 1106 – and it is interesting to compare the two timelines as gradually, battle by battle, siege by siege, their trajectories edge towards one another like ill-fated blips on a radar screen, finally to meet in the (for Alfonso) disastrous battle of Zallaqah in 1086.

By the time Alfonso crowns himself King of almost all of Christian Spain in 1072, Yusuf's Almoravids are already sweeping up the North African coast, their leader's tactical and military genius taking town by town in its stride. By 1077 they are in Tangiers, one of the closest African cities to Andalusia. And yet almost a decade has to pass before the *taifa* rulers, frustrated with ever-increasing tributes from their

Christian neighbours, finally ask the Almoravids to come across the strait and liberate them from Alfonso's expensive 'protection'. The main reason for this delay, despite their shared religion, was the fear which the Spanish Muslims had of their North African neighbours, who had already conquered large stretches of western Africa to reach the Spanish peninsula. It was a fear which, we shall see, was to prove well-justified. Nevertheless, the Almoravids had something the *taifa* rulers desperately needed – *men*, tens of thousands of them. The size of Yusuf's army when it finally arrives, we are told, is almost twenty thousand strong. And yet the bickering nature of the *taifa* rulers, who squabble like children with one another when the powerful Almoravids finally do appear to help them, will be a constant source of frustration to Yusuf ibn Tashufin. In many ways, Yusuf's exasperation with the quarrelling *taifa* kingdoms and their Christian alliances runs parallel to Pope Gregory VII's impatience with the Spanish Christian kings and their Muslim coalitions. Had the two men ever met, Yusuf ibn Tashufin and Pope Gregory VII would certainly have had nothing but utter contempt for one another. And yet, as purists, they shared a common goal: the religious polarisation of a conflict exclusively in terms of belief. Ideologically, of course, the Pope and the Berber were opposed to one another; politically, however, each made the other's task a great deal easier.

The expansion of Castile: from 1072 to the fall of Toledo

Fourteen years pass between Alfonso's coronation and the fateful day in October 1086, when the newly arrived Almoravids massacre the Spanish king's forces at Zallaqah, barely ten weeks after arriving on the mainland. Yusuf's massive force of Berbers landed on the coast in July and almost immediately inflicted upon Alfonso VI the greatest defeat he had ever suffered. In the period up to this point, however, things went from strength to strength for Alfonso, as he allied with one Muslim king after another in an endless chess-game of careful coalitions, moving around the map of Muslim Spain and gradually strengthening his control of the south. What is interesting is that Alfonso VI refrained from conquering any of the Muslim kingdoms outright – which would not have been impossible, given the size of his army – but merely seemed content to play them against one another, or form useful alliances with them in pursuit of a common aim. One of his first allies was al-Ma'mun of Toledo, a strong and familiar figure in Muslim Spain whose inept grandson was to lose Valencia (and his head) in 1092. Alfonso knew al-Ma'mun well because he had stayed in his court as a guest, essentially as a king in exile, for nine months in 1071; rumours that he was later able to capture the city so easily because he had spent his time as a guest inspecting the city's battlements are probably exaggerated.[28] Al-Ma'mun had long had designs on the city of his neighbouring kingdom, Cordoba, and in 1074 we find the Muslim and Christian armies of both rulers marching south towards Granada in an alliance against the newly installed ruler there, the melancholy and somewhat wisftful 'Abd Allah of Granada. Because of the wonderfully poetic memoirs he has left us, historians have been a good deal kinder to 'Abd Allah than his contemporaries ever were (in the end, we are told, he was betrayed by everyone except his mother). Certainly in 1074 the city of Cordoba appeared to be attractive to a number of neighbouring Muslim rulers, and al-Ma'mun lost no time in paying a Christian army to help him take it. Within three months both Castilian and Toledan soldiers were camped in the territories of Granada itself, with Alfonso demanding *parias* from poor 'Abd Allah of thirty thousand gold dinars. The Christian king even finds a local Muslim noble who dislikes 'Abd Allah enough to start building a defiant castle, financed by Alfonso of course.[29] In the end 'Abd Allah, surrounded by Muslims in league with Christians against him, agrees to pay the money, even if this is not enough to save Cordoba. Barely six months later, the city is betrayed into the hands of al-Ma'mun through a series of tricks ('Abd Allah may have received some cold comfort from the fact that al-Ma'mun would not live long to relish this conquest – he was poisoned in his own city of Toledo as soon as he returned in 1075).

Another of Alfonso's Muslim allies in this period was the famous al-Mu'tamid of Seville, even if 'alliance' is perhaps too simple a word for this strained, shifting and ultimately short-lived agreement. Al-Mu'tamid is probably most famous in the history of literature for the brilliant academy of poets and scholars he established in his court. Coerced as his tributary into 'helping' King Alfonso in his campaigns south, we find the armies of Seville and Castile in the late 1070s moving together along the borders of Badajoz (what is now western Portugal) harassing another Muslim ruler, the enigmatic al-Mutawakkil. Al-Mu'tamid's position was certainly unenviable; like most of the *taifa* rulers, caught between two local superpowers, he had to decide whether to side with Alfonso's Christians or Yusuf's North African Berbers. In the end, he would famously make his choice with the words 'I would rather be a camel-herder in Morocco than a swine-herder in Castile'. The reader, perhaps, should not spend too much pity on him. Al-Mu'tamid certainly had a ruthless streak – he crucified the Jewish envoy Alfonso sent to him in 1082 for asking for too much gold as tribute. His own *taifa* of Seville was also aggressive enough by itself, annexing the kingdoms of Denia in 1076 and Murcia in 1078, so that by the time Alfonso VI was bullying him for more *parias*, he had a kingdom which stretched from the Mediterranean to the Atlantic.[30]

Watching the map of Muslim kingdoms quarrel, collude and change in the period up to Zallaqah is a depressing lesson in military Darwinism. The moment one kingdom's ruler dies and a power vacuum opens up, two or three armies, made up of soldiers from both faiths, appear at the capital's gates as each neighbouring kingdom moves in on the other's weakness to annex it. Cordoba is a good example – between 1075 and 1077 it danced between three rulers ('Abd Allah, the poisoned al-Ma'mun and al-Mu'tamid). One of the reasons why so many Muslim-Christian alliances spring up in this period is precisely because, time and time again, so many individual rulers and nobles saw themselves primarily not as Muslims or Christians, but as Castilians or Aragonese, or as belonging to the Hud or Aftasid dynasty. When the tornado of the Almoravids finally lands in Spain, things certainly polarise – faced with the threat of a twenty-thousand-strong fighting force of Berbers, even Pedro I of Aragon and Alfonso VI of Castile start talking to one another about a coalition. And yet cross-faith alliances, although diminished by the increasingly religious tone of the diatribes, certainly do not disappear. A hundred years later at the battle of Alarcos (1195), Leonese and Castilian kings will still be joining forces with Muslims – this time with the Almohads – against one another.

By 1083, the relationship between al-Mu'tamid and King Alfonso began to dissolve, as Alfonso demanded more and more money from the Muslim ruler. Crucifying the king's Jewish ambassador had only worsened already sour relations between the two kingdoms. When al-Mu'tamid refused to pay any more, the 'alliance' broke down and Alfonso began to send his armies into Seville's northern territories. It also gave the Spanish king an excuse to embark upon a venture which had long been his heart's desire – the capture of Toledo, one of the most important cities of Spain, set in the exact middle of the country. Not surprisingly, it was around this time that al-Mu'tamid first made his famous request, across the sea, to the Almoravids for assistance.

The fall of Muslim Toledo in 1085 was a significant victory for King Alfonso. It was also his last one before the disastrous turn of Zallaqah, a kind of Newbury before his Naseby, a Chancellorsville before his Gettysburg. The city passed into Christian hands after three hundred and seventy-five years of Muslim rule. Alfonso was elated; Christendom rejoiced at the passing of the first centre of Islam into Christian rule for a century; Pope Gregory VII would also have been happy at the news, had he not died the very same day. The city, as was the case in many sieges of the period, fell with little violence. An agreement was negotiated with the enormous army waiting to enter it and, on 25 May 1085, Alfonso marched at the head of his soldiers into what would be the centre of a New Castile. Historians have already commented on the unusually tolerant and generous conditions offered to the city's Muslims, who made up possibly over half of the population (the other half consisting of Jews and Mozarabic Christians). For a variety of economic reasons, Christian kings of the *reconquista* were often keen to persuade Muslims to stay on in the cities they conquered; some Muslim commentators suggest the king gave out over 100,000 gold dinars to Muslim farmers as an incentive to stay when the city was taken. Alfonso's first choice of a Mozarabic Christian, fluent in Arabic, as governor would also have calmed all the various groups in the conquered city, Muslims, Mozarabs and Jews. The famous argument over what to do with the city's main mosque – the local bishop wanted it converted into a church straightaway, while both the king and his Mozarabic governor were strictly against the idea – also suggests a more conciliatory attitude towards Islam on Alfonso's part, one which was more interested in tribute than re-conquest.[31] We know that many of the nobles and clerics in Alfonso's court, including his own queen and her archbishop, were deeply unhappy at this absurd respect for the Moors' temple.

What the fall of Toledo also did, however, was dangerously swell Alfonso's confidence. According to some commentators, as soon as the king of Castile took the city, he began to taunt Yusuf ibn Tashufin with charges of cowardice, challenging him to invade Spanish soil and even offering to send a boat to bring his army. Although stories of such swaggering are probably exaggerated, what is clear in hindsight is that Alfonso completely underestimated the strength and resolve of his North African enemies. It was an oversight that would cost him ten thousand men.

The battle of Zallaqah (1086) and the end of the taifa period

On 23 October, 1086, the newly landed forces of Yusuf confronted and scattered the Castilian army which had come out to meet them on the plains of Zallaqah in southwestern Spain. Alfonso badly misjudged the size and resilience of the Berbers in front of him and, after a frontal assault, found himself surrounded on both flanks by the enemy. The Christian contingent suffered almost ten thousand dead, most of the casualties occurring during the chaotic retreat. The king barely escaped with his life and fled under cover of night, eventually finding refuge in the town of Coria, over a hundred kilometres to the north. Bishops, nobles and knights all counted among the dead. In the aftermath of the battle, cartloads of heads were wheeled from town to town as macabre trophies of the Castilian defeat. This brief intervention of the Almoravids, culminating in the battle of Zallaqah, changed everything. Although the North African forces of Yusuf and his Almoravids essentially hopped across the straits, delivered their defeat and then almost immediately returned to Morocco (leaving behind a large cavalry as a reminder of their visit), the rout of Alfonso's armies changed the entire dynamics of the Spanish peninsula.

As the historian Reilly points out, Zallaqah destroyed neither Alfonso's army nor his reign. Although ten thousand fatalities is a fearful number, Zallaqah was by no means Alfonso's Waterloo – the king would go on, for the next twenty years, to maintain a successful defence of his own kingdom, even if further setbacks were to come. What the crushing defeat of Zallaqah did, however, was embolden the *taifa* kings. Suddenly, the Muslims of Valencia, Seville, Granada began to look southward as the location of their destiny shifted from Castile to Morocco. The Almoravids had flexed their muscles, scattered the most powerful army in Spain and sent its Christian king galloping back for his life. No one in *Hispania*, Muslim or Christian, was left in ignorance of this fact.

The consequences of Zallaqah made themselves manifest in other ways, too. While it would be a generalisation to say the Christian kings united, there was certainly a new-found feeling of alliance and reconciliation among them in the face of the looming threat of an Almoravid invasion. In the siege tents outside the Muslim town of Tudela in 1087, we find Alfonso agreeing on a truce with Sancho Ramirez of Aragon and his young son, the future monarch Pedro I. The Aragonese, we are told, promised to help Alfonso in the defence of Toledo against a Muslim attack. Zallaqah also brought crusaders, mercenaries and nobles from France and Italy into Spain across the Pyrenees, including small armies from Burgundy and Toulouse. Essentially, the fear of a possible Muslim re-expansion of Andalusia, moving into Aragon and Castile, and perhaps even southern France, spurred both the Papacy and the various Christian kingdoms to action.[32]

The *parias* – the payments of Muslim gold extracted from the *taifa* rulers, one of Alfonso's main sources of income – also gradually came to an end, as Castile's status as sole superpower on the peninsula suffered irrevocable damage. Alfonso certainly tried hard enough to get the *taifa* rulers to resume their payments – and with 'Abd Allah of Granada he even succeeded temporarily; however, two further visits of Yusuf ibn Tashufin, in 1088 and then in 1090, permanently established the presence of the North African empire in Andalusia and with the arrival of this significant (and united) military force in Muslim Spain, the thousands of dinars Alfonso relied on each year simply dried up. By the end of the 1080s, Zaragoza was the only Muslim kingdom which still paid tribute to Alfonso.

Zallaqah – and the Almoravid invasion it ultimately brought about – also produced a series of regime changes in Andalusia, as Yusuf either exiled or executed the *taifa* rulers and replaced them with his own governors. Yusuf was already deeply unimpressed by the *taifa* kings on his first visit in 1086. Throughout his stay, each king had complained to Yusuf about the other rulers and had tried to set the visitor against them. There is therefore a certain irony in the *taifa* kings being deposed by the very army they invited into the country. The unfortunate al-Mutawakkil of Badajoz was executed in 1090. Al-Mu'tamid of Seville finally realised his wish to be, if not a camel herder, certainly a political prisoner in Morocco – he died peacefully in exile in Marrakesh in 1095. As we have already said, 'Abd Allah of Granada was also banished to Morocco along with his brother Tamim for colluding with the Christian king, and it is there that he wrote his famous memoirs, contributing to that great political tradition of autobiographical reflection which only forced redundancy can produce.

With Zallaqah and the end of the *taifa* period, our brief glimpse at Muslim-Christian coalitions during the Spanish eleventh century also comes to an end. This certainly does not mean that such alliances no longer took place; the developments in and around the city of Valencia between 1086 and 1090 would need a book to fully narrate, as the Muslim-Christian armies of El Cid and Alvar Fanez, collaborating with the forces of al-Musta'in of Zaragoza, fight and skirmish with the armies of Mundir al-Hayib of Tortosa and his Catalan allies.[33] Probably one of the last Muslim-Christian alliances of the eleventh century will be the battle of Alcoraz (1096), where the same al-Musta'in of Zaragoza, together with the combined Christian (Castilian) forces of Najera and Lara, will be defeated by the Aragonese in a struggle for the Muslim town of Huesca. And yet the new-found unity of Muslim Spain under their North African conquerors, first in the guise of the Almoravids and then later the Almohads, will diminish such alliances as both sides draw on their religious identities to create a sense of crusader/jihad solidarity against the foe. In 1080, the idea of an El Cid or a King Alfonso having to apologise for the presence of Muslim soldiers in their army is simply unthinkable. When, a century later, Ramon Berenguer IV uses Muslim aid in his Pallars campaign, he has to publicly request forgiveness for his misdeed.[34]

Probably one of the most famous phrases a historian has ever used to sum up the conflicts we have been reviewing is Elena Lourie's oft-quoted description of medieval Spain as 'a society organized for war'.[35] When we review the bewildering play of alliances between Zaragozan kings and Castilian mercenaries, between rival Muslim nobles whose hatred of one another drives them to pay Christians to assassinate each other, between armies of Catalan mercenaries and Berber factions, what emerges most clearly is how little words like 'Islam' or 'Christianity' help us to understand a very complex situation. What developed in eleventh-century Spain was no 'clash of civilisations', but rather a civilisation fraught with clashes. Although papal outsiders and North African clerics tried to turn it into an abstract war between belief and unbelief, they repeatedly failed. Time and time again, Castilians and Zaragozans, Mozarabs and Granadan Muslims, ended up trusting their neighbours more than a garrison of French knights or Tunisian Berbers.

Sources

'Abdulwahid Dhanun Taha, *The Muslim Conquest and Settlement of North Africa and Spain* (Routledge, 1989).

Aziz al-Azmeh, 'Mortal Enemies, Invisible Neighbours: Northerners in Andalusi Eyes', in Jayyusi (ed.), pp.260–5.

Simon Barton, 'Traitors to the Faith? Christian Mercenaries in al-Andalus and the Maghrib c.1100–1300', in R. Collins and A. Goodman (eds), *Medieval Spain: Culture, Conflict and Coexistence in Honour of Angus MacKay* (London: Palgrave, 2002).

Ross Brann, *Power in the Portrayal: Representations of Jews and Muslims in Eleventh and Twelfth Century Islamic Spain* (Princeton University Press, 2002).

Brian A. Catlos, *The Victors and the Vanquished: Christians and Muslims of Catalonia and Aragon 1050–1300* (Cambridge University Press, 2004).

—'Mahomet Abenadalill: A Muslim Mercenary in the service of the Kings of Aragon (1290–1)', in H.J. Hames (ed.), *Jews, Muslims and Christians in and around the Crown of Aragon* (Leiden, 2004), pp.257–302.

Paul E. Chevedden, 'The Artillery of King James I the Conqueror', in P.E. Chevedden, D.J. Kagay and P.G. Padilla (eds), *Iberia and the Mediterranean World of the Middle Ages* (Leiden, 1996), vol. II, pp. 57–63.

M. Fierro, 'Christian Success and Muslim Fear in Andalusi Writings', in *Israel Oriental Studies* XVII.

Richard Fletcher, *The Quest for El Cid* (London: Hutchinson, 1989).

Antonio Duran Gudiol, 'Francos, Pamploneses y Mozarabes en la Marca Superior de al-Andalus', in P. Sénac (ed.), *La Marche Supérieure d'Al-Andalus et l'Occident Chrétien* (Madrid, 1991).

Pierre Guichard, *Les Musulmans de Valence et la Reconquête (xi–xiii siècles)* (Paris, Damas, 1990).

S.K. Jayyusi (ed.), *The Legacy of Muslim Spain* (Leiden, 1992).

Hugh Kennedy, *Muslim Spain and Portugal* (London: Longman, 1996).

Latin Chronicles of the Kings of Castile, ed. J.F. O'Callaghan (Arizona, 2002).

Elena Lourie, 'A Society Organized for War', in *Past and Present* 35 (1966), pp.54–76.

J.F. O'Callaghan, *A History of Medieval Spain* (Cornell University Press, 1975).

B.F. Reilly, *The Kingdom of Leon-Castilla under King Alfonso VI* (Princeton University Press, 1988).

—*The Kingdom of Leon-Castile under King Alfonso VII 1126–1157* (University of Pennsylvania Press, 1998).

Norman Roth, *Jews, Visigoths and Muslims in Medieval Spain: Cooperation and Conflict* (Leiden, 1994).

J.M. Safran, 'Landscapes in the Conquest of al-Andalus', in J. Howe and M. Wolfe (eds), *Inventing Medieval Landscapes: Senses of Place in Western Europe* (University Press of Florida, 2002), pp.136–49.

Chapter Two

FREDERICK II AND THE SARACENS OF SOUTHERN ITALY

'Islam' is not a word which really springs to mind when we think of Italy in the time of Dante – the cities of Milan and Florence, the frescoes of Giotto and the prayers of St Francis, a whole phase of the late medieval just about to enter the first century of the Renaissance. Apart from a vague awareness that Sicily once briefly belonged to the Arabs, most people would greet the idea of Islam in Italy with some scepticism. The Italian thirteenth century is so firmly cemented in its place as the essence and foundation of the European tradition that to mention anything remotely Muslim in the same breath would seem ridiculous.

And yet, for well over a hundred years, *thousands* of Italian Muslims fought in the armies of emperors outside the walls of Verona, Ravenna and Milan; entire regiments of Arab archers and horsemen played decisive roles in the endless wars between the medieval Italian city-states, as well as in the century-long feuds between emperors and popes. Muslim infantry and bowmen, of Sicilian descent, were stationed by their Christian rulers as far abroad as Romania and Tunisia, and even fought in the armies of a Papacy which (we will recall) had threatened excommunication to anyone who 'allied themselves with the infidel'.

The reason for the central presence of Muslim soldiers in the history of thirteenth-century Italy can be summed up in a single word: Lucera. Today a small town in the south-east of Italy, barely a hundred miles east of Rome, it was used by Frederick II in 1224 as a colony for the forced resettlement of over thirty thousand Sicilian Muslims. For the next eighty years they would remain there, a pocket of Islam in the

heart of Italy, barely three days' march from the Vatican. Frederick II
would be the first of many rulers who would make use of Lucera as
a pool of skilled soldiers and indispensable weapon-makers, a function
they would continue to have throughout the countless wars and crusades
of the thirteenth century until the eventual destruction of the colony
(and the murder and enslavement of its Muslim inhabitants) in 1300.
In many ways, our story of Muslim soldiers in the Italian thirteenth
century will be the story of Lucera – and of the emperor who founded
it, the puzzling, enigmatic figure of Frederick II.

Before we begin, however, a couple of difficulties have to be
anticipated for the modern-day reader. First of all, if we are to
understand the strange story of Italy's Muslim soldiers, we will have
to remind ourselves how differently people thought about their identities
eight hundred years ago. In modern history, we have grown so used
to using collective terms such as 'the French' or 'the Germans' – 'the
English won this battle' or 'the Italians took this city' – that it has
become almost impossible for us to imagine a time when these terms
did not exist. The world of 1200, however, is one such epoch: it is a
world where Norman rulers spoke Greek, where German-Latin
emperors spoke Arabic, where English monarchs negotiated in French
and Latin and where French kings of southern Italian realms fought
against alliances of Spaniards, Tuscans, south German princes and
Tunisian emirs.[1] People did not see themselves as 'Italian' or 'French',
but rather as belonging to the city of Parma or Palermo, as being the
subject of a Hohenstaufen or an Angevin. In itself, the bewilderingly
cosmopolitan world of medieval aristocracy is enough to confuse
anyone: Bohemian nobles marrying English princesses, Hungarian
kings wedding French queens, Greek-Byzantine daughters becoming
the wives of Swabian dukes (not to mention Mongolian khans and
Turkish sultans) . . . if we are to grasp any of this, our modern idea
of the 'nation' has to be left at the door. Those little coloured shapes
we divide our map of Europe into simply have no place in the story
I am going to tell.

A second difficulty today's reader will face in our trip through the
Italian thirteenth century has to do with the question of authority.
The events I am going to relate will be easier to understand if a simple
fact is kept in mind: the tension between the Papacy and the emperor.
The Pope had no real armies or navies of his own. Sometimes, when
things got too dangerous, he did not even have a city of his own –
on more than one occasion, a Pope had to leave Rome and stay in

exile outside the city walls because a hostile army had entered it. What the popes did have, however, was enormous symbolic power. They were able to contract and oblige kings to send fleets of ships and entire regiments of infantry to help them, often in exchange for the title of a kingdom or princedom the Pope was willing to approve. For example, if the English king Henry III had been able to afford the credit, he could have bought the throne of Sicily for his son from the Pope for 140,000 marks and an army of nine thousand men.[2] The Pope did this whenever the ruler of a region grew unsympathetic and needed to be unseated. The unhappy relationship between Rome and the dynasty of Frederick II, needless to say, is one such example. Little love was lost between the two parties. The Papacy called Frederick a 'baptised Sultan' because of the Saracens in his armies; Frederick, in turn, described the armies of the Pope as 'a rabble of louts and criminals'.[3] This antagonism between Frederick and Rome is important not just because it drives the engine of our story, but also because of Frederick's stature as Holy Roman Emperor; the Hohenstaufen dynasty Frederick represented was no tinpot dictatorship, but the rulers of a realm already four centuries old (it would last another four), whose carpet of German and Italian kingdoms stretched from Prussia and the Baltic Sea to Sicily and Jerusalem. Exactly who had authority over whom was always a sensitive point. The Pope and his followers liked to see the emperor as the worldly representative of God's power, a kind of temporal assistant to the Pope's superior spiritual authority; the followers of the emperor, on the other hand, saw their ruler as divinely appointed, with the Papacy providing a secondary, spiritual guidance. The disagreement would never really be resolved. And yet in order to understand how three thousand Sicilian Arabs were able to lay siege to the city of Parma on behalf of a Christian emperor, it is a tension the reader must not forget.

Muslim Sicily before Frederick II

Muslims had already been living in Sicily a good four hundred years before Frederick II came to the throne. Given that our story deals with the Muslims of Sicily, it might be worth a few words to explain how Islam came to Italy – and also how it departed.

Ironically enough, the Arabs invaded Sicily in 827 as they had done with Spain a century earlier – at the invitation of its residents, in this case a disgruntled Byzantine governor by the name of Euphemius who had led a revolt.[4] The Byzantine emperor had threatened to cut his nose off and, reasonably enough, Euphemius decided to do a deal across the water with the Tunisian emir instead. The island the Arab invaders found was populated almost completely by Greek Christians and Jews – none of the Latin speakers we now call 'Italians' were to arrive for another two hundred years – and by 902 it was completely under Arab dominion. For the next hundred and fifty years, until the second set of invaders came, Sicily absorbed the culture of Muslim North Africa into its language, architecture and demographics. An Islamic presence in Palermo certainly had an effect on the Italian mainland. It is a curious fact that, although most of us know Rome was sacked at some point in the past by Goths and Vandals, surprisingly few people are aware that a Muslim army actually reached the city of Rome in 846, burning down the basilica of St Peter's and causing Pope Leo IV to build the walls of what we now know to be the Vatican.[5]

The next invasion, in 1061, came from a completely different direction. Five years before their invasion of a cold, rather wet island off the coast of France, the Normans decided upon the conquest of Sicily, a project which took the better part of thirty years to complete. For our own investigations, it is a time which offers the first Muslim-Christian alliances in this chapter; when the Normans arrived in Sicily, they were delighted to find the island's three Arab emirs bitterly quarrelling with one another. Forming an alliance with Prince Ibn ath-Thimnah of Palermo, they went on to capture city after city until, by 1091, they controlled the entire island. As early as 1076, we find Saracen archers already included in the lists of Robert of Guiscard's armies. By 1098, the armies Count Roger was leading across the Messina straits to fight the Byzantines in Calabria were composed mostly of Muslims. From 1130 Roger II used Saracen footsoldiers in his Royal Guard, and by 1174 we even find Saracens participating in the Norman assault on their fellow Arabs in Alexandria.[6]

Unlike its English counterpart, the Norman conquest of Sicily lasted little over a hundred years. Frederick II would be born at the very end of it, barely four years after the death of the very last Norman king. Sicily was where the boy-king would spend his childhood, and certainly where he would learn his Arabic, the Arabic he would later impress his Muslim negotiators with in Jerusalem. The Sicily Frederick inherited, in other words, came with a legacy of Greco-Norman-Arab culture. It seems fair to ask: what were Muslim-Christian relations like under the Normans? How did Greeks, Muslims and Jews live together under Christian administration?

To give the positive side first: the Norman conquerors of Sicily were more interested in control and regulation than conversion and assimilation. One of the first things English schoolchildren learn about the Norman conquest of England is how the French simply took over and adopted many of the existing Anglo-Saxon traditions, and to a large extent Sicily tells a similar story. Tourists today can see, in the Palatine Chapel at Palermo, trilingual inscriptions in Latin, Greek and Arabic engraved into the stone – the three official languages of the court in the time of Roger II. The Norman kings of Sicily were famous for filling their courts with Muslim thinkers, poets and historians. There is room for cynicism here – as the historian Abulafia points out, many second-rate poets from North Africa who couldn't earn a living from their Arab rulers fled to Sicily to compose flattering verses in Arabic to King Roger, who probably didn't understand a word they were saying.[7] Highly respected thinkers and artists from the Muslim world were also present, however – most notably al-Idrisi (d. 1166), one of the most famous geographers of the Middle Ages. He constructed a legendary silver planisphere for the king (now lost), an enormous, 70-section map of the world (which a German scholar pieced together and published in the 1930s) and a classic work of medieval geography with the wonderfully brief title *The Pleasure Excursion of One Who Is Eager to Traverse the Regions of the World*, shortened by later generations to *The Book of Roger* (*Kitab Rujar*). Al-Idrisi also has the ambiguous distinction of being the first Muslim geographer (though by no means the first Muslim) to have set foot in England, whose southern shores he reputedly visited at some time in the 1120s.

The strong presence of Muslim intellectuals in the Norman courts gives a good idea of how significant a force Muslims still were in Norman Sicily, even under foreign domination. Their culture influenced the churches the Normans built, sending sweeping curves into their arches and planting Oriental domes on top of their chapels. Their language absorbed itself into the other languages of the island, so that even today about two hundred Arabic loan-words still exist in the Italian dialect. One of the Norman kings, William II, could even read and write in Arabic. When the Normans first arrived, Sicily had about a quarter of a million Muslims on its soil, with again as many Greeks living alongside them.[8] When the Arab traveller Ibn Jubayr visits Sicily in 1184, he records his admiration at the magnificent palaces of Muslim notables living in Palermo. A little less charitably, he also writes how much the Christian women of Sicily resemble their Muslim sisters – they wear veils and never stop talking.[9]

Ibn Jubayr, on his visit to Palermo, remarks on how Muslims live in different quarters of the city from Christians. Every Muslim civil servant he talks to expresses fear and a desire to go back to North Africa and live in a Muslim country once again. As time went on, Muslims in Norman Sicily acquired more and more the status of chattels. Muslims living and working on Christian lands were increasingly included in the property lists of the estate. A kind of slave-class was being created, one which would fuel the Sicilian *intifada* which was to happen from the 1190s onwards. For all the harmony and co-habitation the multi-faith court of Roger II conveyed, many Sicilian Muslims were uncomfortably aware that the end of Islam in Sicily was approaching. Latin settlers from the Italian mainland – traders and farmers from cities as far as Bologna, Florence and Milan – were beginning to stream into Sicily. What the twelfth century saw, above all else, was the gradual Latinisation of the island, whose consequences were as permanent for Sicily's Greek-speakers as they were for its Muslims. After the 1150s, the Normans began to lose their pragmatic tolerance and instead encouraged conversion to Christianity. Organised massacres of Muslims (and of some Greeks) by the new settlers took place in the 1160s. Even the tolerant Roger II, in his old age, reversed his policies and began to plan for a Christianisation of the island. It says a great deal about the greater cultural similarity between Sicilian Muslims and Greeks that when faced with forced conversion, Muslims opted for the Greek Orthodox faith rather than the Catholic Church. In the 1180s we find a new generation of 'Christian' farmers with names such as Philippos, but whose fathers had been called 'Mohammed' or 'Ahmad'.[10] In this way, through the time-honoured traditions of massacre, conversion and forced emigration, the Muslim population of Sicily in the twelfth century was reduced by 80 per cent.

The character of Frederick II

Frederick II was born at the very end of that Norman century, and in many ways his reign would inherit all of its ambiguities with regard to Islam – multiculturalism and military repression, the admiration of

Islamic arts and philosophy going hand in hand with the rigid control of Muslims themselves. Many historians have already commented on the irony that the man responsible for the eradication of Islam in Sicily was one of its most sincere and outspoken admirers. This is a man who complained to Egyptian sultans about the low birth of the Pope, and yet who was able to kick a Muslim rebel to death with his spurs; a man whose scholarly work reveals an intimate knowledge of Arab philosophy, and yet who was capable of the most brutal treatment and deportation of Muslims in his own realm. A man some thinkers in the Muslim world respected so much they called him *al-anbaratur* ('the Emperor'), and whom some Christians hated so much they called him 'the Sultan of Lucera' – and yet who, acting as champion of the Pope, won back Jerusalem for the crusades almost single-handedly and without any bloodshed.

Five hundred years after Frederick's death, in 1781, the keepers of the Cathedral of Palermo opened the emperor's tomb in the vaults of the church. What they found was astonishing: the skeleton of the medieval German emperor was wrapped in Oriental silk robes, with Arabic letters proclaiming his title embroidered along its hem, and a Saracen's sword clasped in one bony hand.[11] The scene provides the perfect image for Frederick's legacy – Luther hated him, whereas Nietzsche was inspired by his 'peace and friendship with Islam' and considered him one of Germany's greatest 'free spirits'.[12] As we shall see, the history of Italy's Muslims and the endless wars they fought is intertwined in the strange story of the Hohenstaufen dynasty and Sicily's own 'Sultan'.

Everything in Frederick's life seems to have taken place with a rush. He was born just as the Norman legacy of Sicily was dissolving into a war between Sicilian Muslims, Genoan forces, German captains and the armies of the Pope. His father died when he was three, and even as an infant he was plunged into factional politics: at the age of four he was crowned king of Sicily, and at the age of seven he was kept in Palermo for a year as a virtual prisoner by an anti-Papal oligarchy trying to use him for their own ends. He married his first wife at the age of fourteen – a twenty-four-year-old Spanish princess, Constance of Aragon, chosen for him by the Pope – and sired his first son at sixteen, a boy called Henry whom Frederick would one day have to fight a battle against and imprison, keeping him in a jail in Calabria until his early death.

At the beginning, Rome's relations with the young Frederick had been completely different. Pope Honorius III had agreed to act as ward

of the fatherless infant, and had energetically supported his claim as
emperor, eventually crowning him with the title in Rome in 1220. At
the age of twenty-six, Frederick was emperor of the Holy Roman Empire,
ruler of a vast, medieval machine which commanded the allegiance of
northern German princes and southern Italian barons. Today it is difficult
to imagine how two countries so different, separated by a mountain
chain, a language and a good five degrees in climate, could belong to
one entity. For Frederick, however, it was an intimate co-existence:
decisions made in Frankfurt and Swabia could have enormous influence
on faraway cities such as Naples and Palermo. This was Frederick's
imperial dream: to possess a German-Latin empire which would stretch
from the sands of the Mediterranean to the cold shores of the Baltic.
Frederick was a Hohenstaufen – both his father and his grandfather
had been great crusaders, and when the Pope crowned him, he made
sure Frederick pledged a crusade to the Holy Land as a condition of
his title. One wonders that day, as he placed the crown onto Frederick's
head, if the Pope had any idea how hated the name of 'Hohenstaufen'
would become. When, many years later, the last of Frederick's line was
murdered in battle and his grandchildren incarcerated, Pope Clement
IV would give public thanks to God.

We have no way of knowing what Frederick II was really like as a
person – or rather, we know as much as we can know about any
medieval personality. All we have is parchment: either the scribbled
impressions of people who knew him, who hated or loved him, and
of course the things he wrote himself – a handful of official letters
and the famous book on falconry he composed while laying siege to
the Italian city of Faenza. If praise from a hostile commentator can
be said to mean anything, then we know Frederick had a sharp,
unforgiving sense of humour: the medieval chronicler Salimbene, who
abhorred the entire Hohenstaufen clan, writes of how the emperor
would do imitations of ambassadors before they arrived, mocking
their entrances and pretentious addresses. He was a man who could
take a joke – allowing his jesters, our chronicler tells us, to mock him
in a way other rulers would never have tolerated – and would often
make ironic quips using quotes from the Bible, or even entertain
himself by trying to find irreligious passages in the Holy Book.[13] As
we shall see, these charges of scepticism and even atheism against
Frederick II will come up again and again.

Our chronicler mentions two other aspects of Frederick's personality
which do seem to be partly corroborated by other sources: cruelty

and curiosity. There is senseless cruelty – cutting off a notary's thumb because he misspelt Frederick's name, or sending a famous swimmer into the sea off Faro again and again to retrieve a golden cup the emperor kept throwing back in, until he finally drowned. But there are also tales of strange experiments. In one, he fed two men a good meal, and then sent one to bed, and the other out to hunt. Later that evening, he had them both disembowelled to find out which man had best digested his food. In another tale, the emperor apparently kept a number of baby infants in a secluded room and ordered none of their nurses to speak to them, in order to find out what language a child would naturally speak if it never heard its mother's tongue – Hebrew, Arabic, Greek or Latin. The infants all died after a few months, however, so the experiment was pointless.[14]

Of course, such tales may simply be morbid fantasies, spun by the supporters of the Pope in response to the very real respect and curiosity he sometimes showed towards the non-Christian world. This is not to idealise Frederick, but simply to acknowledge an awareness he seemed to have that pagans could have very different beliefs, and that a conventional Christian response to those beliefs was not always the best one. In the 1220s, for instance, when the Jews of Germany were accused of murdering Christian children, Frederick had no hesitation in coming to their defence, declaring he could find no evidence for the accusations, as the law of their own Talmud forbade it.[15]

The interest Frederick showed in Islam, and the court of thinkers he surrounded himself with, is often given as an example of this curiosity. It should be stressed, first of all, that Frederick did not have nearly as many Muslim thinkers around him as the Norman kings a century earlier; what he did have, however, was Arabic-speaking Christians and Jews who had been educated in the great centres of Muslim learning. There was Michael Scot (d. 1235), a Scottish bishop who had studied Arabic and Hebrew in Toledo and was a central figure in the translation of Aristotle and Arab philosophy into the Latin of the West; and Theodore of Antioch, a man of enormous intellect who had studied at the renowned Arab academies of Mosul and Baghdad and was responsible for drafting Frederick's many letters to the Arab world.[16] There was also the Muslim scholar Ibn al-Jawzi, who accompanied Frederick on his crusades and gave him private lessons in logic. Probably the most curious thing Frederick did – which sets him apart from his medieval contemporaries – was issue a set of questions to the Islamic world, in the hope of finding fresh answers to some abiding problems. The questions were sent to the Arab rulers of each land, with the request that some thinker from their own kingdom might be able to furnish a reply. Although four of the questions are philosophical – 'Has the world always existed?' and 'What proof can we find for the immortality of the soul?' – the last one is intriguing. Frederick wanted an explanation of the Islamic *hadith* or holy proverb: 'The heart of the believer is between the two fingers of God'.[17]

It is difficult to imagine a pious Christian monarch like King Louis IX asking such a set of questions, let alone expecting the Muslim infidel to provide him with the answers. Of course, Frederick was no paradigm of 'multicultural' tolerance – he ordered the execution of many Muslims, banned the building of synagogues and even implemented special clothing to be worn by Jews; and yet the questions he puts to the Muslim world – indeed, the fact that he puts them to the Muslim world at all – do offer an interesting glimpse into an otherwise enigmatic character. When, at the beginning of the thirteenth century, the heretical Cathars rebel in the south of France, it is not surprising that the figure they turn to for assistance is Frederick II – the 'Sultan' of Lucera.[18]

The Sicilian rebellion and the founding of the colony (1220–7)

And so, by the time the twenty-six-year-old emperor accepted his imperial title from the Pope that cold November day in 1220, he had little reason to feel complacent. The very man who crowned him was already suspicious of his imperial designs – by November it was common knowledge that Frederick's son had been elected by the northern German princes that April, adding to the impression of a family dynasty bent on European domination. Moreover, half of Frederick's own realm was in revolt; in Sicily, the Muslim population had begun to stage a full-scale resistance to the pogroms and injustices inflicted upon it. It chose to relocate and regroup itself in concentrated areas. By 1220, most Sicilian Arabs were to be found in the west of the island, where towns such as Iato and Entella operated almost as independent states. In Agrigento, Muslims prevented the Christians from performing religious ceremonies, and even held the local bishop hostage for over a year.[19]

The year of Frederick's coronation, 1220, was certainly eventful. In England, a humbled king had returned to fighting his barons barely five years after signing the Magna Carta. It was a year when two great cathedrals were begun (Salisbury and Notre Dame), when a great thinker was born (Roger Bacon) and two great poets died (the German lyricist Eschenbach and the Persian poet Attar). Across the water from Sicily in the Egyptian town of Damietta, a floundering crusader army was about to be sent back to Christendom on terms more generous than they deserved; and a forty-year-old preacher called Francis of Assisi, who had been travelling with them, managed to obtain an audience with the Egyptian sultan (whom we will meet again) and impress – though not convert – him with his fervour.[20]

The year 1220, however, was also the beginning of a great project: that of the complete de-Islamification of Sicily, the removal of every Muslim man, woman and child from the island. It began with Frederick's ruthless repression of the Sicilian uprising. A man called Ibn Abbad had begun to operate a region of self-rule in the rocky hills of central and western Sicily, even to the point of minting his own coins. The emperor was enraged, particularly since it was his own coinage that had been melted down to produce the new Muslim currency. Sometime around 1222, Frederick personally led an enormous imperial army up to the walls of Ibn Abbad's stronghold, the town of Iato. The size of the infantry alone was estimated to be sixty thousand men, although (as the historian Taylor points out) this is clearly an exaggeration. The strength of the resistance was such that, notwithstanding the size of the army, the siege lasted two months, culminating in a fierce assault.

As the story goes, the fighting was so heavy in the first weeks of the assault that Ibn Abbad's men sent a messenger to their leader, saying the size of the enemy's army was simply overwhelming. Ibn Abbad was amazed. He refused to believe the reports, and demanded to hear this from the men themselves. And so the messenger returned with the soldiers, who dutifully repeated the news the messenger had said: that the fighting was fierce, that the emperor's army was enormous, that some of the men were beginning to desert. Ibn Abbad listened carefully, sent the soldiers back to their lines and then, once they had gone, killed the messenger. When news of this reached the battlements, Ibn Abbad's men decided to visit the camp of the emperor and offer him a way into the town.

When the town's local judge – the *qadi* – heard of what was happening, he ran over to Ibn Abbad that night and told him to surrender, unconditionally, in order to avoid the town's destruction.

Ibn Abbad refused, out of pride, but a few hours later appears to have had a change of mind. At the break of dawn he set out, escorted by the *qadi*, for the tent of Frederick II, to offer his surrender. We do not know what exactly was said, only that the emperor kicked the rebel leader so badly that his entire side was gashed open. He was taken to Palermo and, despite pleas for mercy, executed a week later. His sons were dragged to death behind horses.[21]

Iato was the beginning of the end. It was not the end of the rebellion, which would last another twenty years, but it initiated the event around which our story takes place – the founding of a brand-new Muslim colony at Lucera, with its own Shari'a law, mosques and local *qadi*, in the very middle of a Christian realm, a hundred and fifty miles down the road from the Pope. It would be the equivalent of relocating thirty thousand people on foot from London to Newcastle, or from Munich to Hanover. According to the first records, the deportations began in 1223, and continued into the middle of the 1240s, until the last Sicilian Muslims had been rounded up and sent off to the distant colony, never to return. A form of Arabic would continue to be spoken on the island for another two hundred years, principally by North African Jews who had been invited to settle in Sicily by Frederick. The departure of Muslims from Sicily had a disastrous effect on the island's agriculture, as Muslims had proved themselves to be extremely skilled and knowledgeable in the cultivation of the land – a knowledge which now, of course, had been moved elsewhere. Rather cleverly, Frederick brought in Jewish landowners from the African coast to address the problem without having to re-introduce any Arabs into the island. By 1243 – at least as far as Muslim Arabs were concerned – Sicily had been 'ethnically cleansed'.

It is difficult to know what to make of the deportations. On the one hand, they were certainly ruthless, systematic and took place against a background of violence, repression and, as we have seen, massacres. We simply have no way of knowing how many thousands of Muslims were murdered in Sicily in this period. It was also extremely useful for Frederick to have a pocket of Islam, a colony of 'Saracens', right there in the middle of Christendom, utterly dependent on him. As we shall see, the new Muslim town of Lucera would provide the emperor with a royal bodyguard, an elite corps and thousands of skilled archers and light cavalry, Muslim soldiers which would be used not just by Frederick but also in the Christian armies of his Hohenstaufen and Angevin successors. The deliberate isolation of the place – hundreds of miles away from any other Muslim border – along with the strict travel controls imposed on its inhabitants, seems to underline this strategic purpose.

On the other hand, historians have pointed out how the founding of Muslim Lucera, while remarkable, is not without precedent; the Normans often deported rebels from one end of Sicily to the Italian mainland, and in earlier times the Byzantines had resettled countless communities of Bulgarians, Albanians and even Armenians in the Apulia of southeast Italy.[22] What is more striking, however, is the level of autonomy Frederick allowed the Muslims in their new town, and the rigour with which it was protected. The emperor made careful arrangements with local nobles and the churches in the area, allowing the purchase of houses and land for the settlers. Almost immediately, some of the wealthier Muslims began to lease or buy land from their Christian neighbours – a few even owned second and third houses in the nearby cities of Foggia and Troiano.[23] Whenever conflicts arose between Christians and Muslims over land disputes, Christians who attempted to impede Muslims from lawfully using their land were ordered to leave them in peace. For their own internal affairs, Muslims had their own courts and their own *qadi* or judge, in whose jurisdictions there are no records of any Christian intervening.[24] An Egyptian ambassador who visited Lucera in the 1250s was surprised to find Islam practised publicly in the town, and Muslims occupying prominent places in the royal palace.[25] Lucera truly was a 'Little Islam' in the middle of Italy, and word quickly spread around the Muslim world that the Christians had allowed a province of Islam to be created in the heart of their realms.

Lucera remained a Muslim town for around eighty years, until Charles II ordered its sudden destruction in 1300. Of course, Lucera had been a Christian town before the Muslims arrived; Frederick had first passed through the town in 1221, two years earlier, and it was probably then that he first had the idea of it as a future Muslim colony. When Muslims began to arrive in greater and greater numbers, many of the local Christians left to re-settle in the surrounding area. Frederick personally ordered the local bishop to leave. The main cathedral of Lucera was left in a gradually worsening condition. Records show, some time after the Muslims came to the city, that the church bells were taken down and stored inside the castle.[26] A number of Lucera's Christians remained, however, and it is not an exaggeration to say some sense of unity and co-operation developed. The most important proof of this is the way the town's inhabitants, Christian and Muslim, fiercely resisted the army of Charles d'Anjou in his siege of the town in 1269. When Charles finally captures the city, both Christian and Muslim fighters are executed in their thousands.

Other clues to how Christians and Muslims lived together in Lucera can be found in daily life. The Muslim colonists probably spoke better Italian than they did Arabic, although both languages were in use. Muslim officials can be found quite high up in the town's administration – a Muslim soldier with the Christian name of Riccardo, for example, was captain of the city, and some Muslims were even asked to convene as witnesses in Christian court cases.[27] Although the eating of pork is forbidden in Islam, there is evidence that Muslims raised pigs in Lucera, which means they probably ate them alongside their Christian neighbours; we certainly know that they made and consumed wine, as both Christians and Muslims had wine shops in Lucera's castle.

There was also friction, however. In order to build more houses, Muslims occasionally used materials taken from disused churches which had been abandoned by the Christian population. When Pope Gregory heard of this, he was furious: 'They are building schools for the sons of Hagar from the stones of Zion'.[28] As this appears to have happened on more than one occasion, the issue developed into a long-standing row between emperor and Pope. Frederick himself, in order to build the royal palace of Lucera, had demolished some buildings in nearby Barletta which belonged to the Knights of the Templars, an order of crusaders he was forever at odds with.

The question remains: what did the Muslim inhabitants of Lucera think of the Christian rulers they fought for – Frederick and the kings who came after him? It remains almost impossible to say. The city the Muslims of Sicily were given, at the end of a long and weary journey, was neither a Promised Land nor a gulag. Together with Jews they were considered 'slaves of the court' (*servi camerae*), although to be fair this term was as protective as it was oppressive. Whatever we may think, it remains an amazing fact that, throughout the thirteenth century, Ramadan was openly celebrated on the streets of an Italian city so close to Rome. Both Frederick II and the Hohenstaufen rulers who briefly followed him certainly spent a great deal of time in Lucera; King Conrad died, we are told, surrounded by his Saracen bodyguards, and when King Manfred effectively declared war by killing a papal auxiliary, the first place he fled to was his 'Saracen palace' at Lucera. All of which suggests the Christian kings did not feel threatened by their Muslim subjects or see their town as hostile or alien. Lucera's Muslims were willing to fight for the Hohenstaufen, fiercely and sometimes over-enthusiastically, as far as the northern towns of Italy, and even on crusade against their own Muslim brothers (a contingent of Saracen soldiers would be among the troops Frederick took to the Holy Land in 1228). Of course, as a minority of thirty thousand in a country of probably two million Christians, it would not appear that they had much choice.

Frederick in the Holy Land (1228–9)

Apart from putting down the Sicilian uprisings and relocating Muslims to Lucera, Frederick II also had something else on his mind at this time – the promise he had made to the Pope to assist in a crusade on Egypt. The 1221 attack on the Egyptian town of Damietta had been a complete fiasco; riven with factions and quarrels from the very beginning, it had been led by a cardinal called Pelagius – a man widely described by historians, in a rare and refreshing moment of consensus, as 'pig-headed'. The Egyptians had simply sluiced water into the fields where the enormous army of crusaders had camped, effectively turning them into marshes; the captured Christians were sent packing on the boats they had come in, and were not even given the masts of their ships. They had been lucky to escape with their lives.

It was a crusade Frederick II should have accompanied – as he had promised to do at his coronation – and the thirty-year-old monarch still felt a public obligation to fulfil his vow. It should be remembered that, contrary to popular opinion, the presence of the crusaders in the Middle East was no brief spree, no month-long mission or trip to the Orient. Crusader states in the twelfth century were fairly permanent affairs. Jerusalem, for example, had been occupied by the Franks for very nearly a century – until the brilliant military leader Saladin, an Iraqi Kurd by origin, won back the town for Muslims in 1187. Well-established crusader states and principalities, administrated by Franks, ran all the way down the Syrian coast. It was to the daughter of one of these nobles, who held the title of King of Jerusalem (on paper, at least), that Frederick got married in 1227, his first wife having died some years earlier. The girl was called Isabella and was fifteen years old. Marrying her made Frederick implicit heir to the Kingdom of Jerusalem, a fact he was so happy about he stamped it on his coins. Isabella did not live to see her seventeenth birthday – she died in childbirth. For the rest of his life, her father would claim she was murdered.

The Egyptian sultan St Francis of Assisi had tried to convert was a man called al-Malik al-Kamil, a nephew of the great Saladin. A gifted tactician and a fair negotiator (with Christians, though not with his own relatives), he had been responsible for the routing of the crusaders from Damietta. The news of Frederick's marriage – and the implicit claim to Jerusalem which came with it – brought unease to the Muslim kingdoms. Al-Kamil had a lot to worry about: the Kurdish dynasty he belonged to was squeezed between the growing and ever-threatening power of the Franks in the West, and the terrifying threat of the Mongols in the East. To make matters worse, the huge crescent of land his dynasty controlled – stretching from upper Egypt, through Palestine, Syria and Iraq, to southern Turkey – had been divided by his father into three kingdoms, one for each of his sons, all of whom were now quarrelling with one another. Al-Kamil had been given Egypt, while his other two brothers (al-Mu'azzam and al-Ashraf) had been given Palestine, Syria and much of what we now call Iraq, but what in Arabic was known as *al-Jazeera* or Mesopotamia.[29]

Al-Kamil's relationship with his brother in Damascus was so bad that he began to court the idea of an alliance against him with Frederick, whom he saw as the most accessible face of the Christian West. The Egyptian sultan had already heard a great deal about Frederick and his 'Oriental' manners – the Muslim soldiers in his guard, his interest in Islam, his knowledge of Arabic, his quarrels with the Pope. In 1225 the sultan had sent one of his ablest ambassadors to Palermo, a man called Fakhr ad-Din.[30] He was a statesman who would eventually become a friend and confidante of Frederick, and a key envoy between the emperor and the sultan (the two men, for all their famous alliance, were never to meet). Although on opposing sides, and despite their obvious cultural differences, the German-Latin emperor and the Kurdish-Arab prince had one attitude in common: a wholly political approach to the city of Jerusalem, free of any religious symbolism or fervour. In 1226 the Holy City was in the hands of al-Kamil's brother, al-Mu'azzam, but this did not stop him rather cheekily offering it to Frederick in return for (as Nietzsche would later put it) 'peace and friendship'. Al-Kamil's animosity towards his brother, coupled with a fear of the Mongols and their enemies in the East, led him to see a Latin buffer state in Jerusalem as a temporarily preferable ally. Frederick, for his part, was encouraged; he had received the green light he'd been waiting for. In 1227 he prepared to set sail for the Holy Land, with dreams of winning back Jerusalem in his head. He had little idea of what was going to happen next.

A whole array of different forces – pilgrims, nobles and German mercenaries – began to stream into the southeast corner of Italy under Frederick's supervision, slowly collecting into one crusading force. The Fifth Crusade of 1221 had been so disastrous – a duke of Bavaria and even the Latin king of Jerusalem had been among those taken hostage – that many felt the Sixth Crusade simply had to succeed. As Frederick's Muslim soldiers were among the contingent that sailed with him, it is difficult not to wonder how they felt among their peers on such an apparently Christian venture. It was not the first time Sicilian Muslims had undertaken such campaigns, and it would certainly not be the last. They were going to wage war, alongside thousands of French- and German-speaking Christians, against their fellow believers. Did they see it in those terms? The questions are torturously difficult to answer. When the crusaders filed into the churches of Brindisi and Bari to pray for victory before they embarked, what did the Muslim soldiers do? Wait outside? Have a drink in a tavern somewhere? Were they perhaps in collective denial about the paradox of their actions? Or are we wrong to ask such questions, wrong to exaggerate what is nowadays the much-talked about role of 'Islam'? Perhaps the Italian-speaking, Sicilian-born, Hohenstaufen-serving 'Saracens' in Frederick's army simply saw their Muslim faith as just one peripheral aspect of their whole identity.

Whatever we may conclude, the crusade itself was running into problems. Just when the various armies were beginning to embark, disease struck. A form of cholera or typhoid appears to have swept through Apulia, delaying the armada's departure and killing many.[31] Frederick's crusade vow appeared to have been broken a second time as fever stalled his plans for several months. The newly elected Pope Gregory IX responded, quite simply, by excommunicating him. Frederick was amazed. He responded angrily by denouncing the current Pope and the curia. Things were soon to get much worse.

Excommunication, as the historian Abulafia drily points out, was a standard occupational hazard of any medieval emperor.[32] The Hohenstaufen's endless struggles with the Papacy had already involved numerous excommunications and reconciliations, and would bring many more in time to come. The act downgraded Frederick's campaign from a crusade to a mere imperial expedition. This would cause

problems when Frederick finally reached the Holy Land, as orders
such as the Templars would not be allowed to support him officially.
When Frederick finally marches through Palestine, the crusaders
already stationed there will have to travel a day's journey behind him.

The fleet of ships finally sets sail at the beginning of 1228, moving
along what are today the Greek and Turkish coasts. After an abrupt
stop in Cyprus, where he effectively collects ten years of tribute from
the unfortunate ruler by threatening to arrest him in the middle of a
banquet, the emperor with his flotilla of ships arrives in the Latin
kingdom of Acre on the Syrian/Palestinian coast. Although
excommunicated, the crusaders he finds there are happy to see him;
surviving on the coast only thanks to Venetian seapower, the arrival
even of Frederick's relatively modest sixty ships is a welcome sight.
It is in Acre that Frederick famously asks al-Kamil's ambassador who
their caliph is. Fakhr ad-Din replies, explaining how the Caliphate is
basically the descendant of Mohammed, a title passed down from
father to son. 'A fine idea,' agrees Frederick. 'What we do, instead,
when we choose our caliph,' he tells the astonished envoy, 'is take a
man from the gutter, with no relationship or blood-bond to the Messiah
at all, a man so ignorant he cannot even make himself understood.'[33]

Frederick had good reason to hate the new Pope. No sooner had
he left his kingdom to embark upon his crusade, than Gregory ordered
his armies to attack Frederick's realm. Forces sympathetic to the papal
cause, led surreally enough by Frederick's father-in-law, were beginning
to gather together for an assault. The Apulian barons in the southeast
of Italy were actively encouraged by the Pope to rebel. Gregory even
began to spread the lie that Frederick had died at sea – the Pope knew
this was an untruth, for he was being kept informed of the emperor's
progress on a regular basis. Even for an institution as Machiavellian
as that of the Papacy, to invade the territories of an absent crusader
was an extraordinary gesture, and one which made a number of
monarchs feel uneasy. It was a situation which must have made Frederick
wonder if he should not turn back immediately and defend his kingdom.

The developments which greeted him in Acre, too, reveal not
everything was proceeding as planned. Al-Kamil's brother, essentially
the reason why the sultan had invited Frederick into the Holy Land
in the first place, had died, rendering Frederick's services wholly
useless. Al-Kamil no longer needed a crusader army to fight against
a deceased sibling; Frederick's army of three thousand, now marching
towards Tyre, was (as one Arab chronicler put it) an embarrassment

to him. The Egyptian sultan had not necessarily acted in bad faith; the death of his brother, however, had completely wrong-footed him, and thanks to his own quick thinking and his dead brother's inexperienced and diplomatically inept heir (the poor boy was practically swept aside by his two uncles) al-Kamil suddenly found himself in charge of a whole stretch of land from Palestine to Damascus.[34] The invitation to Frederick had been an emergency call which, as it turned out, was no longer necessary.

Frederick did not give up. He had already invested so much energy in the crusade: the payment for the mercenaries, the disease, the difficult sea voyage, the excommunication . . . the emperor simply could not return to Italy empty-handed. Some historians have also suggested an element of megalomania in the emperor's thinking – he did, indeed, entertain fantasies about playing some apocalyptic role as *imparator mundi* in his conquest of Jerusalem. And so began one of the subtlest and most accomplished set of manoeuvres in his career: first of all, he embarked upon a charm offensive, sending the Bishop of Palermo to the sultan's court with a whole package of gifts, including his own horse and a jewelled saddle. He sent the sultan a message:

> You know that I am the mightiest king of the West. You have written to me about my coming; the Pope and the other kings of the West have crossed the shores of my lands and are already attacking my targets. If I now return empty-handed, I will lose face. This Jerusalem is the root of their faith and the goal of their pilgrimage; the Muslims have destroyed it and for them it has no further use. If the Sultan – may God protect him – were to decide, to lend me control of the city and with it the right to visit the other holy shrines, this would show his wisdom and I could hold my head high among my fellow rulers. If the Sultan wished, I would even be willing to renounce the tax revenues on this land, and hand them over to the Sultan's treasury.[35]

Then he waited. Unlike the pig-headed cardinal who refused to 'deal with the infidel', Frederick's subtlety lay in understanding the need for al-Kamil's honourable reputation as well as his own. The sultan could not simply hand over Jerusalem to the Franks; neither could he allow a Holy Roman emperor to wander around Palestine with his crusader army, particularly since it was an army which had come at his own invitation. Frederick's playing of the 'honour' card is a clever move, one which allows both parties to empathise with the other's needs, to understand the other's position. It was a gesture the obstinate cardinal, seven years earlier, had been unable to make.

Amazingly, a deal was done. Jerusalem would be handed over to the Christians for ten years, along with a strip of land leading to the sea, and a handful of carefully marked corridors to places such as Nazareth and Bethlehem (the complicated map depicting this is eerily similar to the complex contours and boundaries of today's Israeli-Palestine agreements). Muslims would be evacuated from the city, although they would still be allowed access to the Dome of the Rock – the mosque of Jerusalem and one of the holiest sites in the Muslim world. The Franks would under no circumstances be allowed to move outside their areas, nor rebuild the walls of the Holy City. Jerusalem was to remain defenceless. After ten years, five months and forty days (the maximum amount of time allowed by Islamic law for Muslim property to remain in non-Muslim possession), the city would be handed back to al-Kamil. Frederick signed the treaty, in the presence of the sultan's envoys as well as the bishops of Exeter and Winchester, one Sunday afternoon in February 1229. He later told his aide Fakhr ad-Din: 'If I didn't fear to lose face among my own people, I would never have bothered the sultan with any of this. For me, personally, neither Jerusalem nor anywhere else in Palestine is worth the trouble.'[36] The *imparator mundi* was sick of the whole business. Years after his adventure in the Promised Land, Frederick allegedly claimed to have found nothing in it more beautiful than his own lands of Apulia and Calabria.

Before he left the Holy Land, Frederick made one last request: a visit to Jerusalem, and a look inside the Mosque of al-Aqsa, the venerated Dome of the Rock. The sultan agreed, and arranged for a local *qadi* – the judge of the Palestinian town of Nablus – to give him a guided tour. The Arab reports of Frederick's visit are so interesting, and have become so legendary, that they are worth a re-telling. Arab witnesses who saw the emperor in person report a short, balding man with red hair who – in the classic phrase of one unsympathetic chronicler – 'would not have been worth twenty *dirhams* in a slave market'.[37] The impression Frederick gave his Muslim audience was that of being a 'materialist', one to whom 'Christianity was a game'. The *qadi* takes the emperor to the mosque and shows him inside; it was a building which had been captured from the Franks years earlier, and around its walls in Arabic was the inscription: SALADIN CLEANSED THIS HOLY CITY OF THE IDOLATERS (*mushrikin*).[38] The term *mushrikin* in Arabic does not simply mean 'idolater' or 'polytheist', but was also used as a derogatory reference for Christians. Frederick, having understood everything, mischievously asks the *qadi*: 'Who are these *mushrikin* then?' The *qadi* is too embarrassed to reply.

The show continues. Over by the doors of the mosque, wire netting is draped over the entrance. Frederick asks his guide what the nets are for. The *qadi* explains that the nets are used to keep birds out of the mosque. Frederick laughs: 'And now God has brought the pigs in!' By this time, one can only wonder what the *qadi* is thinking. Outside the mosque, by the door, the emperor finds a priest (it remains unclear whether it was an Arab or a Frankish Christian) handing out Bible passages on the steps. Frederick knocks the poor man to the ground, calls him a dog and threatens to kill him if he ever finds him near the mosque again.

On his first night in Jerusalem, al-Kamil had given orders that, out of respect, no prayers should be called from any minaret in the city while the Christian emperor was staying there. The *qadi*, however, forgot to tell the *muezzins* (the men who give the call to prayer out loud five times a day), and that night the sounds of the city's prayer-calls could be heard as normal while the emperor slept. Next day, the *qadi* rebuked his men, and told them to keep quiet the following night. On the second morning, however, we are told the emperor called in the *qadi*. 'Where is the man who yesterday gave the call to prayer?' asked Frederick. The *qadi* explained what the sultan had ordered him to do. 'If you visited my country,' the emperor told him, 'do you think I would order my church bells to be silenced for your sake?'. Chroniclers insist Frederick gave out money to the *muezzins* and keepers of the mosque after this, as an act of compensation.

The results of Frederick's bloodless crusade had a mixed reception back in European Christendom. Those who had unrealistically expected the emperor to win back the Holy Land for them were disappointed with what was, effectively, a ten-year lease. Most historians of the crusades wisely note the dramatic difference between the crazed, intolerant, unrealistic fervour of the Christians in their home countries, and the cannier, more pragmatic approaches of the crusaders who actually ended up spending years, in some cases entire lives, in uneasy co-existence with the Muslims they had gone to conquer. Not that the crusaders who took over administration of the newly ceded territory were entirely happy. Before leaving, Frederick, still angry at the Pope, handed over key positions not to any of the Church's orders – to the Templars or the Hospitallers – but to his own men, an act which sowed the seeds of a great deal of strife. Frederick tried in vain to act in Palestine as though he were in Palermo, and appeared unwilling or unable to realise the cold, hard truth: the Latin East was its own kingdom, with its own mini-history, even its own particular view of authority, and the Latin barons who had been in control of the Arab towns for well over a century saw Frederick's empire as a rather distant, abstract regime. Tension was mounting between the emperor and the crusader barons even as Frederick was making his way back to the coast. Rumours circulated that the Templars were planning to assassinate him, or that the emperor was about to kidnap the grandmaster of the Templars and take him back to Italy as hostage.[39] When Frederick finally boarded his ship in the harbour of Acre, ready to set sail for home, he was pelted with offal by a crowd of the town's butchers.

Frederick's achievement, for all its modesty, was remarkable in many ways: because it occurred without bloodshed, because it took place while his own lands were being attacked by the very Pope who had sent him, and because of the crucial role his own familiarity with the world of Islam played in his reception. Although this has been exaggerated – Frederick's Arabic was nowhere near as good as is claimed, nor was his court as replete with Muslim thinkers as the Norman courts of fifty years earlier – there is no doubt that the Hohenstaufen's cultural openness towards Muslim culture played a significant part in his successful negotiation with the Muslim world, and certainly in Frederick's deal with al-Kamil. The fact that Frederick had Muslim soldiers in his retinue did not go without notice – it was one of the first things Fakhr ad-Din had reported back to his sultan on his first visit to Frederick's court. Years later, when King Louis IX of France launched his own crusade on Egypt in 1249, rumour has it that Frederick sent a secret embassy (disguised as a merchant) to the Ayubbid rulers, warning them to prepare themselves as an attack from the French king was imminent. The fact that Arab historians were willing to report and believe this says a great deal about Frederick's own standing in the Muslim world.

And so Frederick departed from the Holy Land in 1229, leaving a Jerusalem full of quarrelling crusaders behind him. He would never go back, although what was to happen was predictable enough. The end of the ten years' peace brought a renewed attempt to keep hold of the city, but the crusaders, weakened by internal dissension, were overcome and the city was re-taken by Muslim forces in 1244, fifteen years after Frederick's departure. It would never be taken back. From a Western point of view, it is significant that one of the crusades' last successes – for this is what Frederick's result was – would be realised not through military strength or superior firepower, but simply by sitting, waiting and eventually talking.

Quarrelling with the pope: the campaign against the Lombard League (1230–50)

The next part of our story is complicated, and will require some energy and effort to absorb. It is a chronicle filled with endlessly quarrelling cities, over-ambitious merchants, a whole array of sieges and sackings and slaughters, all fuelled by regional rivalries centuries old. There are difficult, multi-faceted relationships to keep in mind, bonds between bishops and towns, between emperors and tyrants, between popes and distant monarchs, all of which were constantly mutating and developing according to the baroque mechanisms of power and the delicate machinery of shifting alliances.

The last twenty years of Frederick's reign (1230–50) would see a concerted war against the cities of northern Italy – embodied in an alliance called the Lombard League – and, as time went on, a Papacy which increasingly took their side against the emperor. The period is significant for us because in it we will see an unprecedented use of Muslim soldiers in Frederick's armies: the Saracens of Lucera. Military records, even taking into account their exaggerated numbers, tell us Frederick's Saracens were a *key* component in his campaign, a central factor in his operations. Their presence was recorded both in the emperor's own registers and also by his enemies. Seven thousand Muslims were said to have participated in the battle outside Mantua in 1237; in the sieges of Brescia and Parma, thousands of Muslim archers took part. At the decisive battle of Cortenuova, between seven and ten thousand Saracens are estimated to have been present. One chronicler records, in 1237, the despatching of over ten thousand Muslims to the city of Ravenna.[40]

Before we get too carried away, we should recall that Lucera had a Muslim population of about thirty thousand. The Lucera scholar Taylor suggests, instead of the regularly cited seven or ten thousand, perhaps two or three thousand Muslim soldiers is a more believable number. This is still a significant figure when one considers the relatively small size of the armies of the period – the King of England's forces at this time, for example, would not have had more than ten thousand men.[41] Reading the records of Frederick's enemies, we learn that the Saracens were a conspicuous force – all the more so because they brought elephants with them. The gossipy chronicler Salimbene records seeing elephants with wooden towers on top of them being used outside the walls of Cremona, and elephants were also a part of the siege tactics at Montechiari and Brescia. Frederick doubtless enjoyed making full use of the foreign and exotic to terrify the citizens of these towns; in his enemies' diatribes against him, the fact that he used 'the infidel Saracen' in his armies against them would become a standard refrain. For Pope Gregory, it was tantamount to forming an alliance with the devil.

When Frederick returned from his crusade in 1229, he was returning for many of his subjects from the dead. The entire sweep of his realm, from Foggia to Palermo, was in rebellion, convinced by Pope Gregory's rumours; the armies of his father-in-law (the father of the deceased Isabella) were already on the edges of southern Italy, encouraging the cities of Lazio to throw off their imperial yoke. Frederick's miraculous re-appearance did a lot to quell the revolts, as he had hoped. Intimidated, the Pope's armies retreated to Capua north of Naples, where (we are told) Frederick directed an army of several thousand Saracens against the enemy, and by the end of October the rebellion was crushed.[42] With some towns, Frederick showed little mercy – the city of Sora was razed to the ground, and its entire population, men, women and children, put to the sword as an example to others. Nevertheless, although the emperor could have marched on Rome and invaded the papal states, what Frederick wanted above all else was peace – peace and absolution. The Pope, with the emperor's victorious armies unchallenged and practically on his doorstep, was in no position to continue hostilities.

One September evening in 1230, a dinner is arranged for just three men, a meal any medieval historian would have given his right arm to attend: Pope Gregory, Frederick and an aristocrat-mediator (the German Hermann von Salza) sit down at the same table to dine and talk. Given the kinds of things the two men had already said about one another, it must have been a tense meeting. And yet the result is a happy one for the emperor: he is absolved, and allowed back into the folds of the church. At least, until the second time Pope Gregory excommunicates him, eight years later.[43]

Over the next five years, a number of separate developments begin to take place, events which will intertwine themselves as our story progresses. Lucera's Muslim population continues to rise – as that of Sicily continues to fall – with a steady stream of deportations arriving from Palermo. The Italian cities of the north, in particular Milan and Vicenza, begin to grow increasingly restless for independence from their German emperor, and a war starts to look increasingly likely. In a small hill town in the south of Italy, Frederick draws up a constitution re-worked from Roman and canon law, which some elements in Rome interpret as another affront to their authority. Frederick, clearly a busy man, somehow finds the time and energy to marry a third time, this time an Englishwoman, the sister of Henry III – a bride, once again, by the name of Isabella. Pope Gregory also begins to quarrel with Frederick over a variety of different things: the emperor is not protecting the church in Sicily diligently enough, he is allowing Muslims to damage churches and use their materials to build mosques, and he isn't doing enough to convert the Saracens he already has in his enclave at Lucera.[44] There is also the slightly bizarre case of the nephew of the Emir of Tunis, who flees his uncle in 1236 and takes refuge in the town of Lucera. Pope Gregory is somehow convinced the young man wants to convert to Christianity, and yet is being prevented by Frederick from coming to Rome to be baptised. Although Frederick continually denies this unlikely claim, it becomes a genuine source of tension. And finally, throughout all of this, far away in the north of France, a small boy is growing up in the region of Anjou; it is a boy Frederick will never meet – when he dies, the young man will be on crusade in Egypt, alongside his brother the King of France – and yet it is a child who, when he grows up, will be responsible for the imprisonment and execution of the emperor's offspring, and the ultimate extermination of the Hohenstaufen line.

The Lombard League – a name nowadays familiar because of the Italian politician Umberto Bossi, who used it to found a political party in the 1990s – was basically a group of medieval cities which allied themselves with one another in a bid for self-rule, independent of the Holy Roman Empire. They were cities run either by local aristocrats or by an elite merchant class, and their history is complicated to tell for many reasons. First of all, it was not always the same group of cities – some of them, such as Cremona, changed sides, while others, such as Ferrara, came over against the emperor when they were dismayed by Frederick's support of local tyrants such as the infamous despot of Verona, Ezzelino. Secondly, the relationships between the cities themselves were constantly shifting – the Pisans hated the Genoese, Cremona resented being bullied by Milan. Finally, even within the same cities pro-papal and pro-imperial factions were present, making the whole web of alliances even more complicated. For both Frederick and the Pope, the Lombard League was a kind of chessboard where, at least until 1238, they enacted a level of secret war against one another, supporting hostile elements here and electing antagonistic bishops there. The situation is of interest to us because the landscape of northern Italy will form the battleground for Frederick's Saracens throughout the last twenty years of his reign.

Frederick, we will remember, saw himself as the true and incontestable manifestation of divine rule. It is difficult not to stress this too much: those who revolted against the emperor were not, in his eyes, simply rebels but *heretics*. The ruthlessness he had shown towards Ibn Abbad, the Muslim he had kicked to near-death with his spurs, was the same inclemency he would show towards those Lombard cities unfortunate enough to fall to his armies. In the siege of Brescia, Frederick hanged hundreds of the city's captured inhabitants from the tops of the attacking siege towers, to prevent the defenders from smashing them down (the defenders replied in kind by hanging large numbers of Frederick's captured troops by their arms from the city's battlements, often dangling them in the way of his battering rams).[45] For Frederick, the war on the cities of the Lombard League was a virtual crusade; in his propaganda, he even painted it as the initial phase of a holy war which would go on to cleanse the whole world – a rhetorical trick, to be fair, used by several popes and emperors to sell their grudges as universal causes and their local wars as the beginnings of wider crusades against a sea of unbelief. Exactly how much religious zeal Frederick himself applied to the numerous battles and sieges he participated in during this time remains debatable – in the siege of Faenza, he spent the summer of 1240 correcting the Latin translation of an Arabic treatise on falconry, while some sources suggest an entire camp of his infantry was once sacked by the enemy because he had gone away on an afternoon's hunting.[46]

The last fifteen years of Frederick's reign – until his death in 1250 – would be taken up with endless numbers of such sieges, waiting encamped for months outside small Italian towns such as Faenza or Brescia, trying to break their resolve. That he employed Saracens in his armies was remarkable, but not wholly strange; a brief look at the composition of the emperor's military campaigns tells us he had mercenaries from south Germany, as well as whole contingents of volunteers from French and Spanish kingdoms, and some soldiers from Hungary and Latin-held Greece. In his campaign against Milan, there were even a hundred English knights in his service, not too surprising now that Frederick was married to the sister of the English king.[47]

The Muslim soldiers in his army were mostly archers. There were also some light cavalry, and a significant proportion of infantry, but it is as archers that the 'Saracens of Lucera' were infamous. Although they were fighting in a time when the crossbow was being introduced, most of Frederick's Muslim archers continued to use a 'composite bow' – basically a simple bow, strengthened with a second piece of wood or bone to give it greater power and distance. A thousand archers could produce a rain of arrows upon an enemy charge – the two or three thousand archers who helped Frederick take the castle of Montechiari (near Mantua, northern Italy) in 1236 would have produced one such shower of arrows more or less every minute. Military historians of the Middle Ages tell us how archers were used to break up spear-bristling squares of pikemen or *fanteria* and dissolve them into disorder, so that heavily armoured cavalry charges could be sent in against them.[48]

We see this in one of Frederick's most convincing victories, the battle of Cortenuova, which took place on 27 November 1237. On the edge of Lake Como, at the foot of the Alps, it is probably the farthest north a Muslim infantry ever fought on the Italian mainland. Even today, eight centuries later, it is remarkable to think that over three thousand Arabic-speaking Muslims, fighting not as mercenaries but as official subjects for their German emperor, would passionately take part in the civil wars of the Italian cities as far north as the cold plains of Lombardy. If the picture of Italian Muslims, in the epoch of Dante and Aquinas, fighting the soldiers of Milan and Bologna against the backdrop of the Italian Alps, seems so strange to our modern eyes, it is a consequence more than anything else of our own historical ignorance; the simplistic 'Christian Europe' we have all fallen so in love with, which gives us a tingle between the shoulder blades every time we visit a cathedral or listen to a fugue by Bach, has relied on the airbrushing out of any trace of Islam or Judaism from our great European tradition. Until this process is reversed, the idea of Arabs fighting for the cities of Cremona and Ferrara against the armies of Milan is always going to sound absurd.

At Cortenuova, the emperor's Muslim archers were to intervene significantly at the end of the battle, 'emptying their quiver' as Piero della Vigna, Frederick's most gifted propagandist, would later put it. Frederick had been stalking the rebel army of the Milanese for two days, following it carefully as it made its way along the other bank of the river Oglio. The Milanese simply had no idea he was shadowing them; towards late afternoon they started to cross the river. A small cavalry contingent of Frederick's larger force charged ahead and unexpectedly collided with them, gaining a considerable advantage with their surprise and driving the stunned Lombards back across the river. Full-scale battle followed as the Milanese took a spirited stand together around the wagon of their precious *carroccio*, the collection of saints' remains and holy relics which they always took with them into battle, the medieval Italian equivalent of a Roman standard. At first Frederick's troops were simply unable to break the fixed wall of spear and armour set against them. Only when the Saracen archers began to saturate the Milanese ranks with arrows did their resistance begin to break, and by the fall of evening they had suffered terrible losses. During the night most of the rebel army fled, so that in the morning, when Frederick's forces prepared themselves anew for another day of pitched battle, they arrived to find the camp completely deserted.

How did Frederick's Muslim troops get along with their fellow soldiers? What were relations like between Muslim and Christian in the Hohenstaufen armies? The paucity of records makes it difficult to say, although we do know that most Muslim companies were often commanded by Muslim captains, a practice which continued up until the end of the century. The fact that Muslim soldiers constituted the main body of Frederick's personal army – immediately after the battle of Cortenuova he took a small group of them with him on his way to Soncino – does suggest a semi-privileged status for some of them, although we should be wary of exaggerating this. We have at least one record of a dispute between Muslim and Christian soldiers – vaguely described, many years after Cortenuova, at the battle of Benevento (1266) – in the service of Frederick's son, Manfred. The Saracens, one source tells us, didn't fight in this battle with complete dedication (*non furono in fede*) because of a quarrel with some Christians the evening before.[49] The fact that such an event is remarked upon at all does suggest its infrequency; moreover, from Hohenstaufen sympathisers, there are also positive remarks upon how, in later years, the Saracens sacrificed their best men to the defence of the realm in the last pitched battles the Hohenstaufen fought: San Germano, Benevento and, of course, the final siege of Lucera itself.

What *is* remarked upon frequently is the lack of discipline among Frederick's Saracens. Sometimes they were too eager, too unorganised, sometimes they charged too quickly or didn't wait for the signal to attack. A good example of this is the heavy defeat the emperor suffered at the siege of Parma in 1248. Parma was a city which had been loyal to Frederick's cause, but a year earlier had suddenly decided to join the alliance of the Lombard League instead. As a consequence, it found Frederick's army camped outside its walls. On the morning of 18 February, Frederick took a large number of his German cavalry and a good half of his Cremonese infantry further up the river Po to block reinforcements for the besieged city; outside the city of Parma lay the attackers' camp of Vittoria, filled with (we are told) four thousand Saracen archers, but little infantry or cavalry. The defenders of Parma cleverly pretended to send out a large section of their forces on a sortie; the remaining German cavalry and Cremonese footsoldiers ran off in pursuit, leaving the camp practically defenceless. The Saracen archers swallowed the bait, too, believing Parma now to be completely without arms, and charged madly in, hoping to sack the rebel city and reap its spoils. Too late they discovered the trap: they were pounced upon by a whole set of soldiers lying in wait, not to mention the returning cavalry and a sea of angry inhabitants – men, women and children, we are told. The hasty Saracens were not only driven back, but the city's forces managed to penetrate the attackers' camp, laying it to waste. Archers' daggers and buckle-shields were no match for heavy cavalry and broadswords. Frederick's Muslims suffered appalling losses.

Undisciplined or not, the Saracens of Lucera featured in every battle Frederick fought. They became associated with his name, and gradually formed a key part not just in his campaigns, but also in the propaganda battle with the Pope which was to occupy the final decade of the emperor's life. Throughout the 1240s, we see an imperial regent who is militarily secure (by 1244 Frederick's armies even controlled Rome, causing the Pope to flee to France) but riven with uncertainty in political, diplomatic and economic terms. His protracted wars with the Italian city-states were costly; to finance them, he was forced to buy Venetian gold with endless ships of Sicilian grain. His diplomatic standing might also have been better. Acts such as hijacking a papal fleet filled with cardinals and bishops in 1241 – in today's terms, roughly analogous to kidnapping a conference hall full of ambassadors to the UN – gained Frederick little sympathy among the royal families of Europe, and only served to worsen his image as a tyrant of the church. And yet it was Frederick's association with 'Mohammedanism' – one can't help feeling – and the doubts this aroused concerning the integrity of his faith, that seems to have decided the emperor's guilt in the minds of many. The excommunications Pope Gregory and his successor, Pope Innocent IV, delivered to Frederick were couched in some of the most demeaning language a Pope was ever to use about a sovereign head of state. Frederick was called a sodomite, an atheist, someone who allegedly claimed that 'Jesus, Moses and Mohammed were all impostors'. He was accused of building an Oriental harem at Lucera – an accusation which, perhaps, had more validity, given the camels, elephants and leopards he was continually bringing there, as well as the African dancing slaves he kept for the palace's entertainment.[50] To be fair, neither had the emperor's extramarital activities entirely discouraged this reproof. However, although officially Frederick's excommunications had less to do with Lucera than infringements on papal authority (such as a claim to the island of Sardinia), it is difficult not to see the emperor's Muslim city, so close to Rome, as a continual provocation. The example of Muslim Lucera, with its *shari'a* law, its Muslim royal guard and its prayer calls (all a hundred and fifty miles down the road from the Vatican), contradicted the entire papal concept of crusade.

Frederick died on 13 December 1250 at the age of fifty-six; his end came suddenly and in the midst of a campaign which was, perhaps, beginning to turn in his favour. It is a sign of the hatred the Papacy nurtured for Frederick that they considered him, in all seriousness, the Antichrist. In this they followed the prophecies of an old Calabrian monk, Joachim of Fiore, and labelled him a true enemy of Christ, and a heralder of the End of the Age. To this day, the pseudo-apocalyptic echoes surrounding Frederick are curious to observe; years later, many of his subjects still appeared to believe he would return from the dead – even, according to one rumour, from the heart of Mount Etna, where his spirit was said to reside. A number of impostors claiming to be Frederick appeared in the years following his death, one of whom – sources tell – was captured by King Manfred and tortured horribly. Salimbene, our hostile chronicler, insists he himself couldn't believe it when he heard the reports that Frederick was dead – even though he

was standing right next to the Pope when he said it.[51] Supporters of
the Pope reported the stench of Frederick's corpse was so strong that
it could not be carried to Palermo to be buried with the other kings,
and that as soon as the emperor died a mass of worms swarmed out
of his rotting carcass – all testimony to the hatred he inspired in the
faithful of the church. Of course, we should not idealise Frederick II;
in the end, all things considered, he was a despot, even if a somewhat
unusual one. In the last year of his life, he imprisoned on suspicion
of treason his closest and most talented statesman, the rhetorical genius
Piero della Vigna, causing him to commit suicide, through self-mutilation,
in the solitude of his prison cell. Even if the alleged Antichrist outlived
a fair number of popes, it is ironic that the Papacy would ultimately
have the final, conclusive laugh: within twenty years of the emperor's
death, not a single legitimate heir to his dynasty would remain alive.

After Frederick: from Manfred to the battle of Benevento (1266)

What happened to the Hohenstaufens after Frederick's death? What
happened to Lucera and its Muslims? Who was responsible for the
end of Frederick's dynasty – indeed, for the end of the Holy Roman
Empire in Italy – and how was the Papacy so triumphantly involved?
In answering these questions, the scope of our investigations suddenly
broadens out, in a flash, to include the whole span of the Mediterranean
from Aragon to Asia Minor: the intrigues and plots of the Byzantine
Empire, a Papacy driven by the Mongol threat to dialogue with
Constantinople, the resentment of a disgruntled Spanish king, the
Christian sympathies of a Tunisian emir and a ruthlessly pious
nobleman from the Anjou of northern France. All of these elements
would somehow, over the next fifty years, blend together to bring
about the deliverance of Constantinople from a second Latin sacking,
the beginning of centuries of Spanish rule over southern Italy and,
last but not least, the effective end of Islam on Italian soil.

Muslim soldiers found themselves in the armies of most of the battles
from this period – occasionally, even, on both sides of the conflict.
Saracens helped the anti-papal Ghibellines keep hold of Siena in the
battle of Montaperti (1261), helped to conquer the city of San Germano
by secretly stealing into it and opening the main gates (1254), and died
in their thousands at the battle of Benevento (1266). Even after the

Hohenstaufen were vanquished by their French nemesis the Angevins, Saracens fought for their new rulers in the towns of Albania and Romania against the armies of the Byzantines, and also helped the Latins in central Greece, where they came up against Turkish mercenaries fighting for the Greek emperor Michael VIII. In Sicily and Calabria, Lucera's Muslims were regularly despatched as soldiers for the Vespers War (1282–1302), and, most interestingly of all, they would have represented Charles of Anjou's military presence in the crusade on Tunis (1271–2), bringing war under a Christian banner to the very shores from which their Muslim forefathers had come to Sicily, centuries earlier. I should add, and by now it cannot come as a surprise, that on the Muslim side the crusading armies would have found among the enemy a good number of Christian soldiers belonging to Frederick of Castile.[52] Christians and Muslims, once again, lined up against Christians and Muslims.

Manfred, Frederick's illegitimate son, was the last Italian ruler to employ significant numbers of Muslims in his service. In many ways he carried on the traditions of his father – not just the keeping of a Saracen bodyguard, the retention of an 'Oriental' palace at Lucera or a fondness for hunting, but also a series of more substantial continuities: a cultivation of Islamic thought (the Arabic commentaries of Aristotle were translated by the scholar Hermann into Latin at his court) and solid relations with the Muslim world (the Egyptian Mameluks' ambassador was received with full honours in 1261, staying on in Apulia for a number of months as a pampered guest – the king even received a giraffe from Sultan Baybars as a sign of good will).[53] The report of the ambassador, in fact, offers an interesting – though probably exaggerated – view of Manfred's court:

> I went as ambassador to Manfred from the Sultan in ramadan 659/August 1261, and was entertained by him in the highest honour in a city called Barletta in Apulia, which is in the Long Country [Italy], next to Spain. Near the town where he lived was a city called Lucera, whose inhabitants were all Muslims from the island of Sicily; they hold public prayer there on a Friday ... most of [Manfred's] officials and courtiers were Muslims, and in his camp the call to prayer, and even the canonic prayers themselves, were openly heard.[54]

Of course, Manfred also kept another tradition of the Hohenstaufen alive: a barely suppressed (and carefully reciprocated) antagonism towards the Pope.

Manfred came to the throne in 1254, after the brief reign of one of Frederick's legitimate heirs, King Conrad. Although Conrad actually had a son (more of which later), Manfred took the opportunity – based on rumours of the little boy's death – to usurp the throne, ultimately crowning himself King of Sicily in 1257. It was a crown the Papacy never accepted, and for the next decade they would dedicate their energies to removing it from him.

At first, things seemed to be quite different. Pope Innocent IV, in the last year of his life, appeared to make friendly overtures to Manfred, the twenty-two-year-old monarch. He was given the title Prince of Taranto, and was even made vicar of the mainland's southern provinces. When the Pope came to meet him in September 1254, Manfred walked out to meet him halfway across the river Garigliano, leading the Pope's horse ahead as he talked to him.[55] But the handsome young ruler and the elderly pontiff had ultimately incompatible aims; not two months would pass before the peace broke down. In unknown circumstances – reportedly a roadside skirmish – Manfred killed a papal aide, and immediately fled to the palace of his trustworthy Saracens at Lucera, who opened the gates for him and swore their loyalty to the new monarch. The move was irreversible; Manfred was excommunicated in 1255, and war came rumbling once again to the cities and hill towns of Italy. Throughout the lands of Europe, Lucera's name was heard as 'crusading' tithes were requested in an effort to finance a campaign against Manfred; in England, the only thing which persuaded the kingdom of Henry III to contribute was the rumour that the campaign would be waged against a fortress of Mohammedans who had somehow made their nest on Christian soil.

Finances were gathered, mercenaries were hired, an army was formed. The Hohenstaufen and their Saracen allies would be exterminated for good. In late 1255 a Roman cardinal led an enormous army of over fifty thousand men on Lucera, winding through the valleys of Campania and Lazio. It was a papal expedition which ended in absolute failure; double-agents in the Pope's army kept Manfred informed of the campaign's movements, allowing him to cut off supply lines and practically starve the enemy into surrender. A humbled cardinal had to sign a peace treaty with Manfred, which his superior immediately declared invalid. It was a humiliating experience for the new Pope.

The years leading to 1262 were Manfred's 'up' years – everything seemed to go right for him. Most of the areas known as the Papal

States – essentially the middle chunk of Italy – were under his control by 1257; by 1262 he had literally married off his daughters to East and West – to a Byzantine despot and the future King of Aragon, a marriage pact which would have unexpected consequences in the years to come. Manfred must have seen his destiny as following in his legendary father's footsteps. In a manner not unlike that of certain Western governments today, the son of Frederick also pursued a successful policy in northern Italy of supporting local despots and oligarchies who were sympathetic to his anti-papal cause, as his father had with figures such as Ezzelino, the dictator of Vicenza.

The high point of this policy came on 4 September 1260, on a small hill called Montaperti just outside the city of Siena. A significantly smaller force, supported by Manfred's Saracens and German mercenaries, managed to save the town from a reported army of over thirty thousand pro-papal Florentines and their Tuscan allies.[56] The Siennese army, even helped by the German knights and Luceran Muslims Manfred had sent ahead to assist his pro-imperial allies, was barely two-thirds the size of the Florentines' force. The Siennese, however, had a trump up their sleeve: a traitor in the ranks of the Florentines. After the first day of pitched battle, their commander ordered an apparently suicidal counter-charge towards the Florentine ranks. In reality it was no *kamikaze* charge but a signal – a secret supporter among the Florentines' commanders, Bocca degli Abati (Dante would immortalise his name thereafter), saw the charge, walked over to the legion's standard-bearer and cut off his hand. The standard fell, chaos ensued, and thousands of Florentines fell in the slaughter. The battle of Montaperti made Siena a centre of anti-papal factions for years to come. As Siena was his home town, Pope Alexander VII cannot have been too happy. The victory meant that by 1261 Manfred was effectively in control of Italy.

Manfred was convinced the Hohenstaufen cause was finally on the point of being won: he had military authority on the Italian mainland – his armies marched freely across the territories of the Pope – and with his marriages and alliances was on the way to obtaining symbolic recognition, if not from Rome then certainly from the other rulers of Europe and the East. But the Vatican had not remained idle. From 1255, it would spend the next seven years searching for a new king of Sicily to replace Manfred, employing the three skills it had honed to perfection over the centuries – arrangement, negotiation and endorsement. Like an unhappy group of shareholders looking for a new director, Pope Alexander combed the royal families of Europe, looking for a monarch keen enough – and wealthy enough – to take on the job.

The chance to become King of Sicily – which, in real language, meant the task of defeating Manfred – was first proposed to the brother-in-law of the English king, Richard of Cornwall, who turned down the offer, saying it was like being offered the moon, on the condition that one lifted it down from the sky.[57] Then followed the expensive fiasco with the King of England himself; Henry III, having heard the Kingdom of Sicily was being offered by the Vicar of Christ to anyone who was willing to bid for it, saw the island as the perfect domain for his infant son, but four years of financial difficulties (and a dozen English barons) eventually persuaded the foolish monarch to pull out of the project. Finally, the Pope turned to Charles of Anjou, the brother of the King of France. For the crown of Sicily, Charles was more than happy to accept the bank-breaking terms of the offer: ten thousand gold coins a year to the Papacy, the promise to supply three hundred ships whenever the Pope required, and a vow never to become Holy Roman Emperor or contradict the Pope's commands in any way.[58] There were rumours that it was Charles' wife who, desperate for a more impressive title than merely 'Beatrice of Provence', pushed him to agree to the offer; given the kind of ruthlessness Charles was to show to his enemy, it seems unlikely his ambitions needed any uxorial encouragement.

History has not been kind to Charles of Anjou. This is not merely because his brother, Louis IX, was one of the most famous kings of France (French explorers named the American city of St Louis after him). Set against the dashing, handsome young figures of the Hohenstaufen who were themselves idealised by Romantic poets such as Heine, he has emerged as a stern, rather conservative figure – 'a grim, unfeeling brute', in the words of one historian.[59] His murder of child-monarchs and exploitation of crusade-fever for his own personal ends are difficult to deny; the French ruler did so well out of the failed crusade on Tunis in 1271, effectively bagging a trade deal and ten years' tribute out of the unfortunate emir, that many crusaders openly expressed their resentment, while some even suspected the deal had been the real reason for the crusade. And yet, as we shall see, Charles was not massively different from the Hohenstaufen rulers he eventually replaced. It is an oft-commented irony that although the Angevin ruler initially called the Saracens in Manfred's army 'devilish', it did not stop him using them in his own regiments once he had taken over the realm.

As the Pope orchestrated the end of the Hohenstaufens, bringing together through Charles the various nobles, factions and mercenaries into a single army to face the hated Manfred, another development was also taking place. The threat of a Mongol invasion had become much more real with the advances of the Tartars into Eastern Europe. Barely two decades earlier, the Mongols had swept a Polish army aside at the battle of Liegnitz (1241) in southern Poland, and had been kept from advancing further into the German kingdoms only through the sudden death of their khan. The shock waves of the defeat were felt in Rome just as much as Byzantium, and even though the two churches had bitterly split two centuries earlier, there was a sense of urgency in the Vatican that some form of reconciliation, some kind of united front, should take place. This pseudo-ecumenicalism, initiated more by circumstances than any spirit of forgiveness and understanding, would forever frustrate Charles, whose eye was greedily on Constantinople as a conquerable source of wealth and trade, certainly not as an ally.

Charles' campaign came down through Italy like an avalanche, drawing pro-papal allies to it as it passed town after town, and intimidating Manfred's sympathisers. The year was 1266: somewhere in the Italian landscape Charles' army was passing through, the greatest thinker of the Christian Middle Ages, Thomas Aquinas, was beginning his masterpiece, the *Summa Theologiae*; in the small town of Vespignano, a child called Giotto was born, and fifteen miles down the road, a one-year-old Dante Alighieri was probably screaming for his mother's milk. For Manfred, the year 1266 would have a darker significance, even though his confidence seems to have prevented him from giving defeat, let alone death, the slightest consideration. When Charles' army arrived unchallenged in Rome, Manfred brashly declared: 'The bird is in the cage'.[60] Even though waverers were already beginning to join Charles' campaign – encouraged by five cardinals' symbolic crowning of the French prince in Rome – Manfred appears to have underestimated the gravity of the moment. Instead of advancing on Charles' camp in Tivoli, south of Rome, essentially taking the battle to him instead of waiting passively for the pretender to arrive, Manfred did something incredible: he turned back into his own kingdom to spend a month hunting with his courtiers.

The bird did not stay in the cage. Having regained Rome without so much as a skirmish, Charles moved down into Campagna, towards the boundaries of the Hohenstaufen's kingdom. In these closing moves of the Angevin-Hohenstaufen game, there is a genuine mood of finale, as one senses an extraordinary dynasty is about to come to an end. Charles' army gradually rolled down towards the city of Benevento, on the river Calore, swallowing up castle after castle on its way. Time was not on Charles' side: his army, hungry and tired, was already beginning to show cracks in its loyalty. He was keen to attack, and attack quickly. Reinforcements for Manfred were beginning to gather in the north – all the Hohenstaufen ruler had to do was sit and wait. As the scholar Runciman relates, when Charles' army finally made its way down the mountain pass towards Benevento on the morning of 25 February 1266, they would have seen a forbidding sight: the whole array of Manfred's infantry, cavalry and reserves, an army of well over ten thousand men, waiting for them in front of the city, with the river – and, crucially, a single bridge – between them.[61]

Manfred chose to attack the next day, carefully filing over the bridge to meet the opposing army on the plains in front of the city. In one sense, the battle of Benevento illustrates the tired adage that a well-disciplined army, no matter what its size, will always defeat an undisciplined one. Unlike Charles' army, Manfred's troops were more diverse – first came his Saracen archers and light infantry, then mostly German heavily armoured cavalry, and behind these a collection of Italian mercenary regiments and (as it would turn out) unreliable Italian nobles, along with some two or three hundred light-armed Saracen cavalry. Such diversity may have been a factor in the poor communication which followed. The large presence of Muslim and German troops, and relative paucity of local reserves, was largely due to Manfred's own lack of trust in his subjects' allegiance. The German cavalry were well over a thousand strong, and their heavy plate armour – Benevento was one of the first battles in which such an innovation was used – would have presented a strange, terrifying sight as they charged full speed towards the French ranks.

The battle was over by the end of the day. Commentators report the Saracen infantry initiating the attack upon Charles' front ranks without waiting for the command; the Muslim soldiers seemed to have some success, until Charles ordered his Provençal horsemen in to disperse the Saracens, a move which quickly drove them back. The

German cavalry must have seen this from afar and, acting on impulse
to assist their Muslim comrades, led a heavy charge into Charles'
flanks, again without waiting for Manfred's orders. Although massively
outnumbered, their plate armour initially proved resilient to any weapon
the French soldiers could swing at them. The sight must have been
a deeply disturbing one for the enemy – hundreds of steel-skinned
men on horseback, shrugging off the blows of swords and axes as if
they were sticks and staves. At some point in the conflict, however,
one of the officers in Charles' army noticed how the underarms of
the German knights were exposed whenever they raised their weapons
to strike. Suddenly ordering all his men to aim their blows at the
knights' armpits, the tide of the battle turns, and the German contingent
begins to suffer heavy losses. Moreover, because they have charged
too soon, without waiting for the order to attack, the battalion of
Italian mercenaries and Muslim cavalry bringing up their rear have
not yet filed over the bridge to help them. The French forces, having
decimated the German cavalry (barely a sixth of them would survive),
fall upon Manfred's troops as they prepare to gather for a charge;
this, combined with a third attack by Charles on the army's flanks, is
enough to send Manfred's remaining forces streaming back over the
bridge in disarray. By late evening, all was lost. Although he could
have fled, Manfred famously chose to stay with his retinue, and his
Saracen guard, and fight on to the last man. After exchanging surcoats
with his friend Tebaldo, he drew a sword and plunged into the melee.
Days after the battle was over, his corpse was found in the middle of
the battlefield by a wandering soldier. Charles allowed the ruler an
honourable funeral, burying him at the foot of the bridge of Benevento;
once the army had moved on, it was later said, the local archbishop
ordered the body to be dug up and re-buried outside the boundaries
of the kingdom.

The tale of Manfred's young wife and children is equally sad; the
queen, when the news of her husband's death reached her in the
palace at Lucera, took her two boys and fled to the coast to find a
ship to Greece. She was caught by Charles' men at the seaside town
of Trani, and would die in prison five years later, not yet thirty. Her
two young boys would meet the same fate of lifelong imprisonment
– apparently, they were still behind bars in 1309.[62]

Regime change: Lucera's Muslims under Charles of Anjou

In many ways, as far as our history of Muslim-Christian alliances goes, the end of the Hohenstaufen dynasty should be the end of our story. There was nothing very 'exotic' about Charles of Anjou – he didn't speak Arabic or build 'Oriental' palaces or maintain a Muslim bodyguard. There was no danger of him making any alliances with the 'heathen'; if he had any interest in other religions at all, he certainly kept it to himself (although, to be fair, his court did translate the Persian sceptic al-Razes into Latin). Indeed, the only thing 'Oriental' about the Angevin newcomer was his ambitions – he almost immediately declared war on the Emir of Tunis (an old ally of Charles' enemies, the Aragonese), and carefully began his plan to re-conquer Constantinople from the Greeks.

Charles' pragmatism, however, and the extraordinary dimension of his ambitions – the domination of the Mediterranean world, no less – probably explain in part the strange tolerance he showed towards the Muslims of the Hohenstaufen who had now become his subjects. When the Lucerans petition for surrender in 1266, immediately acknowledging Charles as their new sovereign, he shows them remarkable mildness, ordering his officials not to sack the city and to allow the Muslims to keep their own law. Some have suggested that the Lucerans effectively bribed their way out of their threatened destruction; we have a number of sermons from the period rebuking Charles for accepting the Saracens' gold.[63] There may also have been a sense in which Charles, like Frederick, saw the Muslims of Lucera as a useful fighting force in times to come. Whatever the reason, Lucera did not share the fate of other (Christian) cities which, faithful to Manfred, tried to resist the triumphant Angevins; the Sicilian city of Augusta, for example, was mercilessly dealt with.

For Lucera, the brief peace which followed in the years 1266 and 1267 was merely the calm before the storm. The city's Muslim inhabitants would probably have resented the sudden appearance of French-speaking officials and the punitory taxes they brought, silently lamented the demise of their Hohenstaufen masters, but also breathed a sigh of relief that the unenviable fate of a sacked city had not been bestowed upon them. Some of the Muslims who had fled north to Abruzzo had been rounded up and sent back to Lucera – Charles, evidently, was careful to follow his predecessor's policy of keeping all his Saracens in one place.

In 1268, however, everything changed. Word arrived in Lucera that the grandson of Frederick II – the little boy rumoured to have died – was marching into Italy from the north with an army of Hohenstaufen sympathisers behind him, preparing to take back the realm Charles had so rudely seized. The grandson, called Conradin, was fourteen years old. Lucera, encouraged by the possibility of the return of the Hohenstaufens, forgot its peace with the Angevins and immediately staged an uprising.

We have to remember that Lucera was a fully fledged royal city, with a large number of soldiers among its male population and an impressive armoury in the vaults of the castle. The Muslim soldiers of Lucera had fought all over Italy for Frederick and Manfred; they were no unruly farmers, but skilled and experienced veterans. The uprising at Lucera was no spurt of rebellion, but the initiation of a full-scale war of independence. Charles took it seriously enough to demand a horse and a soldier from every house in the realm to fight it. Even Amalfi, way over on the other coast, was asked to contribute to the army he immediately sent to besiege the Muslim city. Pope Clement IV declared the war on the city a crusade, although curiously enough Charles – in his official language concerning the uprising – never makes any reference to the Lucerans' Muslim faith, choosing instead simply to call them 'traitors' (*proditores*).[64] This may have been partly because the rebels of Lucera were not only Muslims – the Saracens' Christian neighbours were also united with them against Charles, and would fight alongside them to the end.

In 1268, Lucera's Muslims finally broke out beyond the limits which had been set for them for decades. In a series of guerrilla activities, bands of Lucerans raided several smaller towns in the area, stealing food, burning buildings and mutilating Angevin sympathisers. Charles' forces were not by any means morally superior: when they caught hold of one Luceran rebel, a man called Vallone, they removed his eyes and later hanged him in his home town.[65] And yet, for all the ferociousness of their uprising, the rebels' end was approaching quicker than anyone had expected. In 1268, at the battle of Tagliacozzo, Charles defeats the army of Hohenstaufen sympathisers and – in an act of ruthlessness which would be remembered by poets and chroniclers for centuries to come – orders the execution of their fifteen-year-old sovereign. The boy is decapitated in front of a large crowd in the market square in Naples.

With the last hope of the Hohenstaufen gone – and the prospect of a return of the status quo now effectively vanquished – spirits must have been low in Lucera. Charles personally led an army against the city in 1269, a long, difficult siege which caused tremendous hardship for the town's inhabitants. By the end, we are told, the Lucerans had begun to eat grass. When the city finally surrendered, in August, Charles' troops did not occupy the town without a fight from some of the Christian and Muslim inhabitants. One chronicler records the death of over three thousand Saracens, while another reports Charles' particular anger with the Christians who had taken the Muslims' side during the rebellion. All of the Christian collaborators were put to death.[66]

The destruction of Lucera

With the end of the siege of Lucera comes the end of Frederick II's Muslim-Christian legacy. It is tempting to idealise the fact that members of both faiths died in the final takeover of the city – a temptation, most probably, it would be wise to resist. Psychologists tell us how situations of war or imminent death produce extraordinary sensations of solidarity in social groups, and perhaps it was one such situation which brought Lucera's two religions together during the siege. Perhaps there was a political identity – a sense of *fidelità* to Manfred, a common aversion to the Angevins – which enabled their collaboration; or maybe it was about language – fighting alongside the Italian-speaking neighbour you can understand, against the French-speaking aggressor you cannot. Or, finally, perhaps the whole essence of the Muslim-Christian resistance at Lucera came from something as simple as co-habitation; human beings who had spent so many years living next to one another, that they were not going to allow anyone – neither a French nobleman nor a meddlesome Pope – to push them out of their city.

Whatever the reason, Lucera did not have the chance to rebel again in the three remaining decades that destiny allotted its existence. As I have already said, the end of Manfred's reign certainly did not mean the end of Muslim soldiers serving in the armies of the sovereign: Lucera's Muslims, in reduced numbers, fought for Charles of Anjou and his son, Charles II, all over the Mediterranean – in the Balkans against the Byzantines, in Tunisia against the Arab emir,

and in Sicily against the coalition forces of the Spanish Aragonese
(a coalition instigated, irony of ironies, by Manfred's daughter).
Whether they fought for Charles with the same enthusiasm remains
a moot point: there are numerous cases recorded of Muslim soldiers
deserting their positions in Albania or Sicily and fleeing back to
Lucera. This may well have more to do with family needs at home
rather than any disavowal of loyalty. There is, perhaps, a sense in
which some Angevin commanders did not trust the Saracens as
much as the Hohenstaufens had; on at least one occasion, when
Muslim archers were being ferried across the Adriatic from Italy
to Albania, the wary commander did not send them all in one boat,
but split the Saracens up into groups of ten and sent them across
in different ships.[67]

Throughout the 1270s, 80s and 90s, Lucera continued to thrive,
unaware it was soon to be brutally crushed. The death of Charles in
1285 did not disturb any continuity in the relatively tolerant attitude
displayed towards the Muslim city. Some Muslims, especially those
who chose a career in the military, appeared to do particularly well
in the period. A good example of this is 'Abd al-'Aziz (in Italian,
Abdelasio), a Muslim officer and noble who owned property and
houses inside and outside Lucera, and even leased farmland from
abbeys and monasteries. This is significant, when one considers the
fact that as late as 1294 the bishop of Lucera was said to be living
in poverty. The historian Taylor reports that Charles II gave the
Muslim officer a fiefdom in 1296, in a ceremony witnessed by one
Giovanni Pipino – a dark irony, given the fact that the very same
Pipino would oversee the destruction of Lucera barely four years
later.[68]

A more ominous sign of things to come could have been discerned
in the messages coming from Rome. There was an increased awareness
of the need to convert the Muslims of Lucera to the true faith; although
conversion to Christianity was definitely *not* a condition of advancement
in Charles' army, the increasing number of Luceran Muslims with
Christian names – such as Riccardo or Pietro – does suggest a trend
was beginning, in much the same way Jews in central Europe would
convert to the Protestant or Catholic faiths. The renowned Christian
thinker Ramond Lull, a mystical esotericist and one of the Middle
Ages' most brilliant apologists, had been planning to visit Lucera in
1294 to preach an evangelical sermon there. Lull had already preached,
earlier in the year, to some Luceran Muslims who were held prisoner

in Naples, although it is not clear whether the famous philosopher ever made his visit to the Muslim city itself.[69] The fervour of conversion was part of the general *Zeitgeist* of the 1290s – in Sicily, thousands of Jews were forced to renounce their faith. Jewish quarters of cities, such as that of Salerno, were re-named in order permanently to erase any trace of the non-Christian in the city's memory. In Lucera, a similar version of erasure was to take place.

The order for the dismantling of the colony came suddenly in the summer of 1300. Charles II, a monarch who unlike his father had never been on crusade, declared his desire to improve the status of the Christian faith in the region and authorised his officials to remove those in the city who had failed to respond, eight weeks earlier, to an invitation to convert. The operation lasted little over a month. Giovanni Pipino led men into the city to either abduct or, in many cases, murder the inhabitants. Widespread massacres took place, and as no trace of any Muslim architecture exists in Lucera today, we can assume the mosques and Koran schools of the city were completely destroyed. We know that some resistance took place, as Giovanni later requested compensation from Charles II for the loss of some of his men during the operation. As tens of thousands of Muslims were living in Lucera at the time, it is difficult to know how many survived. Large groups of refugees were shifted to relocation centres in the countryside – although here they were often robbed and massacred by locals, as in the case of 150 Muslims at Venosa. Ill feeling in the poorer provinces against the wealthy Saracens of Lucera was high. Unscrupulous Christians took the opportunity of purchasing large numbers of slaves in the ensuing mayhem – women and girls were sold off all over Apulia. On a more positive note, we also have records of Christians who either hid Muslims from the operation or bought them as slaves with the clear aim of protecting them. A monastery in Benevento was ordered by the Vatican to hand over a Muslim knight it was keeping hold of. A choir leader from another church in Troia appears to have bought a Muslim couple and their six-month-old baby in circumstances which indicate a desire for their safety.[70] However, the overwhelming evidence points to a local population, a Papacy and a king who are relieved to have rid Italian soil of the 'unclean doctrine of Mohammed'.

One of the most striking things about Frederick's Muslim colony – apart from the speed with which we have forgotten it – is the number of anomalies it throws up for our cosy, Christian picture of an Italian Middle Ages. For today's reader (and for myself, before researching this period), words such as 'Arab' and 'Florence', 'Muslim' and 'Milan' simply do not fit, and the idea of a period in history when they were profoundly connected strikes most of us as fantastic. To be honest, I am not sure how this resistance to the unthinkable in history can be overcome. Episodes such as the Muslim city of Lucera should make us question the Christian Europe we have all so readily downloaded and installed in our heads, programmes which move into action automatically whenever the word 'Islam' springs up in conversation. In the attitudes of the Hohenstaufen and their supporters towards the Saracens on their side, what is interesting is how un-exotic they were, how little special attention was actually given to the Muslims in their armies. For Frederick and his followers – and, one suspects, even for Charles of Anjou – the principal identity of the Saracens of Lucera was as subjects of the king; in the end, their Islamic faith may well have had little more weight than a regional accent.

Sources

David Abulafia, *Frederick II: A Medieval Emperor* (Penguin, 1988).

—*The Western Mediterranean Kingdoms* (London: Longman, 1997).

—*Medieval Encounters, Economic, Religious, Political 1100–1350* (Ashgate, 2000).

—'The End of Muslim Sicily', in J.M. Powell (ed.), *Muslims Under Latin Rule 1100–1300* (Princeton University Press, 1990).

Aziz Ahmad, *A History of Islamic Sicily* (Edinburgh University Press, 1975).

Giovanni Amatuccio, 'Saracen Archers in Southern Italy' E-HAWK June 1997. www.idir.net.

The Chronicle of Salimbene de Adam, J.L. Baird, G. Baglivi and J.R. Kane (eds) (Binghamton, NY, 1986).

Pietro Egidi, *La Colonnia dei Saraceni e la sua distruzione* (Naples, 1915).

F. Gabrieli, *Arab Histories of the Crusades*, trans. E.J. Costello (London: Routledge, 1969).

—'Friedrich II und die Kultur des Islam', in G. Wolf (ed.), *Stupor Mundi: Zur Geschichte Friedrichs II von Hohenstaufen* (Darmstadt, 1982).

J. Göbbels, *Das Militärwesen im Königreich Siziliens zur Zeit Karls I von Anjou* (Hiersemann: Stuttgart, 1984).

H.L. Gottschalk, *Al-Malik al-Kamil von Egypten und seine Zeit* (Wiesbaden, 1958).

Eberhard Horst, *Der Sultan von Lucera* (Freiburg: Herder Verlag, 1997).

J.P. Lomax, 'Frederick II, His Saracens and the Papacy', in John V. Toran (ed.), *Medieval Christian Perceptions of Islam* (London: Routledge, 1996).

Amin Maalouf, *The Crusades Through Arab Eyes*, trans. J. Rothschild (Zed Books, 1984).

Piero Pieri, 'I Saraceni di Lucera nella storia militare medievale', *Archivo Storico Pugliese* 6 (1953).

Enrico Pispisa, *Il Regno di Manfredi* (Sicania: Messina, 1991).

S. Runciman, *The Sicilian Vespers* (Cambridge University Press, 1958).

Kurt Victor Selge, 'Die Ketzerpolitik Friedrichs II', in G. Wolf, *Stupor Mundi*.

Douglas Sterling, 'The Siege of Damietta', in D.J. Kagay and L.J.A. Villalon (eds), *Crusaders, Condottieri and Cannon: Medieval Warfare in Societies Around the Mediterranean* (Brill: Leiden, 2003) pp.101–132.

Julie Taylor, *Muslims in Medieval Italy: The Colony at Lucera* (Lexington University Press, 2003).

Peter Thorau, *The Lion of Egypt: Sultan Baybars I and the Near East in the Thirteenth Century* (New York: Longman, 1987).

J.F. Verbruggen, *The Art of Warfare in Western Europe*, trans. C.S. Willard and R.W. Southern (Woodbridge: Boydell Press, 1997).

Chapter Three

TURKISH-CHRISTIAN
ALLIANCES IN ASIA MINOR
1300–1402

For our next chapter, our attention shifts a few hundred miles east and a few decades onwards – from thirteenth-century Italy to fourteenth-century Greece and Asia Minor (what we now call Turkey). It is a chapter which involves the dissolution of one empire, and the explosive appearance of another. Depending on the reader's viewpoint, this could be the melancholy story of the gradual demise of Byzantium, the Greek-speaking eastern half of the former Roman Empire; the final decades which saw a former imperial power, which once commanded towns stretching from the Crimea to the North African coast, reduced to an impoverished, strife-torn city-state, led by an emperor who was often little more than a vassal of the sultan. For such a reader, our chapter will narrate a sombre countdown to the final siege and capitulation of Constantinople – the Christian capital, the 'second Rome' – which after 1453 would take on the name of Istanbul. When Mehmet II finally enters the Hagia Sophia, the holiest church of Constantinople, in 1453 and symbolically smashes the altar of the cathedral, he brings to an end a thousand years of Byzantine rule.[1]

Alternatively, this chapter could narrate the exciting new beginning of another dynasty – the Ottomans – and an empire which would spring from a small tribe of Turkish pastoralists in the northwest corner of Turkey to eventually span one of the largest empires the world had ever seen; in this version of the tale, the melancholy would be replaced by marvel, promise and awe, as a dynasty grows which would stretch as far as Ukraine and Algeria, Hungary and Yemen, establishing an administration that was to last well over six hundred years. For such a reader, the 'fall' of Constantinople becomes the *conquest* (an important word in Turkish – *Fatih*) – not the tragic end of a Byzantine millennium, but the glorious foundation of a wholly new Ottoman project.

It is a commonplace among historians that one man's victory is another man's massacre, that someone's triumph is always going to be another's catastrophe. The year 1453, quite simply, signifies a beginning for many Turks, and an end for many Greeks. What I shall try to do in this chapter, by focusing constantly on the endless alliances between Turks and Christians (Catalans, Greeks, Serbs) in this period, is to show how these two viewpoints are not the only ways of understanding the history of the region. Identities do not change overnight, even when their lands are conquered by other peoples; the Greek-speaking regions conquered by the Turks, as we shall see, played a significant part in the evolution of the Ottoman Empire, not just accounting for the overwhelming Christian presence in its military, but also forming a crucial cultural and political influence on the Ottomans themselves. The hybridity of Ottoman culture – the fact that it was always willing to incorporate foreign elements and cultures into its structures – has gradually come to be seen as part of its success. A similar tale can be told in terms of Byzantine culture, particularly those Byzantine Greeks who lived in the 'frontier' areas of Asia Minor, and who lived for generations alongside Seljuk and Ilhanid Turks, sharing idioms and food, inter-marrying, in some cases even having common places of worship.[2] To understand the Ottoman conquest of Asia Minor and Constantinople as a historic struggle between Islam and Christianity is, as we shall see, to misunderstand wholly an extremely complex series of processes. When half of the Turkish armies have Christian soldiers in them, and half of the Byzantine armies involved consist of Turkish mercenaries, then it becomes clear we need to find another way of talking about this history.

Although the number of nationalities and ethnic groups involved in this period are legion – from Mongols and Turkmen to Hungarians, Berbers and even the Anglo-Saxon bodyguard of the Byzantine emperor himself, the Varangians – the powers I shall be dealing with are essentially three in number: Turks, Byzantines and Latins. All three are complex entities, riven through with differences, cultural overlaps, ethnic variants and complicated histories. In order to understand how a Byzantine emperor can willingly give his daughter to a Turkish sultan – and spend four days enjoying himself at the wedding banquet – we will need to spend a little time examining the context of each 'player' in turn.

The Latins: Catalans, Venetians, Genoans

The role of the Latin kingdoms and states in the demise of the Byzantine Empire is not a pretty one: their divisions, feuds and willingness to profit – at the expense of Greeks, fellow Catholics or Turks – from any crisis which came their way does not make pleasant reading. The crusaders' sacking of Constantinople in 1204 led to four days of murder, rape and pillage. Bursting into the Orthodox church of St Sophia, the soldiers found a prostitute off the streets and seated her on the patriarch's throne, with a fake sceptre in her hand, as the Whore of Babylon. The subsequent sixty-year occupation of Constantinople – it was only liberated from the Latins in 1261 – crippled the empire, and made sure it would never really return to its former greatness. Given the kinds of things Venetians, Genoans and Catalans did to Greeks on their own soil, it is hardly surprising to hear the last prime minister of Constantinople say: 'Better the Sultan's turban than the Cardinal's hat'.[3]

Although united by a common Catholic faith, the Venetians, Catalans and Genoese had little more than contempt for one another. The fierce competition between Venice and Genoa, in particular, for the valuable trade routes through the straits of the Bosphorus ensured the two would forever remain rivals; even in the last days of Constantinople, we are told, surrounded by an army of nearly sixty thousand Ottomans, quarrels would still break out among the Genoans and Venetians fighting from within the city walls for its defence. Throughout the fourteenth century, as the rival trading powers of Venice and Genoa grew in wealth and influence – and as Constantinople grew poorer and poorer – the former imperial capital often became a helpless backdrop to clashes between the two Italian powers, clashes in which the unfortunate Greeks were forced reluctantly to take sides.

In 1300, the presence of Latins, and in particular Italians, in the eastern Mediterranean was an established fact. Rather like the crusader states formed in Palestine and Syria, the Latin control of large stretches of the former Byzantine Empire, including Athens and the Greek mainland itself, was largely a consequence of Western European ambitions and the after-effects of three major papal crusades. Crete was controlled by Venice, as were some of the bigger Greek islands such as Naxos, while an entity called the Latin Duchy of Athens – run by one of Rome's most powerful families, the Orsini – had established itself around the Acropolis, a duchy the Catalans were later destined to conquer and administer (as we shall see) until 1388. Although some Latin rulers, such as Prince William of Achaia, were fluent in Greek, for most Byzantines the presence of Venetians, Genoans and Catalans on their soil was a foreign and occasionally brutal occupation. Even today, there is a saying in modern Greek: 'Not even the Catalans would have done that'.[4] It comes as no surprise, therefore, to learn that Byzantines such as Andronikos were more than happy to hire Turkish mercenaries against them. In his siege of the Latin-held Greek city of Ioannina in 1292, records tell us over fourteen thousand Turkish cavalry assisted thirty thousand Byzantine troops (clearly exaggerated numbers, although the proportions are probably accurate).[5] More importantly, the Latins were also willing to make Turkish alliances in their wars against one another. The Catalans' desire, for example, to push the Italians out of their occupation of the Greek peninsula led them to make a whole series of military collaborations with the Anatolian Turks on the other side of the Aegean.

Although we have said the Latins were seen largely as foreigners by the occupied Byzantines, some mention should be made of the Genoese colony-cum-city of Pera, which sat on a hill opposite the walls of Constantinople. For anyone walking around the heaving centre of today's Istanbul, with its population of over fifteen million, it is difficult to imagine a time when the metropolis was not one but two cities. And yet here Genoese and Greeks lived alongside one another in relative harmony, operating at the centre of a fourteenth-century trade hub in which ships travelled from the coasts of the Black Sea, through Constantinople, to ports as far away as Southampton and London. The Genoese presence in Byzantium was therefore a centuries-long, significant, if ambiguous one. In 1453, when the Ottomans lay siege to Constantinople, the Genoans of Pera can do nothing but watch on helplessly as the city finally collapses.

The Byzantines: divisions of dynasty, region, class and religion

All kinds of things divided the Byzantines, to such an extent that even the approach of an invading army was unable to unite them. It is a standard practice of most Byzantine histories, at some point, to remark with astonishment at the number of civil wars the empire was able to have with itself, even with its frontiers shrinking thanks to the ever-encroaching presence of enemies all around it. Such amazement is not always intelligent: the Byzantines, like all imperial subjects, were made up of very different groups, belonging to very different regions and classes. That a Greek-speaking peasant who has toiled all his life under Byzantine rule might wonder whether things will really be any worse under the Turks is, perhaps, not that astonishing.

Before we begin to examine what divided the Byzantines, perhaps we should first note that the word 'Byzantine' is a word no Byzantine would have used to describe himself. The subjects of Constantinople, Thessaloniki and Trebizond called themselves Romans (*rhomaioi* – a sense still present in the Turkish word for Greeks today, *Rum*). They called the Turks either 'Persians' or 'Barbarians', depending on whether they were in alliance with them or not. The three main cities of the empire just mentioned were geographically quite distant from one another – Trebizond, today's Trabzon, lies on the northeastern border between Turkey and Georgia. For the last two hundred years of the Byzantine Empire, it was effectively a separate state (and later an independent empire), a provincial capital cut off from Constantinople by a whole sweep of Turkish coastline. People in Constantinople could be quite snobbish towards it: some Greek historians called the rulers of Trebizond 'barbarians', and even gave their patriarch a Turkish nickname, insinuating that he was not really a Greek.[6] This sense of distance and disaffection between Constantinople and its provincial sister states is important – it will explain why the Ottomans found it so easy to recruit Christian allies in their campaigns against the capital of Byzantium. When the Turks made their first serious advances into Byzantine Asia Minor, as we shall see, they were helped by disillusioned Greek provincials, weary of an indifferent and inward-looking Constantinople.

Trebizond, being the farthest east of the Byzantine city-states, also offers the most interesting example of Muslim-Christian co-operation on all levels. The architecture of churches, as Spain and Sicily have already shown us, is always a good indicator of inter-faith influence and co-existence; the central church of Trebizond, for anyone wandering around it today, looks like a cross between a Byzantine monastery and a Seljuk mosque.[7] The Christian stonework is filled with Muslim floral plaques and the kinds of geometrical, multi-faceted cornices found in the columns of *medrese* or Koran schools. Military tactics are also revealing: the Greeks of Trebizond employed a kind of horse archery identical to that of the Seljuks, shooting from the saddle, so that to one Spanish traveller they appeared to be indistinguishable from Turks.[8] Inter-marriage between Greek-Trebizond and Turkish nobles was also common; as Byzantine territories shrank – and Turkish ones expanded – marriage became an increasingly attractive way of avoiding invasion. When the ruler of Trebizond married off his sister to the leader of the Turkish Akkoyunlu tribes in 1352, the Turks stopped raiding his lands (now that he was, effectively, part of the family). Naturally, the women had to convert to Islam, although this was seen as a small price to pay for peace and stability in the kingdom.

In other words, there was no such thing as a typical Greek. For an empire as diverse as that of the Byzantine, its inhabitants would differ from one another as starkly as the inhabitants of the Shetland Islands would differ today from those of Cornwall, or as people in Barcelona would from those in Granada. More than any geographical distance, there was a difference in the level of familiarity with Turks. Greek speakers living in the 'frontier' areas of the empire, in the porous border regions where Turks and Greeks had been living together for centuries, had different ideas about Ottoman occupation than Greeks living in areas where there were no Turkish settlers. Byzantines and Turks were living together on the shores of Lake Beyşehir (in the middle of western Turkey) as early as the 1100s, a fact which means that by 1350 they had been sharing the same communities for over two hundred years. In the town of Eskişehir (today in northwestern Turkey), Turks had a marketplace next to a bath, where Christians sold water-glasses and other goods.[9] In contrast, for Greeks living on the European coast, the 'barbarians' would be no neighbours but thieves and plunderers who would periodically appear on the horizon to raid and storm their town.

Political divisions also existed in Byzantium, and were every bit as destructive as regional divisions. For the last two hundred years of Constantinople's life, two prestigious families dominated the political landscape – the Palaiologoi and the Kantakouzenoi. Although the emperor was almost always a Palaiologos – the Kantakouzenos family never held the imperial throne but for one brief decade – the Kantakouzenoi had an immense pedigree in the city, and held some of the most important positions in the administration of the empire. Probably the most important member of the Kantakouzenos clan ever was John VI Kantakouzenos, the subject of our chapter, a brilliant statesman and valuable chronicler who abdicated the imperial throne at the age of sixty-two and spent the last thirty years of his life as a monk. The two families usually interacted quite well with one another – several famous friendships and marriages occurred between them – but when they quarrelled, both sides proved willing to go to any lengths to protect their interests, lengths which included bringing Turkish troops into their armies to fight for them. Not surprisingly, these feuds between the two Greek dynasties will play a central role in producing some of the most substantial Muslim-Christian alliances in our chapter.

In a sense, the tension between these two important families highlights another, perhaps more predictable, difference among the Byzantines: that of class. For one period at least, the Kantakouzenos family was seen to be the more elitist and out of touch with the people, while (oddly enough) the ruling Palaiologos dynasty enjoyed more popular support on the streets. For any socialist medieval historian embarking on the unusual quest for pre-modern revolutions, the Zealots of Thessaloniki offer an unusual example of a planned popular uprising. Peasants and under-privileged farm workers organised themselves into a violent political movement (remarkable for 1347) and threw the representatives of the then-emperor Kantakouzenos out of the city, setting up their own non-aristocratic administration. When Kantakouzenos sent his soldiers to the city, they were refused entry. This bolshy spirit of the Thessalonians was no brief disturbance, but the beginning of a much more permanent resentment of the ruling classes – it continued well into the 1380s, when some of the Zealots actually suggested doing a deal with the invading Turks rather than their Byzantine rulers. Emperor Manuel II was exasperated by the independent-mindedness of his subjects. Writing in 1383, he complained to a friend how even the lowliest peasants of the city were 'like walking dictionaries'.[10]

It was class – or, more correctly, the ruling classes' fear of a popular, empire-wide insurrection – which partly accounted for the high number of foreign mercenaries in the empire's armies. For a territory which was constantly under threat, the Byzantines displayed a surprising reluctance to encourage popular sentiment against the enemy – be it Bulgarians or Turks – partly because it felt the defence of the empire was the 'job' of the army, not dangerously large groups of peasants. When, in northwestern Greece, a populist leader by the name of 'the Pigherd' gathered three hundred locals together in 1304 to fight

against the Turks in Asia Minor, the government did not encourage
his intiative but put him behind bars for nine months.[11]

The final division which sowed conflict among the Greek speakers
of Asia Minor and, to some extent, enabled the Ottomans to recruit
and play one faction against another, was religion. Of course there
was only one religion among the Byzantines, that which we call the
Orthodox church, but the subject of religion in Byzantium provoked
disputes in three ways: arguments over property and power between
the patriarchy and the non-religious authorities (emperors, governors);
religious debates over specific theological issues which then took on
political meanings; and finally, an inability to decide on a common
position with regard to the Western Catholic church – an institution
whose help they badly needed against the Turks, but against which
they still nurtured incredibly deep feelings of mistrust and resentment.
There are endless arguments reported between the patriarchs and
Byzantine emperors about who owned what and who had the right
to sell it to someone else; in Thessaloniki, for example, we find the
church leaders angrily refusing to give their buildings over to the
authorities, even when they were told it was necessary for the defence
of the city.[12] In 1303, the military defences of the empire's boundaries
were so poor that Andronikos II contemplated the radical plan of
giving a square of land to every soldier, so that they would at least
stay and defend it against the Turks. Due to opposition, the plan was
never realised. Neither, we can imagine, were the ecclesiastical
authorities too happy when Kantakouzenos used church finances to
pay for Turkish troops against his (Christian) rival, John V.

Although weirdly esoteric debates such as the controversy over the
hesychia (the mystical stillness which enables the believer to glimpse
momentarily the divine light of the transfiguration) were able to divide
the Greeks quite significantly – for no one appears to have loved a
good religious controversy more than the Byzantines – it was the
question of the West which caused the most bitter splits and conflicts.
Rome's offer to help Constantinople against what it perceived to be
the tide of Islam which was threatening to sweep over it had a number
of very unpleasant strings attached – not just trade and political
concessions, but most significantly a 'return' of the Orthodox church
to the true doctrine of the Catholic creed. It is impossible to over-
state the violent feelings of opposition this aroused among most Greeks,
who (with some justification) saw the Latins generically as a collection
of pirates and cut-throats who had robbed and plundered their lands

for well over two centuries. Michael VIII was the first emperor to attempt a union with the Catholic church – which meant, in real terms, Greek bishops travelling to Rome and kissing the Pope's hand as their spiritual leader – and the resulting dissent very nearly cost him his empire. Disobedient patriarchs who refused to agree to any alliance with the West were banished, exiled, even threatened with blinding. And yet, even as the Ottomans inched nearer each decade, reducing the once-glorious Byzantine Empire to basically three Greek city-states, the need for Western help could not bring the Byzantines to agree on a common position. With an army of sixty thousand Ottomans at the gates, the minister of Constantinople could still prefer the turban to the cardinal's hat.

Who were 'the Turks'?

It is no easy task to relate the population shift of a people-group from the plains of northern China, down through the hill regions of Uzbekistan, and then finally across and into the pastures of central and western Turkey. Probably the most important fact to emphasise is that by the time of our chapter's events (1300–1453), the ethnic group known generically as Turks, speaking a central Asian language wholly unrelated to Arabic and Persian but filled with loan-words from these languages, had been occupying much of the Byzantines' former territories in Asia Minor for around two hundred years.

Rather like the Byzantine Greeks, there was no such thing simply as 'the Turks'. Although united by a more or less similar language and a Sunni Muslim faith, Anatolia (as we shall term the mainland of present-day Turkey) was a patchwork of principalities in 1300, each at one another's throats. The Turkmen states of Saruhan, Germiyan, Karas and Aydin all had uneasy relations with one another, and often chose to ally themselves with their Christian neighbours in raiding one another's territories. The mighty Ottoman Empire had its origins as one such principality, a modest hill tribe led by a man called Osman ('Ottoman' translates the Turkish word for 'followers of Osman', *Osmanli*). It is hard to believe that this small square of territory, situated in northwest Turkey, would one day command respect and even tribute from the courts of Elizabeth I and the Doge of Venice. The lightning speed of the Ottomans' growth from tribe to empire, from shepherds and raiders to engineers and empire-builders, took everyone by surprise – including, most significantly, their Byzantine neighbours, who for much of the thirteenth century had been anticipating trouble from a completely different direction.

At this point, without wishing to complicate matters or make anything too 'academic', I have to mention a modern historical debate. It is a debate which has more to do with the politics of modern Turkish nationalism – and hasty Western misconceptions of Islam – than with the historical facts themselves. For many years, one of the main reasons given for the astonishing success of the Ottomans' rise to power was, in a word, Islam. Many prominent historians, both Turkish and Western, insisted not only on the wholly Turkish and Muslim origin of the Ottomans, but also that it was the idea of the *gazi* – the holy warrior of Islam who spreads the true faith and wages a jihad against his neighbours – that was the secret of their extraordinary growth.

Over the past thirty years, a number of leading historians have begun to seriously question this thesis. Partly because the job of a *gazi* was to wage war on non-Muslims – and, as we have just seen, some of the Ottomans' earliest wars were in collaboration with Greek unbelievers and waged against their fellow Muslim believers. With the help of the Christian Byzantines of Harman Kaya, the early Ottomans swallowed up their hated (Muslim) rivals, the emirates of Karas and Germiyan, in the 1320s and 1330s. In fact, one of the leading *gazi* referred to in sagas was an unconverted Christian Greek, Köse Mihal (who became a Muslim at the end of his life), a central figure in the growth of the Ottoman state and a close hunting-companion of Osman himself. In an early Turkish medieval epic, the *Battalname*, one of the protagonist's closest friends is a Byzantine. Moreover, the word *gazi* or 'holy warrior of the faith' simply does not feature as prominently as tradition would have us believe. Since many of the sagas and epic poems concerning the birth of the Ottomans were written well over a hundred years after the events took place, basing our conception on them is like trying to understand the English Civil War only by reading books about it written in the nineteenth century – in the end, you learn more about the historians' epoch than the history itself. Many of the later Ottoman poets, embarrassed by the mention of Christians in the founding of their Muslim empire, simply airbrushed any non-Muslims out of the poems they were writing for their sultans. Our simplistic, 'football-match' understanding of the history of Asia Minor – essentially Greeks versus Turks, with one group pushing the other out in much the same way oil displaces water – is partly a consequence of this re-writing of history.[13]

What is most ironic is that the secret of the Ottomans' startling success, far from being any kind of Islamic call to jihad, actually appears to have been the reverse: the early Ottomans were not particularly Islamic at all, and appeared to have no problem doing convenient deals with any neighbour, Christian or Muslim, if it helped them get ahead (the reader will have to decide for themselves how to respond to this strategic multiculturalism). As the ethnologist Lindner points out, tribal groups can often be quite open to the arrival of new elements, if their incorporation is beneficial to the group as a whole.[14] Unlike the later Ottoman Empire, there appears to have been no particular pressure to convert to Islam during the first century of the Ottoman expansion. There are records of Christian judges in Ottoman Bithynia (northwest Turkey) in the 1340s, while registers for the charity hospices in cities such as Bursa record them as being open to all religions – Muslims, Christians and Jews. When, in 1326, the Ottoman Sultan Orhan asks the chief minister why his Greek city finally decided to surrender to the Turks, he receives the reply:

> We surrendered for a variety of reasons. For one thing your state is growing bigger and bigger every day . . . For another, your . . . state took all our villages. They submitted to you. We understood that they were comfortable. We realised that they didn't miss us. We, too, desired that comfort.[15]

What the text shows is that the early Ottomans were more interested in absorbing cities than laying them to waste. If this meant tolerating their Christian practices and allowing them a measure of autonomy, then so be it. The most important point to be underlined here is that the conquest of Byzantine territories had as much effect on the Ottomans as it had on the Greeks. What followed was a *modus vivendi*, a way of living together which should not be idealised into some utopia of blissful tolerance – when the Turks captured a town, the first thing they did was convert the central church into a mosque – but simply be seen as the result of two people-groups sharing the same living space. Although not everyone would go as far as one Greek historian, who has called the Ottoman Empire a 'Turkish-Greek empire',[16] Byzantine culture did not simply 'disappear' once the Turks had arrived. Even a hundred and fifty years after the Turks conquered the city of Thessaloniki, the quarters of the city still had Greek names, even though they were inhabited by Muslims.[17]

Medieval Anatolia proved itself to be, again and again, an extremely violent place. Greek cities and settlements, as well as their Turkish neighbours, suffered a great deal throughout the thirteenth and fourteenth centuries. The point is, however, that this violence cannot simply be divided up into 'Muslims' and 'Christians'. The armies and military forces which caused much of this suffering were made up of both parties. The Ottoman expansion into the Balkans tells a similar tale. Even as late as 1472, records from one district show over 85 per cent of the Turks' raiding parties (akincilar) were made up of Christians.[18] The early Ottoman tactic of absorbing foreign cultures – Greeks, Armenians, Jews – into the armies and administrations under its banner makes a black-and-white picture of religious and ethnic conflict in this area extremely difficult. And as we shall see, Constantinople's policy of employing any army possible, Christian or non-Christian, to defend its interests makes the whole situation even more complicated.

As the image of a horde of 'Mohammedan' barbarians surging across the frontiers of civilisation is part of the myth we are trying to dispel, we should finally spend a few moments examining the culture Turks brought with them, and how it mingled with the local traditions and practices they found in their newly conquered lands. The Sufi poetry of Yunus Emre, the Persian parables of Jelaleddin Rumi (known as Mevlana in Turkish), the folktales of Nasreddin Hoja and the highly individual spirituality of Haji Bektash all took place in thirteenth- and fourteenth-century Anatolia. Rumi and Haji Bektash, in particular, reveal the extent of Christian influence[19] – Bektashi followers incorporated Christian practices such as the breaking of bread and the confession of sins into their own Muslim rituals, while in Rumi's *Masnavi* we even find scattered verses of Greek.

In the confusion and instability of Anatolia, many have argued, the unrest and anxiety provided a perfect spiritual environment for conversion. There is certainly something remarkable about the mixing of Christian and Islamic traditions in areas of Turkey such as Cappadocia, and it is not surprising that the Sufi movements were able to make the headway they did in such a climate of fear and uncertainty. What resulted was a curious mingling of faiths as well as cultures – Cappadocian churches where Sultan Masud and Emir Basil are depicted and praised together on the same wall, as well as the adoption of Christian practices such as baptism by some Turks. There are a number of thirteenth/fourteenth-century anecdotes told with a similar spirit – a priest who couldn't exorcise his wife, so a Turkish woman came and broke the spell, or a wandering Derwish (religious hermit) who eats the bread of the Christians, and watches their harvests double as a result. The fact that Haji Bektash, a Muslim holy man, was revered as Saint Charalambos by some Greeks, does indicate a remarkable overlapping of spiritualities. In one poem, the death of a Muslim holy man in the village has Jews, Armenians and Christians wailing and crying: 'Where is our sheikh?'

Muslim Anatolia was also a thriving hub of book production. Although some of the figures we have are clearly fictitious (one scholar was said to have had, in 1431, over 'ten thousand volumes' in his library), a book culture was definitely in full swing. The mosque of Umur Bey in Bursa, for example, had nearly three hundred books in 1455. As early as the 1200s, at least one *medrese* in Konya had already started to produce manuscripts. The northwest Turkish city of Bursa is interesting because its status as a newly conquered capital of the Ottoman dynasty drew scholars to it from all around – including Damascus and Shiraz (Iran).[20] The explosive growth of Ottoman architecture in this period – and the Seljuk and Byzantine influence its half-domes and conches reveal – produced a wave of *medrese*, mosques and bath-houses (*hamamlar*) across Anatolia and the Balkans, starting with the Ottoman complex in Iznik in 1334. The culmination of these architectural efforts is the pearl of early Ottoman architecture, the Green Mosque (Yeşil Cami) of Bursa, with its shimmering Turquoise ceramics and carefully laid blue, yellow and gold interiors.[21] Manuscripts, mosques, poetry and parables – this was the 'barbarian' culture which arrived in Anatolia at the beginning of the twelfth century.

The Catalan company (1303–11): The mercenaries who changed sides

The story of six thousand Catalans, Aragonese and Sicilians who went to Asia Minor to fight the Turks for the Byzantine emperor – and then, halfway through, decided to switch sides and ally themselves with the Turks to fight against the Byzantines – offers a useful introduction to our look at the closing century of the Byzantine Empire. Not simply because it is one of the first Muslim-Christian alliances (indeed, Turk-Latin) of the fourteenth century, but also because it gives us a good picture of the desperate state of the late-Byzantine army, and why it was so often supplemented by Turkish troops.

By 1300, the Byzantines found themselves in a situation which was going to become standard for the next fifty years: threatened and attacked by Bulgarians and Serbs to the north of them, and by various Turkish emirates to the south. Although for the previous thirty years the Byzantines had been more worried about a Latin crusade and invasion of their territory (primarily, as we saw in the last chapter, in the form of Charles of Anjou), the gradual capture of one Greek city after another in Asia Minor was an increasingly disturbing phenomenon.

The emperor, Andronikos II (a man who, in the words of one historian, should have been a professor of theology, but whom 'accident made a Byzantine emperor'[22]), had good reason to be worried. Militarily, the empire had long passed its peak. Andronikos himself had made one of the most disastrous decisions in medieval Greek history – the near-dismantling of the navy in 1285, a move which effectively gave control of the Bosphorus (the straits between Europe and Asia) over to the Venetians and Genoese. Many of the sailors made redundant simply went over to work on Turkish and Latin ships.[23] The number of Byzantine soldiers in the imperial armies who were actually Greek speakers was already small, and was destined to grow even smaller as the century progressed, as the Byzantines relied on an ever-increasing supply of foreign mercenaries.

Who were these foreign mercenaries? They came from all directions. Some were Latins – Catalans, Italians, Frenchmen. Some, as we shall see, were Muslim Turks from the highlands of Anatolia. Two further groups are also worth noting: the Alans and the Tourkopouloi. The Alans were a Christian Turkic/Mongol people, whose origins lay more or less in the region known today as Moldavia, north of Romania. About eight thousand of them were employed by the Byzantine emperor to fight against the Turks (and then against the mercenaries they had employed to fight against the Turks . . .). Andronikos employed them, apparently, because he was tired of his own 'effeminate and weakened citizens . . . and their malevolent attitudes and disposition'.[24] The Alans had a reputation, which they were soon to prove, for being loyal to the master they swore allegiance to.

The Tourkopouloi (the word in Greek simply means 'Turkish people') were also Christianised Turks – that is, Turks who were Christian for one of two reasons. In some cases, they were the offspring of a Greek-Turkish marriage, usually a Turkish father and Greek mother, a phenomenon much more common than records were willing to acknowledge. The term 'Tourkopouloi', however, was also used to describe Turks who stayed on in Byzantine territories and adopted the Christian faith after the retreat of the Seljuks in 1264. Their presence was acknowledged in records of the time – for example, the Christian Turk Nikephoras Rimpsas led the Turkish contingent of the Byzantine army against the Latins in the Thessalian campaign of 1273.[25] In 1300, both of these groups – the Alans and the Tourkopouloi – were to play, as mercenaries, a significant part in Byzantium's attempt to halt the growing incursions of the Turks into its lands.

In 1302, in the town of Nicomedia (today's Izmit), a band of Turkish warriors under the leadership of a Turk called Osman inflicted a significant defeat upon a surprised Byzantine army. For Byzantium, it was a gloomy sign of things to come. Even Andronikos' contemporaries could see the loss of Asia Minor to Turkish rule, along with all its Greek cities and states, was becoming an inevitability – even if the ultimate capitulation of Constantinople itself was still an unimaginable prospect. A radical solution was needed to the Turkish threat. It is at this point in the narrative that Roger de Flor and his Grand Catalan Company enter.

The tale of Roger de Flor and his mercenaries reads like something out of a Kipling short story. A former Knight Templar who had fought against the Saracens in Palestine and had been thrown out of the order for blackmailing refugees, de Flor had subsequently pursued a career in the Mediterranean as a professional soldier, fighting for Aragon against the Angevins. His German father had been one of Frederick II's falconers. In 1302 he wrote to the Byzantine emperor, offering his services and those of his mercenary employees. Andronikos II agreed, eager for any help from any quarter and not imagining de Flor's company to number any more than 1,500 men. De Flor was offered four months' pay in advance and even got the emperor's niece into the bargain. One year later, a fleet of well over a dozen ships, carrying nearly seven thousand men, arrived in Constantinople. 'We did not instruct you to collect and bring such a multitude', complained Andronikos.[26]

The Catalan mercenaries were skilled combatants and experienced strategists. They were also a violent bunch. Fights broke out with the Genoans almost as soon as they arrived. The money for the ships the Catalans had hired to take them to Constantinople – money de Flor had loaned from the Genoese – became the subject of a quarrel, then a violent dispute, then a small-scale war, with running battles between Genoans and Catalans through the streets of the city. All this took place in the first week of their arrival. In the end the emperor himself had to intervene to settle the dispute, as the clashes had reached the royal palace. The city breathed a collective sigh of relief when de Flor and his men finally left Constantinople in the winter of 1303 to start their campaign in Asia Minor, attacking the people they were supposed to attack, and accompanied by a large company of extremely unhappy Alan mercenaries.

Whatever we might say about The Grand Catalan Company, and their unruly, uncontrolled, thuggish behaviour, one thing is acknowledged by all sources – they beat every single army they came across, sometimes defeating forces three to four times larger than their own. Their pillaging and plundering were undisciplined, but as a fighting unit they were highly organised. In the space of just five months they drove the Turks from the city of Philadelphia, forced them to abandon the siege of Magnesia (today in the mid-western part of Turkey), and then marched all the way down to the borders of Armenia before coming back to Constantinople in late 1304.[27] Of course, they were also highly paid: some of their officers' salaries were significantly more than their Alan counterparts, a fact which partly accounted for the disastrous relations between the two groups of mercenaries. Quarrels and fights broke out with increasing frequency between the Alans and the Catalans; in one skirmish, de Flor's men killed the son of the Alan chieftain, along with much of his three-hundred-man bodyguard. The Alans eventually left the Catalans later that year, with the explanation, in the famous words of one chronicler, that they 'preferred death to Roger de Flor'.[28]

Apart from their quarrels with other Byzantine mercenaries, one of the problems with de Flor's men was that they often pillaged the very cities the emperor had paid them to protect. In Magnesia and Philadelphia, the Catalans tortured local Greeks to reveal to them where the townspeople had hidden their treasure. In many ways, the solution Andronikos had invited into Asia Minor turned out to be as bad as the problem. A second drawback was the superficiality of the campaign: although the Catalans had been highly effective in defeating the various Turkish armies they encountered, they could only move on after a battle without leaving any men behind, and so the territory was often re-conquered as soon as the mercenaries had disappeared.

There were other factors which gradually led to the Catalans abandoning their allegiance to their Byzantine employers and collaborating with the Turks against them. Andronikos' poor finances did not help the situation. De Flor complained they were not being paid, and it is a reflection of the emperor's financial desperation that he had tried to fool the mercenaries with fake coins. Roger de Flor's own delusions of grandeur also have to be taken into account. By late 1304, the falconer's son had convinced himself he was the heir to the 'kingdom of Anatolia', a title Andronikos was happy to bestow upon him, as the Byzantines had practically lost control of Asia Minor anyway.

One final cause for the Catalans' change of sides was the son of the emperor Andronikos (who ruled with him as co-emperor in the Byzantine practice), Michael IX, who was three years older than Roger de Flor and bitterly resented his military prowess. Whatever skills and talents Michael IX may have had, commanding an army was not one of them; in 1302 he led a disastrous campaign to protect the city of Magnesia (modern-day Manisa in western Turkey), whereby half of his army had deserted by the time he reached there. Michael IX was so unnerved by this that he secretly fled to Pergamon in the middle of the night. When his army woke up next morning and found he had gone, they packed up camp and followed him.[29]

When the Catalans discovered there was no more money to be obtained from Andronikos, they came back to Constantinople in 1305, stopping short of advancing on the city and instead establishing a base on the peninsula south of the capital – Gallipoli. The Byzantines, in other words, were faced with the peculiar prospect of being attacked by the very army they had financed to protect them against the Turks. Even more ironically, the Catalans had actually struck up a friendship with some of the Anatolian Turks, and had incorporated them as co-workers into the Company. It is illuminating to read the warm terms in which one of the Catalans' chroniclers, Ramon Muntaner, describes the decision to accept the help of the Turks, whose chief is unintelligibly communicated to us as 'Ximelich':

> With that we received [the Turks], who joined us with eight hundred horse and two thousand foot. And if ever people were obedient to a lord, they were to us; and if ever men were loyal and true, they were to us, always, and they were very expert men of arms. And so they stayed with us like brothers and they always remained near us ...

... and so ... we raided [the Byzantine] empire at our ease; for when the Turks and the Turcopoles went on forays, those of our men who wished went also, and much honour was shown them ... And so it could never be found that there was any strife between us and them.[30]

Although it is moving to see such sublime moments of inter-faith collaboration and cross-cultural communication between Muslims and Christians, the people we are talking about here were murderers, pillagers and rapists. The Catalan episode was a disaster for the populations of Asia Minor, and a setback for the Byzantines themselves. Nevertheless, it is interesting to see the extent to which a sense of 'brotherly' solidarity (we will encounter the term again in the story of Umur Pasha and Kantakouzenos) was able to exist between very different cultural groups; the Catalans, Aragonese and Sicilians the Turks found among the mercenaries would have been much more culturally different from them than the Byzantine Anatolian Greeks they were raiding together.

What happened to The Grand Catalan Company in the end? After the strange death of their leader Roger de Flor – murdered while visiting Michael IX, a visit whose reasons still appear to resist explanation – the Catalans, along with their Turkish allies, took their revenge upon the emperor's son, inflicting a crushing defeat on the Byzantines at the battle of Apros (now on the Turkish-Greek border) in July 1305. If we are to believe the chronicles, an estimated 2,500 Catalan/Turkish cavalry overwhelmed a numerically superior force of over fourteen thousand Greeks. One of the factors which contributed to the Catalans' victory was the thousand or so Tourkopoloi of Michael's armies, who – possibly reluctant to fight their fellow Turks among the Catalans – changed sides halfway through the battle.[31]

After their victory over Michael IX, The Grand Catalan Company spent the next two years raiding and pillaging Thrace. By 1307 their number was six thousand Spaniards and three thousand Turks. Eventually, they decided to move south into mainland Greece, which was occupied by the Latin forces of a French duke, Walter of Briennes. In fact, the entire region was called the Duchy of Athens, and had been under colonial rule (there is really no other word for it) by the Western Europeans since 1204. Looking at the kinds of Latins who had mini-principalities in Greece – dukes from Lecce, Angevins from Naples, French counts and Venetian traders – offers a sobering view of the miserable length of foreign rule many Greeks had to live under. In characteristic fashion, the Catalans started out by fighting for the French duke, but by 1311 had a change of heart and turned on their former employer. At the battle of Kephissos, The Grand Catalan Company (once again) defeated an army significantly larger than itself – and composed of the very finest French aristocracy in Greece – to lay the foundations for the Catalan Duchy of Athens, which was to last until 1388.[32] For the next seventy years, the kingdom of Catalonia, on the other side of the Mediterranean, would have a bastion of power and influence in the heart of the Byzantine Empire.

Before leaving the Catalans to talk about a Byzantine ruler and his close friendship with a Turkish bey of Aydin, some mention should be made of the brief but substantial period of Turk-Catalan alliances that sprang up during the period 1318–29 against Venice and its dependencies in other parts of the Greek peninsula. As I have already said, there was constant friction between the Venetians, the Genoans and the Catalans. Nothing expresses this mutual animosity more sharply than the various alliances which Alfonso, the new Catalan Duke of Athens, forged with two Turkish emirates on the coast opposite him – the emirs of Menteshe and Aydin. What is even more curious about this alliance is that it had to be kept secret. Military collaboration with the infidel gave the Catalans a bad name, and Alfonso tried his best to ensure no one found out about his understanding with the enemies of Christ – even to the extent of telling the Turks occasionally to attack some of his islands. In 1327, the Turks of Aydin sacked one of Alfonso's islands, Aigina, just to make it look like they were attacking all the Christian lands – and not merely the Venetian territories that Alfonso had asked them to raid.[33]

Unsurprisingly, Alfonso's tricks were ultimately discovered. The Venetians were already sceptical towards the Catalans and their designs on the territories Venice held in Greece, and it was no secret that Catalans and Turks had long enjoyed a 'special relationship'. In one 1322 history, the Venetian scholar Sanudo actually advocates a crusade against the Turks and Catalans, mentioning *Turchorum* and *Saracenorum* in the same breath as *Cathalanorum*. The Pope felt the same way. The Vatican had been trying to organise a league against the Turks in 1327, although the Angevins were lukewarm, Venice was already trying to re-establish commercial relations with the Turks and the Byzantines appeared to be reluctant to join, and more willing to sign treaties with the emirates of Saruhan and Osman. The Latin archbishop of Thebes had even advised the Pope, in drawing up the terms of the crusade, to view the Catalans as 'schismatics' and allies of the infidel. In other words, for Rome the Catalans had become merely a different kind of Turk.

And so what we have in the eastern Mediterranean at this time, far from any war of faith against faith, was a bewilderingly complex play of different forces and mechanisms, each with mini-histories of their own: a collection of Latin states occupying Greece from very different parts of Europe – Catalonia, France, Venice – each struggling to usurp the other, and fully prepared to use Muslim help to do so; a Turkish emirate quite happy to deal first with the Venetians, then with the Catalans, then even against both with the Byzantines; and a Constantinople trying to ascertain, in the midst of all the trade routes, military tensions and naval raids, from which direction the greatest threat was coming, while simultaneously trying to sort out its own internal power struggles. From this confusing situation will emerge the quite remarkable figure of John VI Kantakouzenos.

The friendship of Umur Pasha and Kantakouzenos (1335–48)

Although Kantakouzenos' Turcophilia, as it has been called, was striking – he was certainly the first Byzantine emperor to acquire a Muslim son-in-law – affectionate relations between the rulers of Constantinople and their Turkish neighbours were certainly not without precedent. When the Mongols defeated the Muslim Seljuk ruler Kaykawus II in 1261, he fled to Byzantium for safety. The choice of haven was hardly surprising; five years earlier, the Byzantine emperor Michael VIII had been driven out of his court by his own political rivals and had fled to the Seljuk capital in Konya, where he served Kaykawus for a short time as a leader of foreign troops for the Muslim ruler.[34] The rare tale of the decent and popular general Philanthropenos, who treated his defeated Turkish enemies so honourably after the re-capture of Philadelphia in 1295 that he incurred criticism for his humanity from the imperial court, also shows how Kantakouzenos' friendship with the Turks was no strange, singular episode. Philanthropenos treated the Turks he captured so well that his army soon had a significant Turkish contingent. When, thirty years later in 1323, the Anatolian Turks were again laying siege to the same city, Constantinople famously sent the same general – now an old, blind man – to negotiate. The Turks, remembering the

kindness Philanthropenos had shown thirty years earlier, gave up the
siege and withdrew.[35]

Of all the alliances that sprang up between Byzantines and Turks,
the decade-long friendship and military alliance between Umur of
Aydin and John VI Kantakouzenos (alternatively spelt 'Cantacuzene')
seems to merit particular attention. It was a relationship born out of
the needs of realpolitik, of course, and yet there seems to have been
a definite element of personal sincerity present in the alliance –
according to one otherwise unsympathetic chronicler, Kantakouzenos
and Umur were akin to 'Orestes and Pylades', the close companions
of Greek mythology.[36] On many occasions, Umur would honour his
friendship to Kantakouzenos, even when the opportunities were hardly
the most profitable for himself. This may be a testament either to
Umur's loyalty or Kantakouzenos' much-famed powers of persuasion
(probably both). Kantakouzenos was, after all, the kind of man who
could board a pirate ship heading east and persuade the corsairs to
turn around and join him in raiding an enemy's city in the opposite
direction.

What should also be said is that other Turkish-Byzantine alliances,
although there were quite a few of them, did not always go so well,
particularly when they were founded on pure political necessity, but
without any deeper element of mutual sympathy. The obvious example
is one of Kantakouzenos' opponents, Anna of Savoy (the wife of the
deceased emperor he had allegedly 'usurped'). In response to the
effectiveness of Kantakouzenos' own Turkish allies, she formed her own
alliance in 1346 with one of their rival Turkish emirates, the Emir of
Saruhan, with little success. When they arrived in Thrace to help her,
they immediately started to raid and pillage the very areas they were
supposed to defend, and eventually went over to Kantakouzenos' side
– all proof enough that simple 'deals' were not enough to ensure a sound
alliance.[37] The two parties actually had to like and respect one another
as well; in the case of Kantakouzenos and Umur, as we shall see, the
relationship went beyond mere cordiality and diplomatic hospitality –
from the very start, the two were calling one another 'brother'.

Umur and Kantakouzenos first met in 1335 in what is today the
western Turkish town of Karaburun. Kantakouzenos was nearly forty,
Umur probably around twenty-five.[38] The age difference may explain
the respect Umur consistently showed his Greek counterpart, although
the fact that Kantakouzenos could speak Turkish – and their mutual
distrust of the Latins they had come to Karaburun to fight – clearly

contributed to their immediate understanding. The Turkish report of
the meeting narrates it so: 'They talked, wished each other well, and
became brothers' (*gorişip esenleşip kardaş olur*). The version must be
fairly accurate, because in the memoirs Kantakouzenos wrote as an
old man, he gives an equally warm version of events:

> I had already corresponded with Umur and shown him my good will
> and, when Umur came to Phokaia, I met with him for a short time
> . . .
>
> When I got out of the ship, he immediately welcomed me and
> entertained me and showed me great courtesy. I spent four days with
> my friend, and managed to persuade him to see the [Byzantine]
> emperor as his lord and myself as one of the most important nobles
> in the area. And so I forged with him an unbreakable bond of
> friendship.[39]

The situations of the two men, however, were quite complex, and
it might be worthwhile to spend a moment describing them. It would
certainly take a separate chapter to relate the complicated power
struggles which Kantakouzenos had seen in the past fifteen years of
his life up to this point – and things were not going to become any
simpler as time went on. Like most royal histories, Byzantine feuds
often involved family struggles – father against son, nephew against
uncle, even grandfather against grandson. Kantakouzenos was a kind
of Kennedy figure in the Constantinople of the 1320s, young, rich,
politically eligible and belonging to one of the most powerful families
in the Greek-speaking world. He had been the best friend of the young
emperor Andronikos III, a close companion from his student days,
and the friendship had brought him into the brief power struggle
between the the youth Andronikos and his grandfather, Andronikos
II. In 1330, five years before Umur and Kantakouzenos' meeting, the
old emperor had finally agreed to give up the throne and pass it on
exclusively to his grandson. Andronikos III had tried, on several
occasions, to persuade Kantakouzenos to rule with him as co-emperor,
but it appears the vice-regent didn't want the job.

Byzantium's power struggles, as I have already said, are often
considered remarkable, arising as they do in a time when the influence
of the Turkish emirates in Asia was growing day by day. Armies of
Turks, newly converted Muslim Greeks and angry, disaffected Byzantine
Christians were beginning to capture town after town on the Asian

coast. Conversion to Islam abounded. The Greek patriarch, in 1338, even had to write to the people of Nicaea (today's Iznik) to order them not to give up their Christian faith.[40] Amid all of this, in a situation of apparent crisis, the rival emperors of Byzantium engaged in several protracted and time-consuming civil wars with one another, wars in which Kantakouzenos was centrally involved. For this reason Kantakouzenos, although a major statesman and a gifted writer, has had an ambiguous reputation among his chroniclers – both contemporary and subsequent – not only as the egoist who preferred to divide Byzantines among themselves rather than let go of the throne, but also as the Greek whose use of Turkish allies basically established them on the European side of the Bosphorus, and laid the foundations for the eventual fall of Constantinople itself. Kantakouzenos' knowledge of Turkish and the obvious ease with which he could dialogue and interact (and, of course, inter-marry) with the 'barbarians', for some historians, amounted to consorting with the enemy. The very fact that Kantakouzenos referred to the Turkish troops in his army as 'auxiliary infantry' (*symmachia peze*), while other historians simply called them 'mercenaries' (*mistophoroi*), says a great deal about the different perceptions people had of his own Muslim alliances.[41] The suspicion, as one historian finally put it, was that 'Kantakouzenos loved the Turks just as much as he hated the Romans [Byzantines]'.

In any case, by the time Kantakouzenos met Umur, he was co-emperor in all but name. His long-standing friendship with Andronikos III caused problems with the emperor's wife, who was popularly said to be jealous of Kantakouzenos' familiarity with Andronikos, although these problems would only emerge in a concrete form after the emperor's death. The young Turkish ruler Kantakouzenos met, though, in 1335, was by no means an inexperienced and impressionable youth. Umur of Aydin was the ruler of a relatively young Turkish emirate on the western coast, one which at the time had just as much power and prestige as its neighbouring Muslim territory, that of the Ottomans. Fate, however, along with a rare moment of unity on the part of Venice, Genoa and Rome, would soon transform it into one of the also-rans of early Turkish history – by 1390 the Ottomans had swallowed it up whole. When Umur met Kantakouzenos, his father had just died the previous year, bequeathing to him a princedom – the Emirate of Aydin – made up of several cities, including the wealthy port of Smyrna, today's Izmir.

It is not too surprising that Umur and Kantakouzenos got along. A contemporary of Umur's, the Orthodox monk and historian

Gregoras, bestows unusual praise on Umur's humanity and good character, and considers him (for a Turk) a man not completely devoid of 'Hellenic civilisation'.[42] Umur's court certainly confirms this impression of a place where the representatives of all three religions could be found. In fact, an anecdote reinforcing this comes from an unexpected direction: around 1331, the famous Arab traveller Ibn Battuta passed through the court of Aydin on his way to Constantinople. His report is full of praise for the court and its hospitality towards him, but on his last day there he sees a Jewish physician come into the chamber of the sultan. Ibn Battuta, clearly used to a different treatment of Jews in his native Tunisia, is horrified to find the dignitaries of the court standing up to salute the Jewish doctor, who then has the audacity to seat himself near the sultan, and above the Koran-readers. 'You God-damned son of a God-damned father' the traveller shouts out, 'how dare you sit up there above the readers of the Koran, and you a Jew?' The Arab traveller's anger is a good indication of the extent of multi-faith relations in Turkish-controlled Anatolia, even if we should not exaggerate this too much. Ibn Battuta, while passing through the emirate of Aydin, also bought himself a couple of Greek slaves.[43]

Umur's Turks had spent the previous ten years raiding Latin and Greek territories both in the Aegean and on the Black Sea, as well as trying to take the last remaining Byzantine towns in Asia Minor. As we have already seen, they had profited from a number of alliances with the Catalans. In 1335, however, the West was beginning to move against them. Encouraged by an unusually evangelical Pope – John XXII had already established bishoprics for the first time in Armenia, Iran and India – a union of Venetians, Genoans, Cypriots and Frenchmen had regained control of the Aegean with a fleet of forty ships and attempted to re-take the city of Izmir from Umur in 1334. In fact, Umur was meeting with the Greeks because the Genoans had grabbed an island from them (Lesbos) in the Gulf of Izmir and was holding hostage there the son of another Turkish emir, Saruhan.

The negotiations appear to have gone well. One of the Turkish emirs agreed to send a fleet of ships to help the Greeks – primarily because it was his son who was being held hostage by them. Umur also seems to have been persuaded by Kantakouzenos to join in the attack. Even though the young Turkish ruler had led several expeditions against Byzantine territories, the Greeks' enemy of the moment was definitely the most serious threat Umur's own realm had to face. United against the Latins, it was not too surprising that an 'unbreakable bond of friendship' was formed. One other interesting condition: Kantakouzenos also asked Umur to stop attacking the Greek city of Philadelphia, in the middle of his realm. Umur appears to have consented, but also warned that his campaigns would need to have another target, if he was to stop raiding Byzantine ones.

What followed was, to modern readers (if not to contemporary sources) a slightly bizarre deal. Kantakouzenos cleverly found convenient targets to send Umur and his Turks against, a tactic which was good news for Byzantium, but bad news for Albanians and Bulgarians. As these two groups had been putting pressure on the empire's northern borders, Kantakouzenos simply directed his ally Umur to attack them, accompanied by his own Greek troops and with a promise of significant plunder and booty to take back with them. In the spring of 1338, an infantry regiment of two thousand Turkish footsoldiers, alongside a Byzantine auxiliary troop, left the Byzantine city of Saloniki for the foothills of Thrace to attack a force of Albanian bandits.[44] The attack went well; the bandits were overwhelmed by the lighter-armed Turks, and eventually withdrew, leaving so much plunder (cattle, goods, human slaves) behind them that Umur and Kantakouzenos' troops were unable to take with them everything that was left.

This practice of Turks fighting directly alongside, and occasionally even intermingled with, Greek soldiers would become a common practice for the next ten years. In a later battle (Peritheorion, 1345) fought against the Serbs, reports give a clear picture of how Kantakouzenos' Christian/Muslim army was arranged. On the left flank stood the heavy (Byzantine) cavalry of Asen, Kantakouzenos' brother-in-law; in the centre was Kantakouzenos' own picked guard of mixed Byzantine and Turkish troops; and on the right flank were Umur's Turkish archers. The fact that Turkish and Byzantine troops could fight so closely together – and not simply divided up into sections according to ethnic status, as was standard practice – does suggest an unusually high level of co-operation and communication between Greeks and non-Greeks. Certainly Kantakouzenos' own guard – and the fact that they were fighting quite intimately alongside one another – discourages the idea that Umur's Turks were some kind of wild, savage force that a Byzantine emperor occasionally summoned to his side to win a battle or take a town.[45]

Such an idea that Turkish troops, fighting on behalf of Greeks, were somehow alien or frightening would also be contested by another fact: the gradual homogenisation of military tactics, equipment and uniform in medieval Byzantine history. As the military historian Bartusis points out, the centuries-long mixing of Norman, Italian, Turkish and nomadic influences – detected, for example, in the styles of weapons or armour – had by the fourteenth century produced a manner of warfare which was definitely becoming standard, quite regardless of whether the army concerned was Turkish or Byzantine. Drawings and descriptions of Byzantine soldiers, for example, reveal a very definite Islamic influence in their dress and weaponry: curved swords and daggers, Seljuk-style helmets whose backs extended down to the shoulders. A curved sabre seen in a Serbian painting even appears to resemble similar weapons used in fourteenth-century Mameluk Egypt.[46] The upshot of all this, naturally, is that the Turkish 'barbarians' who came to assist the Byzantines didn't have horns on their heads; their outward appearance would not have been physically that different from the Greeks they had come to help.

Up to now, Kantakouzenos had only used Turkish troops against non-Greeks – against the Genoans and to repel the Albanian bandits in 1338. In 1341, however, an event took place which would bring a costly civil war to the court of Constantinople for the next thirty years: the emperor Andronikos III died of an illness, at the age of forty-five. It was to be a civil war that would see the use of Turkish troops on both sides. The death of the emperor sent waves of instability rippling out into the shrinking empire, as the deaths of sovereigns invariably do. Almost immediately, from five different directions, Byzantium's neighbouring states responded to the news. From the northwest, the Serbian emperor began to make incursions into Macedonia; from the north, the Bulgarian tsar started to demand the extradition of political prisoners from Constantinople; south in Asia Minor, Orhan and his Ottoman emirate continued their expansion, absorbing town after town at the expense of the gradually crumbling Byzantine Empire. Even Umur of Aydin, on learning the news, prepares a series of raids against Byzantine territories to profit from the emperor's death (until Kantakouzenos stops him in the nick of time and, in a masterful moment of persuasion, convinces his 'brother' to attack the Bulgarians instead).[47]

All this would have been bad enough if the political classes of Constantinople had been united. Naturally, they were not. The emperor had left behind a somewhat vulnerable nine-year-old boy, John V Palaiologos. Kantakouzenos was unsure whether to declare himself emperor, or simply regent of the child. The emperor's widow, Anna of Savoy, a forceful and assertive figure, had never really liked Kantakouzenos and now suspected him of having designs on her husband's empty throne. To make matters worse, a former 'friend' of Kantakouzenos called Apokaukos, wholly unrelated to either of the two powerful families, was plotting his own campaign to become emperor. Finally, a violent wave of social unrest erupted, incited by a frustrated underclass tired of aristocracy and its endless mismanagement of internal and external affairs. In cities such as Adrianopolis (Edirne) and Thessaloniki, people took to the streets, burned down buildings, and denounced anything representing aristocracy and elitism as 'Kantakouzenism'. Historians with bourgeois sympathies paint this episode as a regrettable lapse into anarchy; it could also, however, be seen as a refreshing precedent for popular protest. Whatever we may think, the empire appeared to be falling apart. All in all, it was a bit of a mess.

The consequence of this mess, however, was an increasing reliance on Turkish troops. Umur's friendship facilitated one such reliance; and when Kantakouzenos finally decides that he *does* want to be emperor after all – partly because he envisages handing the throne down to his own son, Matthew – Umur and the Turks of Aydin will be of crucial assistance in his struggle to take power.

In 1341 Kantakouzenos retired to the city of Didymotechion – once one of the most significant cities in Byzantine Greece – and crowned himself emperor. Anna, the deceased emperor's wife, threw in her support with the cause of Apokaukos. A civil war was fully declared. At first, it seems clear Kantakouzenos was reluctant about inviting Turkish soldiers onto Greek soil (he would spend a great deal of time apologising for it to everyone in years to come, including the Pope). Indeed, his first choice of an alliance appears to have been the Kingdom of Serbia – a dangerous choice, since its expansion was threatening the very Byzantine lands Kantakouzenos was struggling for control over. The ruler of Serbia was the legendary King Stefan Dusan, a sovereign who had spent his childhood growing up in Constantinople and who was therefore intimately familiar with Byzantine Greek culture. The two men, who would eventually quarrel and become bitter enemies, formed a brief alliance in 1341. Stefan agreed to help Kantakouzenos march militarily into the city of Constantinople.

The story of Kantakouzenos' collaboration with the Serbs is something of a disaster. The first time Stefan gave him an army of soldiers led by twenty of his best officers, but they were decimated by an outbreak of food poisoning before they could reach Constantinople, and Kantakouzenos ended up leading a small fraction of them back into Serbia. The second time Stefan gave Kantakouzenos (in the Byzantine's own words) a 'useless mob', and by the time Kantakouzenos got them once again to the Serbian border half of them had deserted for fear of never seeing their homes again. For a third time – the situation is almost comic – Kantakouzenos went back into Serbia to get a decent army, and this time received a contingent of quality Latin and Catalan mercenaries, some of whom later became his own personal bodyguard. By this time, however, relations between Kantakouzenos and Stefan were beginning to cool, and as one Byzantine city after another was coming over to Kantakouzenos' side anyway, it seemed he no longer needed Serbian help.[48]

This all stands in stark contrast to the kind of assistance Kantakouzenos' 'blood-brother', Umur, gave him. The aspiring emperor called on his Turkish friend to help him on three occasions – in 1342, 1343 and 1345 – and all three times Umur appeared unfailingly with boatloads of troops, Turkish and Anatolian Greek, both unconverted and newly converted, to significantly decide Kantakouzenos' position: first against the Bulgarians (whom Umur drove away from the gates of Didymotechion), then against Kantakouzenos' rival Apokaukos (whose armies hastily withdrew from Saloniki when they saw Umur arrive to help his 'brother' – with nearly six thousand troops behind him), and finally against the very Serbs Kantakouzenos had once made a brief alliance with.[49]

In 1345, Umur – along with another Muslim emir from the western Turkish coast, Prince Suleiman – arrives on the Bulgarian coast and, with an enormous number of cavalry, helps his Byzantine ally vanquish a Slav adventurer called Momčilo who had been working for the Serbian king. Once the Serbs are dealt with, Umur actually escorts Kantakouzenos up to the very gates of Constantinople, before setting off back home. This is far from the only time that a Turkish army will arrive at the walls of the city – the city one day, a century later, the Turks will be fated to conquer. Umur's military assistance to his Byzantine 'brother' will initiate a whole series of Turkish interventions in the politics of Constantinople, as one sultan after another lends a helping hand – sometimes sincerely, sometimes with the malevolent intent to divide –

in the power struggles of the Greeks. For now, Umur's Turkish troops are simply foreign auxiliaries, there to help a local political ally gain power. One day, however, their presence will not be so temporary.

What we have here, in many ways, are two kinds of Muslim-Christian alliance. The first kind would be that illustrated, for example, by the alliance of Osman (the first Ottoman sultan) and the Christian ruler of Harman Kaya, Köse Mihal – a bond not just between individuals but also between peoples who lived next to one another and who either shared, or at the very least were familiar with, the other's culture. The second kind of alliance would be that of Kantakouzenos and Umur – an understanding, and even close friendship, between military and economic elites, but not one which necessarily reflected any similiar feelings in the Greeks and Turks these rulers represented. Many of Kantakouzenos' subjects would hate him for allying with the Turks (although the citizens of Saloniki, after Umur's troops drove Albanian bandits away from the town in 1338, were full of praise for him). Umur's undoubted friendship with Kantakouzenos, for all its sincerity, did not stop him pillaging and sacking the Thracian coast when he saw fit. The fact that Kantakouzenos, on at least one recorded occasion, encountered in the middle of a battle Turks on the opponent's side who had been fighting for him a few years earlier, also suggests that there are some alliances we should be less idealistic about than others.

The Wedding of Theodora with Sultan Orhan I: A Byzantine Emperor and his Muslim son-in-law

Our story of Umur and Kantakouzenos is not quite over. There is, in the Turkish chronicles, an interesting tale concerning the three beautiful daughters of Kantakouzenos which is worth a mention. Of course, as the historian Kafadar points out, Turkish chronicles do have a tendency to indulge in the fantasy of Byzantine women who throw themselves at the feet of brave, unflinching Muslim warriors. In this case, one of the daughters of Kantakouzenos – Theodora – falls in love with Umur during a festive visit to the Greek ruler's house. Kantakouzenos offers Umur her hand in marriage, but Umur sternly refuses on the grounds that his friendship with Kantakouzenos is so close, it would be like marrying his own family: 'But who can give his daughter in marriage to his brother? The emperor is my brother, his daughter is my daughter, in our religion that cannot be'.[50] Umur even goes so far as to call such a union 'incest' (*haram*). When they are hunting in the forest later on, the insistent daughter approaches him again, and implores him one more time to accept her advances. Umur, in his reply, almost sounds like Sir Gawain:

> 'Go away, have shame before God, leave us', he cried, 'do not be without honour, do not speak to me in this way.'
>
> The Pasha [Umur] hid his face in his hands and covered his eyes, cursing his own weakness. The young woman left, looking behind her, bewildered and confused, her eyes full of tears.[51]

Although it remains unclear how much of the episode actually took place in reality, and how much within the Turkish poet's imagination, most historians seem to feel that some kind of marriage offer was unsuccessfully proposed to Umur by the Byzantine ruler, probably two years before the same girl – Theodora – was married off to Umur's Ottoman neighbour, Orhan.[52] Politically, Orhan was a good choice of son-in-law – his emirate, as we know, was expanding across Anatolia and rapidly becoming the most powerful polity in the region. A useful dynasty to be married to, given the reverse trend of Byzantium's own political and military fortunes. Indeed, for seven years after Sultan Orhan's marriage to Kantakouzenos' daughter, the Ottomans make no incursions into Byzantine territories.

Exactly how Theodora felt about it is a different matter. The marriage took place in 1346; Orhan was nearly sixty, Theodora cannot have been older than twenty-five. Orhan was apparently enraptured by the emperor's daughter; Theodora, if we are to believe the accounts, must have been thinking of the handsome (not to mention younger) Umur whose friendship to her father had prevented their marriage. Umur, in any case, would be killed two years after the wedding took place – he lost his life at the age of thirty-eight, fighting to keep the Latins from re-taking Izmir.

The wedding took place on Byzantine soil, with the bridegroom himself absent from the ceremony. Orhan sent thirty ships of men to escort his young bride from the Thracian town of Selymbria to her new home. There was, it appears, no obligation for the daughter to convert to the Islamic faith. In the procession to the wedding, apparently, the bride's father remained on horseback, while everyone – even Orhan's Turkish troops – dismounted and went on foot out of respect. The wedding ceremony was a grand affair, and celebrated by a large party of Greeks and Turks together. Theodora was displayed (in the Byzantine tradition) in a cluster of silk and gilded curtains. After a long period of music, a silence took place in which Orthodox prayers were recited for the bride, before she was finally taken away to her husband.[53]

Kantakouzenos went over to Asia Minor to meet his Muslim son-in-law – probably for the first time – the following year, visiting Turkish Skutari (today's Üsküdar) just across the water from Constantinople. They appear to have had a good time – Kantakouzenos sat and ate with Orhan, while Orhan's four sons (from his other wives) ate at a separate table. Orhan still seems to have been wary of coming over into Byzantine territory, as Kantakouzenos' offer to return the hospitality to his son-in-law in Constantinople is declined, although Orhan's four sons do go back with him to Byzantium to carry on celebrations there. Theodora also comes along, taking the opportunity to visit her mother for a few days before returning to Orhan's palace. She would remain there in Ottoman Bithynia – by all accounts an exemplary Christian, and one whom (we are told) even encouraged former Christians who had converted to Islam to return to their faith – until Orhan's death in 1360, after which she returned to live with her mother in Byzantium. Did she spend those years pining away for the man who rejected her, the Umur who had been slain in battle? Or perhaps for a young Greek nobleman from her own childhood? Or did she finally learn to love a man over thirty years her senior? We really have no way of knowing.

Inter-faith marriages

In an attempt to show how, on so many levels and in so many ways, Muslims do not belong to an 'other' civilisation, marriage alliances are as important as military ones. More often than not, they went together. Kantakouzenos, in his memoirs, suggests there were what amounted to 'finishing schools' in Byzantine kingdoms such as Trebizond, as well as in Constantinople, where exceptionally beautiful Greek girls (sometimes princesses, sometimes of more lowly descent) were educated and prepared as brides for Mongol, and later Turkish, lords. The purpose was exclusively to 'escape destruction', an aim it seems to have served for quite a while.[54] We certainly know that inter-marriage between Muslims and Christians in this period was not confined to aristocrats, as the presence of endless *mourtatoi* (the offspring between Greeks and Turks) attests. And yet the aristocratic Muslim-Christian marriages are interesting not merely because of their enormous symbolic value – as amazing as it sounds today, the marriage alliances of the late-medieval Byzantines link the aristocracies of Western Europe with the Turkish *kiriltays* of central Asia. They are also important for the highly significant territorial and political implications such unions have for both parties. The endless number of Greek princesses who married Ottoman sultans means, as the scholar Bryer points out, that by 1453 Mehmet II had a much more convincing claim to the Byzantine throne than Kantakouzenos had had in 1345.[55] The mothers of numerous sultans were Greek, including the mothers of Murad I and Bayezid. Such inter-marriages underline what I have been trying to show all along – that Byzantines and Ottomans were *not* two separate, distinct entities, not simply 'Greeks and Turks' or 'Muslims and Christians'. The two traditions were linked together in a number of profound and complex ways, ways which suggest religious identity did not always play a primary, or sometimes even significant, role. Mehmet II's remarkable words, as the sultan visited the site of ancient Troy after the Fall of Constantinople, are revealing for how he saw his own conquest of Byzantium: 'It was the Greeks and Macedonians . . . who ravaged this place in the past, and their descendants have now paid the penalty . . . for their injustices to us Asiatics'.[56] The fact that, in some moments at least, the Turks could see themselves not as Islamic warriors but rather as returning Trojans does show there are many more ways of viewing the Ottoman Empire than simply 'Muslim'.

Between 1297 and 1461, over thirty-four Byzantine and Serbian princesses married Muslim rulers – Mongol, Turkish and Turkmen. Inter-faith marriages certainly pre-date this period, of course; a number of Turkish epics and ballads mention such arrangements, and the Turkmen dynasty of the Danishmenids were often quite happy to include an Armenian genealogy in their own dynastic histories – naturally, with the ulterior motive of justifying their rule over such subjects. At least one Byzantine chronicler has claimed that Osman, the legendary founder of the Ottoman dynasty, was the grandson of a marriage, in the 1140s, between a Seljuk princess and a Byzantine nobleman called John Komnenos.[57] Given the mystery of Osman's origins, we should reserve judgement – although the example is interesting, being one of the few instances when a Muslim princess married a Christian male, rather than vice versa.

Theodora's retention of her Christian faith, in her marriage to Orhan, was something of an exception, although there were other examples of Christian princesses who, married to Muslim rulers, managed to resist conversion to Islam. The most striking is *another* Theodora, this time a good hundred years later, who married a Turkish ruler called Uzun Hasan in 1458 and became his *hatun* or princess. This Theodora not only kept a large Christian household, but also represented her Muslim husband in political dialogue with Western rulers. Even when Christian princesses converted to Islam for their marriage, it was not always certain a genuine conversion had taken place. The Arab traveller Ibn Battuta records travelling in the same caravan as a Byzantine noblewoman who had married a ruler of the central Asian Kipchak tribes; now a converted Muslim, the princess was returning to Constantinople briefly to visit her parents. As soon as the caravan entered Bulgaria – Christian soil – Ibn Battuta was appalled to see her throw off her veil, and start eating pork and drinking wine.[58]

Kantakouzenos' reign and after (1347–1400)

Kantakouzenos spent seven years on the throne, after which the empire returned to its long, hitherto unbroken administration by the Palaiologoi dynasty. The next forty years, however, would see only civil strife between the two families. It was a complicated picture, with the son of Kantakouzenos, Matthew, continuing the struggle against the son and grandson of Andronikos III (Palaiologos). Although both sides did make use of Turkish troops, it was Kantakouzenos who was really seen to be the ally of Orhan and the Ottomans. John V – the little boy who should have been crowned emperor when his father Andronikos III died in 1341 – had grown up to become the military opponent of Kantakouzenos, against whom he made an alliance not with the Turks but with the Serbs and Latins.

And so what we see in Constantinople, effectively, is a game of chess played by two players who are not Greeks; where two rival parties struggle for the imperial throne, each supported by a powerful neighbour (Serbs and Turks), neighbours who are more than happy to see the problem-beset Byzantine state gradually implode. Within this period, the fact of Turkish soldiers fighting alongside Christian troops for one of the two struggling factions (usually Kantakouzenos') becomes so frequent that it is scarcely worth mentioning their presence. While Kantakouzenos is emperor, John V desperately tries to rally help around him to depose the 'usurper'. For a while, he remains unsuccessful. At a battle on the Marica river in 1352, thousands of Orhan's Turks, fighting for Kantakouzenos, overwhelmingly defeat a Serbian army which John V had called to fight for him. At this defeat, allegedly, the Bulgarian cavalry chose to withdraw at the last minute without engaging once in the conflict.[59] In 1356, Orhan sends five thousand Turks to accompany Matthew in a march on the city of Constantinople. The same manoeuvres, with different names and different dates, are played out again and again, as the Ottoman sultans support one Byzantine rival or another. In 1376, Andronikos IV stages a coup and with Turkish and Genoese help he is able to re-take his own throne (although he has to give Gallipoli to the Ottomans as payment). In 1379, John V actually brings a Turkish army (with the blessing of Sultan Murad I) into Constantinople. In 1390, John VII besieges Constantinople with a Turkish and Genoese army; interestingly, although the inhabitants are happy to see John VII appear, they let the Genoese army in through the gates but not the Turks.

This repeated use of Turkish troops by Byzantine emperors – or would-be emperors – shows how dependent Byzantium had become on its Ottoman neighbour. In fact, 'neighbour' is an understatement: by the 1390s, the Ottoman Empire was a sea stretching across the Balkans from coast to coast, and the Byzantine 'empire' a series of tiny dotted islands in that Ottoman sea – Constantinople, Thessaloniki and the Greek peninsula. Unlike the early alliances with Umur and Orhan, which had been more or less between equals, the collaborations of the second half of the fourteenth century were that of an interested and by no means well-intentioned superpower in the internal disturbances of a minor state. After the 1370s, the Byzantine emperors acquired the status of 'vassals' for the sultan, which meant the rather depressing obligation of having to go and fight in the sultan's wars for him. Orthodox countries in other parts of the world found this humiliating. One Russian prince was so disgusted by the presence of a Byzantine emperor in the armies of the Turkish sultan that he declared the Orthodox world still had a patriarch, but no emperor anymore – and struck the emperor's name out of the liturgy. The relationship of a vassal to his monarch was certainly a strange one; several times the sultan would refer to the Byzantine emperor as 'my son' in official documents (Murad I calls Manuel II this on at least one occasion), and in 1403 Prince Suleiman even refers to John VII as 'my father'.[60] And yet there is little doubt that vassalship could be particularly humiliating – especially when the sovereign himself had to accompany his overlord on the prescribed campaign. The learned emperor Manuel II Palaiologos – a man who was not just an emperor, but also a scholar and a poet[61] – was forced to do this in 1391–2, when he found himself with an army of Greeks fighting for Sultan Bayezid I in the middle of eastern Turkey against one of the sultan's Turkmen rivals. From the letters on campaign Manuel II writes back home to his friend, we know that he is deeply depressed at having to serve in Bayezid's armies, and even more distraught at having to attend the sultan's drinking parties in his tent every evening.[62]

Although Constantinople fell in 1453, it should really have been taken fifty years earlier. By 1390, most Byzantines could see the game was over. It was simply a question of time before the unofficial Ottoman dependency – which is what Byzantium essentially was – would become an acknowledged part of the Ottoman Empire. By the end of the century, the strained relationship of vassalhood which had prevented Constantinople's fall was beginning to collapse. The more sedate ruler Murad I was succeeded by Bayezid, whose designs on Constantinople immediately became clear. In fact, Bayezid had already begun a siege of the city in 1402, and would have taken it but for the sudden arrival in the east of Asia Minor of an extraordinary army which had just spent the past seven years sacking the cities of Delhi, Damascus and (very nearly) Moscow. Bayezid's nemesis, known to the West as the infamous Tamerlane, had arrived. When Bayezid left the siege of Constantinople to head into Asia Minor to fight him, he was leaving behind a city he would not see again.

Timur and the battle of Ankara (1402): Bayezid's loyal Serbs, disloyal Turks

At the mention of Bayezid I and vassalhood, we shall finally turn our attention away from Turkish-Byzantine alliances towards Turkish-Serbian ones. Even though vassals are hardly model examples of voluntary collaboration and cross-cultural alliance, the case of the battle of Ankara – where the Ottoman sultan was deserted by practically the entirety of his Turkish troops, but staunchly defended by his Christian Serb vassals – is so unusual it deserves some mention.

The vast military campaigns of Tamerlane, whose real name was Timur, stretched across the world of the fourteenth century from India to Russia, and from China to Iraq. The level of destruction and dimension of atrocity this Mongol-Turk tribal leader was responsible for have made his name a synonym for absolute, unchecked rampage: Timur's armies methodically sacked cities, murdering entire populations often in the cruellest ways – skinning them, burning them or burying thousands of them alive in ditches. Although claiming to be a Muslim – and often rebuking other states for not being Islamic enough – his massacres made little distinction between faiths.

It was this army that arrived on the outskirts of the Ottoman city of Sivas (today in the northeast of modern Turkey) in 1400, on the very edges of Bayezid I's growing empire. The majority of the Ottoman troops who vainly defended the town against Timur were Armenian *sipahis* or cavalry; when the town finally capitulated, they were buried alive in the moat of the city. One Christian chronicler reports how a choir of children came out singing in an attempt to provoke some clemency in the chieftain's heart; Timur simply ordered his cavalry to mow them down.[63] In comparison to the relatively mild rule of the Ottomans, the Armenians must have found their latest Muslim conqueror to be the nearest version of Hell imaginable.

Timur saw Sultan Bayezid as a significant regional power, one whose ambitions could not be allowed to co-exist with his own without some form of tribute or acknowledgement from the Ottomans, which Bayezid (whose ego was easily as large as Timur's) was unwilling to give. The two rulers had already exchanged declarations. Ambassadors had been sent to Bayezid's court with a letter, in which Timur poured scorn on the obscure origins of the Ottoman dynasty, suggesting they were descended from slaves.[64] Bayezid sent the messengers back to Timur with their beards shaved off, and a coarse warning that if Timur dared to come to him, he would sexually molest his wife. The two men would meet soon enough, but not on terms Bayezid would have imagined.

In 1402, Bayezid left the siege of Constantinople without raising it – indeed, the city would be on the brink of surrendering in his absence – and moved southwards with his army to meet Timur in central Turkey, near the modern capital of Ankara. One chronicler suggests Timur, on his way westwards from Sivas to Ankara through the middle of Turkey, had conscripted large numbers of Armenians into his army.[65] If this is the case, then there were Christian soldiers on both sides of the battle which was fought in the July of that year. Bayezid had brought with him, along with his Turkish emirs, his Serbian vassal (and brother-in-law) Stefan Lazarevic.

The story of Prince Stefan Lazarevic is a curious one, and illustrates how being a vassal to a sovereign did not necessarily empty the relationship of any personal sentiment. In Stefan's case, his loyalty to Bayezid I is all the more striking because of two facts: first of all, Bayezid's own character, which was often cruel, erratic and impulsive (in Turkish he is called *Yildirim* or 'the thunderbolt'). More significantly, Stefan's own father had been killed by Bayezid's army at the battle of Kosovo in 1389, the conflict which effectively delivered the Kingdom of Serbia into Ottoman hands. The battle of Kosovo is famous for the assassination of Sultan Murad I (Bayezid's father) in his tent by a Serbian knight, pretending to visit the sultan as a traitor with information to give. After the Serbs were defeated, Stefan's father, King Lazar of Serbia, was brought into the very same tent and executed on the spot. Perhaps, in a rather macabre way, the violent deaths of their fathers provided some kind of empathy between the two men.

Whatever their pasts, Bayezid is reported to have held Prince Stefan in high esteem, bestowing upon him a respect which he did not always accord his other Christian vassals, or even his own Muslim sons. He marries Stefan's sister (although this would naturally be to legitimise his subjection of the Serbs), and appears to have held a special regard both for Stefan and his family members. When, for example, some of Stefan's nobles complain to Bayezid that he is doing a deal with the Hungarians against the Turks, Stefan first allows his mother to travel to Edirne and plead his case with the sultan, and then actually goes himself. Both mother and son are received generously by Bayezid, and the embarrassing situation is resolved.[66] 'I think of you as my eldest and favourite son', Bayezid reportedly tells him. 'Who stands before me in such honour as you? I am already growing old, and soon will die perhaps in battle or of illness – and then your time will come.'[67] Stefan's own role in saving the life of Bayezid's son, Prince Suleiman, at the battle of Ankara and bringing him away from the field of conflict also suggests the Serb's vassaldom was something more than a mere mechanical obedience to an overlord.

This is reflected in the arrangement of the enormous army which meets Timur's even larger force on 20 July 1402. It is difficult to know how correct the figures are. Bayezid's men number 85,000, we are told, whereas Timur's eight detachments amount to well over

140,000 (not to mention thirty-five Indian elephants). And yet what is interesting is that Prince Stefan is given command not of his own troops – which are led by his brother, Vuk – but of the Ottoman army's entire right flank, putting the Serbian prince in charge of Muslim nobles such as Timurtash Pasha, Firuz Bey and Hadjit Il-Bey.[68] The Serbian contingent itself numbers around five thousand men, clad in the singular black chainmail which may have played a part in the distinction with which the Serbs fought (and which appears to be unanimously recognised in all the sources, Muslim and Christian).

The battle takes place on a hot July day, outside the small town of Cubuk, on a high plain strewn with hills and valleys to the northeast of the city of Ankara. Timur cleverly dams the river which would have served as the only water supply for Bayezid's army, so that the parched Ottoman troops have to fight a full-scale battle without water in the middle of summer. The actual battle itself lasts around six hours. At the beginning, Timur orders his archers to release a rain of arrows upon the left flank of the Ottoman army, commanded by Bayezid's son, Prince Suleiman. The flank suffers terrible casualties. At the same time, Timur's Cagatays attack the Serb contingent, who resist the attack effectively, but soon find themselves overwhelmed and forced back to gather themselves around another Turkish noble, Melik Shah.

At this point, an incident takes place which will be inscribed in the memory of Turkish chroniclers for years to come. Bayezid's Muslim princes had long been unhappy, for a variety of reasons, with their Ottoman overlord, and the unsatisfactory conditions of the campaign – along with the secret wooing of Timur – combined to provoke an act of treachery which would cost the sultan his empire and his life. The Tatar cavalry of Bayezid's left flank, situated at the very rear of the army, suddenly take the side of Timur and actually begin to attack the Ottoman army from behind. Chaos ensues as the entire left flank begins to dissolve. Seeing the confusion, the commander of Timur's reserves asks for authorisation to attack the centre of the Ottomans – led by Bayezid himself – and receives permission. The army of Samarkand moves into the fray, pushing hard upon both the centre and right flanks of the Ottomans.

At the same time, the very Anatolian nobles Prince Stefan is leading – the emirs of Mentesh, Aydin, Saruhan and Germiyan – also pass over to Timur's side. The Serbian prince rapidly discovers there is, quite literally, no right flank anymore to lead, apart from Bayezid's own soldiers and his Serbian troops. Abandoned by the Anatolian nobles, the Serbs form a compact defence around Melik Shah, defending their position with a vigour that attracts the admiration of Timur, who from afar mistakes them for Muslim Ishiks. Over on the other side of the battlefield, Ali Pasha, seeing his own decimated and dissolving troops attacked by Timur on the front and in the rear from their allies of two hours ago, decides to call for a withdrawal, in order to escort Prince Suleiman back to the capital of Bursa. Somehow, in the middle of the confusion, Stefan manages to reach Bayezid and asks him to announce a retreat, given the immense carnage that is now taking place, as the sultan's troops are falling all around him. Bayezid refuses.

By now, the Serb prince has understood what the sultan refuses to acknowledge: the conflict is over, the struggle is lost. Stefan rallies his Serbs and decides to cover the retreat of Prince Suleiman as the sultan's son leaves the battlefield for the relative safety of Bursa. The Serbs follow him, leaving Bayezid on a small hill on his own, surrounded by the very last of his army – his Janissaries (the Ottoman's elite guard) and his archers (*sholak*). A number of Bayezid's nobles repeatedly plead with him to flee for safety, but the sultan apparently refuses, rejecting the solution as dishonourable.

When Timur, in the thick of battle, notices the sultan's standard flying above Catal hill, he orders all his forces to concentrate their efforts there. The battle moves into endgame, as Bayezid struggles, surrounded by his small, loyal forces, to resist the overwhelming superiority of Timur's numbers, under what is a truly continuous rain of arrows. By dusk, the struggle is over. Bayezid, his army almost completely destroyed or driven off, attempts to flee on horseback, but is thrown from his steed near the present-day village of Mahmud-Oglan and captured by Timur's men. The tales told concerning how Bayezid is brought to Timur on a pony, or made to wait outside the Mongol's tent as he finishes a game of chess, are probably untrue: Timur receives Bayezid with all the honours due to a vanquished sultan. He dies in captivity, possibly of self-inflicted wounds, a year later. [69]

Although Timur goes on to briefly ravage Anatolia, the battle of Ankara is no death-blow to the Ottoman Empire, even though it constitutes a defeat so great, and so humiliating, that it remains inscribed in Turkish history in a wholly ambiguous way – as a moment of catastrophe, and also of rebirth (some have suggested the defeat was a significant factor in Atatürk's choice of Ankara as the modern capital).

It certainly takes ten years for the Ottomans to recover from the blow, and to resume their interrupted encroachment into Byzantine territory. The Byzantines, for their part, see Timur's crushing of the sultan as a moment of temporary relief, a period of grace which was not fated to last.

Fifty years after the battle of Ankara, the city of Constantinople, the second Rome, the last great polis of the Byzantine Empire, finally falls to the twenty-one-year-old Sultan Mehmet II on 29 May 1453, after six difficult weeks of siege. Its sacking effectively signifies the end of Byzantium. For Greek patriots and Turkish nationalists alike, as well as a long tradition of Muslim and Western scholarship, it is a date which marks the fall of a Christian city to a Muslim empire. For at least the past thirty years, however, a whole range of modern researchers have been trying to emphasise how complex the forces underlying this conflict really were. The story of the fall itself contains countless ironies, paradoxes which ultimately accumulate to belie the notion of a 'Christian' city falling to a 'Muslim' army, of a 'Christian' civilisation giving way to a 'Muslim' one.

The Turks who fought *alongside* the Greeks, for instance, within the walls of Constantinople, have been quickly forgotten. Prince Orhan, a rival pretender to the sultan's throne, had been living for many years in Constantinople as a political exile, with a small army of loyal Turks. In the last days of the final attack, they were given one of the most crucial sections of the city's defences – the sea walls along the harbour of Eleutherius (today the district of Eminönü) – where, assisted by Greek monks, they turned back Ottoman attacks on the city's marine defences. We have, unfortunately, no way of knowing what the rest of the Christians thought of their Turkish co-defenders – whether, as the attack worsened and the siege grew more desperate, people chose to curse them, or felt even greater solidarity with them. The fact that most of the siege's chroniclers mention them without any derogatory reference to their faith suggests the fact that they were Muslims was of little importance. When the Ottomans broke through, Orhan tried to escape in a black robe, hoping to be mistaken for a Greek, but some of the Ottoman troops recognised him and brought him to the sultan. He was decapitated on the spot.[70]

Just as there were Muslims among the Christians defending Constantinople, equally there were Christians among the Muslims attacking it. As in the battle of Ankara, a contingent of Serbian vassal troops (belonging to the despot George) took part in the siege and the final attack, although one commentator has described the indignation of the Serbian troops when they learnt they were being ordered to help the Turks take Constantinople. A large number of the Ottoman troops themselves – especially among the infantry and naval forces – would have been Christian. The *bashi bazouk* or Ottoman mercenaries, notorious for their lack of discipline (the word 'berserk' comes from the Turkish *bazouk*), were mainly from Christian countries such as Hungary, Italy or the Slav kingdoms, and were among the first wave of attackers to try to scale the ramparts of the city.[71]

Ironically, the vizier (or minister) who was most responsible for urging the young Mehmet II to take the great city was a Greek and Christian renegade, the famous Zaganos Pasha, whose daughter had also married the sultan. Zaganos was one of a number of ministers who were almost fanatically devoted to persuading the young ruler to attack Constantinople – in contrast to the Muslim vizier Halil Pasha, whose sympathy for Christians led him in vain to try to soften the sultan's plans. Even more irony can be found in the fact that it was a Christian engineer who constructed the enormous cannon which dealt the final blow to the allegedly impregnable walls of the city. In 1452 Urban, a Hungarian cannon-maker, had offered his services to Emperor Constantine XI, but the Byzantine ruler was unable to afford him. Clearly a man unburdened by any ideological convictions, the Hungarian immediately paid a visit to Mehmet II, who straightaway offered him four times the salary for a cannon that 'would blast the walls of Babylon itself'.[72] The gargantuan artillery-piece the Christian finally constructed, a two-ton monster that could fire large iron balls over a mile before burying them six feet into the earth, was responsible for the demolition of Constantinople's formidable defences – defences which had kept the metropolis safe for just over a thousand years.

Constantine XI, the last emperor of Byzantium, was killed on top of the walls of the city, defending it in its very last moments. What happened to his successors? What fate, in the Ottoman transformation of Constantinople into Istanbul, did the next-in-line to the Byzantine throne meet? As the scholar Lowry points out, Constantine was childless, and so the line of succession would have passed onto his three nephews. Given the political potential of their continued existence within a conquered city, they could easily have been killed; instead, they were taken into the palace service of the sultan and 'Ottomanised'. Within twenty years, we find two of them in some of the most powerful positions in the Ottoman Empire. One nephew (Murad Pasha) became a governor in the Balkans, and died leading an Ottoman army against a Turkmen chief in eastern Anatolia. The other nephew (Mesih Pasha), even more surprisingly, became the admiral of the Ottoman fleet and ultimately the grand vizier of the Ottoman government, the most powerful position in the Ottoman Empire after the sultan himself.[73] In other words, the children of one defunct empire became the seeds of the enlargement of another. This should only surprise us if we view historical conflicts the way we play board-games – where one counter pushes another off a square or takes a piece – and forget the astonishing persistence of traditions, both Christian and Muslim, Greek and Turkish, in the endlessly doubling folds of history.

Sources

M.M. Alexandrescu-Dersca, *Le Campagne de Timur en Anatolie* (London: Variorum, 1977).

Michel Balivet, 'The long-lived relations between Christians and Moslems in Central Anatolia: dervishes, papadhes and country folk', in *Byzantinische Forschungen* XVI (Amsterdam, 1991), pp.313–22.

John W. Barker, *Manuel II Palaeologus* (Rutgers University Press, 1969).

M.C. Bartusis, *The Late Byzantine Army: Arms and Society 1204–1453* (University of Pennsylvania Press, 1992).

M. Braun, *Lebensbeschreibung des Despoten Stefan Lazarevic* (Göttingen, 1956).

A. Bryer, 'The Case of the first Byzantine-Ottoman marriage', in R.H.C. Davis and J.M. Wallace-Hadrill (eds), *The Writing of History in the Middle Ages* (Clarendon Press, 1981).

The Chronicle of Muntaner, trans. Lady Goodenough (London: Hakluyt Society, 1920).

G.T. Dennis SJ, *The Reign of Manuel II Palaeologus in Thessalonica 1382–1387* (Rome, 1960).

V. Dimitriades, 'Byzantine and Ottoman Thessaloniki', in A.M. Hakkert and W.E. Kaegi Jr (eds), *Byzantinische Forschungen* XVI:268 (1991), pp.265–74.

Doukas, *Decline and Fall of Byzantium to the Ottoman Turks*, trans. H.J. Magoulias (Detroit, 1975).

A. Eastmond, *Art and Identity in Thirteenth century Byzantium* (London: Ashgate, 2004).

Enveri, author of the *Duşturname*, trans. Irene Melikoff-Sayar, in *Le Destan d'Umur Pacha* (Paris, 1954).

Pal Fodor, *In Quest of the Golden Apple* (Isis Press: Istanbul, 2000).

H.A.R. Gibb, *The Travels of Ibn Battuta* (Cambridge University Press, 1962).

Rene Grousset, *L'Empire des Steppes* (Paris, 1960).

Keith Hopwood, 'Mudara', in A. Singer and A. Cohen (eds), *Aspects of Ottoman History* (Jerusalem: The Magras Press, 1994).

Halil Inalcik, *Studies in Ottoman Social and Economic History* (London, 1985).

Johannes Kantakuzenos: Geschichte II, trans. G. Fatouros and T. Krischer (Stuttgart: Hiersemann, 1986).

C. Kafadar, *Between Two Worlds: The Construction of the Ottoman State* (University of California Press, 1995).

Dimitri Kitsikis, *Turk-Yunan Imparatorlugu: Arabolge Gercegi Isiginda Osmanli Tarihine Bakis* (Istanbul, 1996).

Aptullah Kuran, *The Mosque in Early Ottoman Architecture* (Chicago, 1968).

A.E. Laiou, *Constantinople and the Latins: The Foreign Policy of Andronikos II 1282–1328* (Harvard, 1972).

P. Lemerle, *L'Emirat d'Aydin* (Paris, 1957).

R.P. Lindner, *Nomads and Ottomans in Medieval Anatolia* (Bloomington, Indiana, 1983).

Heath W. Lowry, *The Nature of the Early Ottoman State* (SUNY Press, 2003).

Klaus Peter Matschke, *Die Schlacht bei Ankara und das Schicksal von Byzanz* (Weimar, 1981).

D.M. Nicol, *The Reluctant Emperor* (Cambridge University Press, 1996).

David Nicolle, *The Mongol Warlords* (Firebird Books, 1990).

Porphryogenita: Essays on the History and Literature of the Byzantine and Latin East, C. Dendrinos, J. Harris, E. Harvalia Crook and J. Herrin (eds) (Ashgate, 2003).

S. Runciman, *The Fall of Constantinople* (Cambridge University Press, 1965).

Aryeh Shmowelevitz, 'Ottoman History and Society', in *Analecta Isisiana* XXXVIII:43 (1999).

Turkish Bookbinding in the Fifteenth Century, J. Raby and Z. Tanindi (eds) (London: Azimuth, 1993).

Istvan Vasary, *Cumans and Tatars: Oriental Military in the Pre-Ottoman Balkans 1185–1365* (Cambridge University Press, 2005).

A.A. Vasiliev, *History of the Byzantine Empire* (University of Wisconsin Press, 1952).

S. Vryonis, Jr, *Byzantium and Europe* (London, 1967).

E.A. Zachariadou, *Romania and the Turks 1300–1500* (London: Variorum, 1985).

Chapter Four

MUSLIMS, PROTESTANTS AND PEASANTS: OTTOMAN HUNGARY 1526–1683

The story, for some people, goes like this: in 1526, the Turks marched into Hungary and held its free, Christian peoples captive for over a hundred and fifty years. The country was laid waste, its people either starved or massacred, held under the rule of the despotic Turk despite all the attempts of their Christian neighbours to free them. On two occasions the Muslim hordes even tried to march on Vienna – the shadow of Islam was about to fall on the heart of Europe itself. On the second attempt, Christendom finally united itself before the Mohammedan foe and repelled the invaders, before going on to liberate Hungary and even drive the Ottomans back to Belgrade. Christian Europe had been saved, the Balkans practically re-conquered (in the most Spanish sense of the word), and the Turkish threat finally put to rest. All of Christianity – Protestant and Catholic, peasant and noble, Slav and German – rejoiced.

The memory of the Turkish siege of Vienna (1683) arises from this landscape of symbols – a Muslim army, bristling with crescents, scimitars and turbans, laying siege to a Christian city at the gate of Europe. Woodcuts from the period show camels and elephants in the camps of the Turk, Orientals smoking their water pipes or tethering their animals, as the spire-dotted city of Christendom waits helplessly in the background. The memory of the Turkish siege was not merely visual: even a hundred years later, Grimm's dictionary tells us, the word 'Turk' still had negative, warlike connotations, even though the Ottoman threat had long since faded. People called their dogs 'Turk', churches still had *Turckenglocken* or 'Turkish bells' where people had gathered to pray for help against the Ottomans. Words such as *türkenzen* (to act like a barbarian) or *turkeln* (to stagger drunkenly) were still widely used, and taverns with names like The Turk's Head were commonplace. Vienna was quite simply the closest the Turks had ever come to their dream of conquering Europe ('On to Rome! On to Rome!' had been their cry). The encounter was a traumatic one for German-speaking Christians at that time, particularly those unfamiliar with Muslim cultures. The philosopher Leibniz was shocked when he heard the news of the arrival of the sultan's armies on the other side of the Danube. He was not alone. Although the Habsburgs had known of the Turkish plans for over a year, no one seems to have quite realised that the 200,000-strong army which set out from Istanbul in the spring would eventually arrive.[1]

Even today, over three hundred years later, the memory of the *Belagerung von Wien* has not quite gone away. According to some political commentators, Austria's late attempts to block Turkey's entry into the European Union – and the large segment of public opinion in agreement with this strategy – sprang not merely from anxieties concerning the present-day Turkish population, further immigration and dissolution of Austrian national values, but also owed some minor influence to the memory of the Terrible Turk, and their near-capture of the city three centuries earlier.

The whole point of this chapter will be to dismantle some of the myths concerning the Turkish march on Vienna, especially the manner in which it is enrolled into some form of East-West conflict between a Christian Europe and a Muslim Orient – an interpretation which is, in the end, nothing more than a Disney version of history. On a variety of levels – from international and diplomatic to local and military, from ambassadors and treaties to footsoldiers on the ground and peasants in the villages – we shall see how Christians and Christian countries were directly involved alongside the Turks in the attempt to take Vienna. From Louis XIV's alliance with the sultan to the 100,000-strong army of Hungarian Christians who assisted the Ottoman attack; from the thousands of Greeks, Armenians and Slavs in the Ottomans' own armies who loyally fought for the sultan to the Transylvanian Protestants and disaffected peasants who, tired of the Catholic Habsburgs' yoke (or of their own Hungarian aristocracy) moved over to the Turkish side; and culminating in the figure of Imre Thököly, the Hungarian Protestant prince who first persuaded the grand vizier to try to take the city – and whose army of Kuruzen fought alongside the Turks and the Tatars as far north as present-day Slovakia.

Coin embossed with the heads of Thököly and Grand Vizier Ibrahim

The intention, it should be stressed, is not to paint the Ottomans as an army of angels (no army, Christian or Muslim, has ever merited the term 'angelic'), nor to sell a picture of their empire as some oasis of tolerance and justice (imperialism is imperialism, be it Turkish or Austrian), nor even to pretend religion had no place in the conflict – on the contrary, words such as 'unbeliever', 'infidel' and *giaur* (Turkish for 'non-believer') were consistently thrown about as common currency. Instead, I have two more modest aims: first of all, to show that the Ottoman presence in the Balkans was not the inferno of absolute tyranny and despotism many cardinals tried to paint it as – in some periods, many Hungarians appear to have preferred the pragmatic tolerance of Ottoman rule to the Catholic fervour of Habsburg domination. Secondly, I shall try to point out that beneath the religious wars of propaganda provided by both sides, an extraordinary level of Muslim-Christian collaboration took place – alliances historians of both faiths were not always willing to acknowledge.

As the events which brought about the 1683 Siege of Vienna really took place in Hungary, our story is, to a large extent, the story of Ottoman Hungary. The story of a country caught, for a century and a half, between two empires, three religions and well over a dozen ethnic groups. The first thing to be said here is that the seventeenth-century Hungary of this chapter – *Ungarn* in German, *Maceristan* in Turkish – was about three times the size of the smaller country we know by that name today. The country called 'Hungary' here covered present-day Slovakia and parts of Austria on its northern border, a long slice of Romania to the south, and a whole stretch of present-day Serbia and Croatia to the west. It was an enormous realm, rich in pasture and arable land, and throughout the 1400s had enjoyed the status of being a Christian bulwark against the encroachments of the Turks. Hungarian kings were called 'champions of Christ' (*atleta Christi*) and their land was seen as the eastern gate of Christendom.[2] After the fateful date of 1526, of course, all this was to change.

An awareness of the different linguistic and ethnic background of what we generically term 'Hungarians' is important in order to understand some of the difficulties they later had with their Christian neighbours. The language, notoriously difficult to learn, is an Uralic (central Asian) language, and has practically nothing in common with any Germanic, Slavic or Latin tongue. The Hungarians (*Magyars*) arrived in the plains surrounding Budapest in the late ninth century – more or less the same time the Anglo-Saxons were converting to Christianity. They brought with them a nomadic steppe culture, and a whole mixture of Turkic and Finno-Ugric influences from the regions of western Siberia. Although it would be unwise to see this Turkic element in Hungary's past as facilitating any kind of collaboration with the Ottomans – by the time Suleiman the Magnificent arrived in Hungary, the Hungarians had been Christians for over five hundred years – it certainly was a factor in some of the cultural reservations they had towards Germans. Moreover, we have records of at least one Hungarian ruler, King Matthias (d.1490), who developed the idea of a Hunno-Hungarian relationship, calling himself a 'second Attila' and even proposing an alliance to Sultan Mehmet the Conqueror on the basis of a common blood.[3]

Whatever we might think, the fact remains that, centuries before the Ottomans ever set a foot in Europe, Hungary was already a place where the very different streams of Latin Christendom, Greek Byzantium and the nomadic cultures of the Asian steppes were beginning to mix. The non-European origin of the Magyars, at least one historian has suggested, may have been the reason why Turks did not seem as alien or as threatening to Hungarians as they were to Germans or Latins – and why, as a result, some Hungarians found it easier to collaborate with them and invite them into their wars.[4]

Islam in Hungary before the Turks (1000–1300)

Since this chapter is concerned with Ottoman Hungary, I shall take a moment to look at the presence of Hungarian Muslims in the centuries before the Turks appeared on the horizon. The number of Muslims living in early medieval Hungary was, in any case, tiny (barely 5 per cent), and these had disappeared (either through conversion, massacre or deportation) almost completely by 1300, a good two hundred years before the Turkish conquest. We know Muslim villages existed in Hungary around 1100 – one has even been excavated – and since there are records of Muslim merchants travelling to Prague and the cities of southern Poland as early as 965, it seems likely there were Muslim communities existing in Hungary at this time.[5] No one seems really sure where the Muslims of Hungary first came from – sources are so scarce. Since there were only Byzantines south of the Balkans, many scholars seem to feel Islam first arrived in Hungary from the east, along a trade route which connected the German empire with Kiev. If this is true, the first Muslims to settle in Hungary might have been Khazar Turks travelling from across Georgia and the Ukraine.

We certainly know that by 1200, a small but well-established population of Muslims had settled in Hungary, adopting Hungarian customs and speaking the language of their 'new' land. A Spanish Muslim traveller met some of them in the 1130s and complained that they did not dress like Muslims but like Hungarians, even to the point of shaving off their beards. They knew little Arabic, says our traveller, and were quite happy to fight against the Byzantines in the armies of the Hungarian king, even when they knew that there were Muslims fighting in the Byzantine armies too. 'The enemies of Hungary are the enemies of Islam', they told him. The word in Hungarian for 'Mussulman' (*böszörmény*) appears around this time, and by 1217 there are reports of Hungarian Muslims travelling to Jerusalem and Aleppo to study Arabic. We know this because a Hungarian noble, captured by the Saracens while in the Holy Land, is freed thanks to the intervention of some Hungarian Muslims who happen to be in Jerusalem at the time.[6]

Hungary's Muslims ultimately met the same fate as that of Sicily's, and more or less around the same time. After 1300 – the year of the destruction of the Saracen colony in Lucera – Hungarian Muslims also drop out of the historical records, apart from the occasional reference to a conversion. Unlike Hungary's Jews, who managed to persist as an autonomous and semi-protected group, Muslims simply disappeared. As they were a tiny, mercantile minority, their demise did not have the kind of effect it had on Sicily. Nevertheless, another two hundred years would have to pass before any mosques were built again on Hungarian soil.

The Hungarians: caught between two empires

Hungary has been called a nation squeezed between two pagans (the German and the Turk).[7] However nationalistic that may sound, it is difficult not to have some sympathy for the lot of the Hungarians in the sixteenth and seventeenth centuries, as they found themselves struggling to manoeuvre between the two juggernauts of the Habsburg and Ottoman empires. In fact, a history of Hungarian diplomacy from this period is a history of necessary duplicity, a shuttling between Istanbul and Vienna, as one monarch after another had to develop dual personalities in order to whisper different things into the ears of the sultan and the kaiser. Often rulers such as King Janos Zápolyai or insurgent princes such as Bocskai had to hedge their bets until the last possible moment between 'German' and 'Turk', even switching sides as the power struggle developed.

To the north of Hungary lay the Habsburgs, an energetically Catholic, Spanish-German dynasty, originally springing from a Swiss castle, flourishing on Austrian soil and moving, through a series of stunningly engineered marriages, into the position it was enjoying by the late 1520s – one of the most dominant forces in Europe. Hungarian history – and their countless collaborations with the Turks – simply cannot be understood without grasping the truly colonial attitudes the court of Vienna was sometimes able to foster towards the 'Magyars' – and the hatred which, in turn, many Hungarians bore for the imperial insignia of the Austrian troops. 'All the laws of the Hungarians should be burned upon their very heads' was a standard phrase among Habsburg diplomats; indeed, when the Austrians finally re-conquered Buda from the Turks in 1686, one of the first laws they drew up was that only Germans and Catholics could have houses in the vicinity of the castle. The Habsburgs' occasionally fanatical Catholicism drove them to murder and terrorise Hungary's Protestants, forcing conversions upon thousands and sending hundreds of pastors either to the gallows or to work as slaves. Unsurprisingly, even in their struggles against the Ottomans, many Hungarians saw the Habsburgs as another problem, not part of the solution. As the great Miklós Zrinyí (d. 1664) wrote, 'If help comes from the Habsburgs at all, it will come slowly, like a cancer'.[8]

To the south of Hungary, of course, lay the Turks. This is hardly the place to idealise the Ottoman Empire, whose soldiers, stationed in most parts of Hungary, would probably have been about as loved as a garrison of British paras in a Belfast suburb or French police in an Algerian village. As we shall see, however, some lesser extent of cultural exchange and mutual influence was still possible between Turks and Hungarians. Moreover, the Ottoman Empire I shall be examining is a very different one from the growing regional power we saw Kantakouzenos dealing with in the last chapter. Two hundred years on from the early days of Sultan Orhan and his hill tribes, the army which marched into Hungary in 1526 was truly that of a world empire. It was an empire which belonged to one of the most famous names in Turkish history, Suleiman the Magnificent (ruled 1520–66), called 'Magnificent' partly because of his conquests, partly because of his radical re-structuring of the Ottoman state, and partly because of the breathtaking sweep of his building programme – mosques, *medrese*, bridges – across the empire. Hungary had the misfortune to be invaded by an empire at the very peak of its power.

Of course, the vast expanse of Suleiman's empire was also one of his problems; a series of wars on the Persian front would forever keep the Ottomans from establishing themselves fully in the northern Balkans. Political revolts, coups and large-scale insurrections in Anatolian Turkey at the turn of the sixteenth century would also distract the Ottomans from their northward push into Europe – their quest for the 'Golden Apple', the mythical European city which, once captured, would signify the end of history and the coming of the (Muslim) messiah or *mesih*. Probably the most interesting developments, in contrast with the Ottomans we saw in the previous chapter, was the establishment of the Janissaries (in Turkish *yeni ceri* or 'new soldiers'), an elite class of soldiers, originally young Christian boys taken from Balkan families and raised as Muslims to become soldiers and statesmen in the very highest echelons of the state. An empire, essentially, built on the education and cultivation of a small class of orphaned apprentices. The institution, originally devised to

146 IAN ALMOND

avoid tribal or family conflicts, by the sixteenth century had formed one of the most powerful political classes in the Ottoman state – one which, from time to time, even had the power to dethrone a sultan or two.

The lot of Hungary was to try to steer a path between these two entities. To begin with, the Hungarian aristocracy was divided on which side to take; some chose the Habsburgs, others more pragmatically opted for a modus vivendi with the Ottomans. The diverse mix of Hungary's own population, and its history as a point of intersection between a variety of different cultures, made this difficult task even more complicated. The immigration of German-speaking settlers during the twelfth and thirteenth centuries accounted for a large number of 'Saxons' in Hungary. Even today, many Hungarian and Romanian cities have alternative German versions of their names – Budapest is called 'Ofen', for example, and Sibiu 'Hermannstadt'. To the west in Transylvania, now a part of modern Romania, significant populations of both Romanians and Székely (another Hungarian ethnic group) colour this mosaic even further. Finally, the question of religion – and the conversion of large areas of Hungary to the Protestant faith – brought further division to the kingdom of Hungary, particularly when the Ottomans chose, rather cleverly, to favour Lutherans and Calvinists over Catholics.

Hungary's peasants: 'the serf hates his lord'

Before we get too carried away with all this talk of nations and peoples – Hungarians, Turks, Habsburgs – another factor has to be brought into the equation. It is a factor which is all too often overlooked, and yet it complicates any simplistic version of the Ottoman conquest: namely, the lot of the peasants.

Hungarian aristocrats were very good at speaking on behalf of their peoples. When looking for soldiers to help the Habsburgs stop the Turkish advance at Rabaköz, the two local counts generously offered to send their own subjects, begging Emperor Leopold to 'let the Hungarian nation express its firm devotion'.[9] Exactly what the 'Hungarian nation' felt about it was a different matter. The lot of the sixteenth-century Hungarian peasant was an acutely miserable one. Hungary itself, for a variety of reasons, had not experienced the kind of political and economic trends Western European monarchies were going through at that time – trends which produced, more than anything else, a growing and healthy mercantile middle class in countries like France and England. On the contrary, at the time of the Turkish conquest Hungary was still in a state of late feudalism, one characterised by an increasing enslavement of the poor.[10] One of the reasons the Turks were able to take and retain control of Hungary so easily was precisely this social tension between the serfs and their 'Christian' masters; peasants who had been beaten and starved by their local betters were immediately expected to answer patriotic calls of Christian unity against the oncoming infidel. As documents from the period show, many serfs understandably concluded things under the Turk couldn't possibly be worse than the atrocious conditions they suffered under their own count or baron. One 1561 letter, from the commander of a Hungarian border fortress to his aristocrat superiors, warns the following:

> I have an additional fear which I wrote to you, Sir, and told you . . . the serf hates his lord. With reason, too, and there is no one in the peasantry to learn the word of God from; they indeed believe the Ottomans are the people of God and the true faith is theirs, and so God is on their side. I am afraid they will not run against the Ottomans but turn against their lords, as they shouted at many places on their way from Hegyesd. 'The barons dare not ask us to fight' they shouted, 'because they are afraid of us, in case we do to them what Székely did [a leader of a peasant revolt in 1514], and they are right to be afraid!'[11]

The belief that the poor might unite with the approaching Turks against their own Christian landlords was no paranoid aristocratic fear, but a tried and tested Ottoman strategy, one which the Turkish forces had often employed in their lightning conquest of the Balkans. As early as 1461, a century earlier than the passage above, we find one Bosnian king complaining to the Pope about the faithlessness of his own peasants:

> The Ottomans are very friendly to the peasants. They promise that every peasant who joins them will be free. The small-minded peasantry are unable to realise the deception and believe that this freedom will last for ever . . . the magnates, abandoned by the peasants, will not be able to persevere in their castles for long.[12]

Although we should not become too enamoured of the Ottomans'
thirst for social justice – as we shall see, they were more than happy
to do deals with rulers who notoriously oppressed their serfs – there
was a sense in which, once the serf converted to Islam, he often had
a better chance at social improvement. The historian Fodor offers us
the example of a Hungarian who helped the Turks take the town of
Orahovica and, after converting and acquiring the new name of
Mustafa, received a piece of land and an income of 5,000 akce a
year.[13] Such incidences were no strange events but regular occurrences
– the Ottoman army, with its enormous Christian influx, grew precisely
from such strategies.

It was not simply the aristocrats but also the Hungarian soldiers
who were responsible for the unwillingness of the peasantry to 'fight
for king and country'. As the soldiers themselves were poorly paid,
they regularly molested and plundered the local peasantry to
supplement – or even replace – their own incomes. No surprise, then,
to learn about the widespread tensions between the border infantry
and the peasantry they were supposed to 'protect'. As one 1633 source
put it, the two groups 'hate one another so much that when they
should be fighting together against the Turk, they end up fighting one
another'.[14] In many ways, the soldier class bore nothing but contempt
for the peasants, and looked down upon them as inferior creatures
whose goods and property they had every right to appropriate as their
own. We should remember that many soldiers had, themselves, originally
been peasants, and had seen a military career as the only way of
escaping the misery of serfdom. With such social tensions present, it
was no surprise that the Turks were able to establish their *pax ottomanica*
in the Balkans as quickly as they did. An old Hungarian peasant song
from the fifteenth century puts it best: 'When the soldiers come into
our village/it doesn't matter where they're from/they are our enemy'.[15]

The seething anger and discontent of Hungary's peasants, in other
words, had three consequences. First of all, many peasants – and even
some of the poorer-paid soldiers – simply refused to fight against the
Ottoman advance. According to one historian, out of the entire sixteenth
and seventeenth centuries, we can only find one large-scale peasant
movement which had clearly anti-Turkish sentiments (the Karácsony
uprising of 1570).[16] Peasant organisations sprang up all over Hungary,
but primarily with the aim of protecting themselves against attacks
either from their own soldiers, or from the ravages of the imperial
(Habsburg) troops. On many occasions, their activities actually

hindered anti-Turkish campaigns. In 1660 in Croatia, for example, unrest between the border infantry and the serfs disturbed a military offensive against the Turks.[17]

A second consequence was – as we saw in the previous chapter with the Byzantines – that the authorities were too frightened to arm the serfs against the Ottomans, for fear of provoking an uprising they would not be able to quash. In the region of Transdanubia, during the 1540s, the military command did not dare employ the locals in a defence of the area against an Ottoman incursion, because the idea of arming the local population was considered to be simply too dangerous.[18]

Thirdly, it sometimes happened that peasant groups actually took up arms with the Ottomans, either receiving help from them indirectly (in 1631, a peasant uprising in East Upper Hungary turned to the Pasha of Eger for help) or even going out to fight on their behalf. One incident illustrates this quite clearly. In 1660, Romanian peasants from the towns of Bihar refused to pay any more taxes, or indeed observe any allegiance to the local nobility. They moved through village after village in a fanfare of trumpets and flags, gathering together in such numbers that the nobles finally fled for their lives to the nearby town of Várad. A local Turkish commander, clearly a man well-tuned to the sensitivies of alliances in war, offered the peasants a year's freedom from taxes for every village that sent three men to the sultan's armies. The trick worked wonders for the Ottomans: the peasants went on to conquer three towns for the Turks, and unsuccessfully laid siege to a fourth.[19]

The battle of Mohács (1526) and the beginning of Ottoman rule

Mohács is, quite simply, the single most important battle in the history of Hungary. For most Hungarians, it has the status of a Hastings or a Gettysburg, a confrontation which decisively changed the history of a nation. The battle (the site of nhich is found today in the far south of the country) signified the beginning of over 150 years of Ottoman rule. Seriously outnumbered by the forces of Suleiman the Magnificent, compelled into battle by a mixture of military pride and ineptitude, and (most crucially) duped into a clumsy, suicidal forward advance through the Ottomans' own clever shielding of their troop movements, the near-entirety of Hungary's military, aristocratic and clerical elite, alongside twenty thousand soldiers, were annihilated in just under two hours. The Hungarians were not even aware the Ottomans had artillery until it opened fire on them. The Hungarian king was slain, as was most of his court. Three bishops left the battlefield alive.[20]

Not everyone was *that* unhappy. It is a fact that the first thing many Hungarians did was celebrate getting rid of Queen Marie of Habsburg.[21] At the vanquishing of the Habsburg-Hungarian army by the Turks, a kind of chaos immediately followed, as Hungarians resentful of their Viennese rulers plundered royal palaces and robbed courtiers, while a whole stream of priests, Habsburgs and German Saxons made its way north, fleeing the oncoming Turks. The capital was reportedly empty within days.

At first, Suleiman the Magnificent appeared to have no desire to colonise the country – partly because he was already looking ahead to the first (ultimately unsuccessful) siege of Vienna, but also because Hungary was too far north for him to control adequately. Instead he found a king from Transylvania – King János Szápolayi – to put on the throne as a not-quite vassal. The newly defeated Habsburgs immediately insisted on their own rival claim to the King of Hungary – Ferdinand I, Spanish-born, clever, modest, never quite able to step out of the shadow of his illustrious brother (the Christian champion of Europe, Charles V), but certainly better than some of the mentally unbalanced grandchildren who were to follow him. What followed, until the death of King János in 1540, was fifteen years of tense, low-level warfare, as the Ottomans carefully supported the relative autonomy of their Hungarian king against the Habsburgs, who had been driven out to the upper edges of Hungary. When the Austrians sent a general to take back Buda in 1530, the Ottomans sent a few thousand troops to help the Hungarians keep it. King János was, in other words, as free as any king dependent on a foreign power can be.

The defeat at Mohács, and the Ottoman annexing of Hungary it precipitated, was seen by many in Europe as another Muslim encroachment upon the sacred lands of the Holy Roman Empire. One way of refuting this Cross-versus-Crescent mythologising is to emphasise the Hungarian collaboration, willing or not, in the Ottoman annexing of Hungary. Another factor, however, which has to be taken into account, is the high number of Christians in the Ottoman armies themselves.

Of the Turkish garrisons which came to occupy and eventually take over Budapest, well over a *third* of the soldiers and administrative staff were Greek Orthodox subjects of the Ottoman state.[22] This fact will only come as a surprise to readers unfamiliar with the history of the Ottomans and the enormous military machine they ran to control and consolidate their sprawling, multicultural empire. The extent to which Greeks were successfully integrated into the Ottoman project can hardly be overlooked, and is worth a few words if we are to understand anything at all about the part they played in the Turkish military.

This 'Ottomanising' of Greek speakers had a long history, beginning in the very early centuries of the Empire, and culminating in the 'Phanariots' of the eighteenth and nineteenth centuries – Greek citizens from the Phanar (Fener) district of Istanbul who formed one of the most powerful and influential administrative classes in the Ottoman Empire. The Ottomans took the Greek Orthodox with them wherever they went on their conquests – even to Persia and the Holy Land (the German poet Goethe would consider them 'slaves' of the Turks). Although many Greeks quite naturally hated Turkish rule, it was not uncommon to find a large degree of cultural assimilation to the type of *homo ottomanicus*. By the middle of the seventeenth century, colloquial Greek had a large number of Turkish words within it – even the Ottoman sultan was referred to, in the Greek fashion, as *basileus*.[23] We encounter priests who appear to express genuine admiration for their local pashas, and also genuine mourning at the death of Mehmet IV (there were even scandalous cases of Orthodox priests converting to Islam, usually because they had fallen in love with a Turkish girl).[24] The significant Greek presence in the Turkish garrisons sent to Hungary clearly reflects this assimilation of Greeks into the Ottoman state.

The Christians who fought in the Ottoman armies were not simply Greeks, but also Serbs, Bulgarians and Romanians. If we take a look at the roll-call registers of Ottoman soldiers stationed on the banks of the Danube in the 1550s, about twenty years after the battle of Mohács, the presence of Christian-Slav soldiers among the lists of names is quite striking. Out of over 6,200 soldiers listed, well over 1,200 are Christians. In Pest two artillery companies were under the command of Christians, mostly Eastern Orthodox Serbs who had passed into the service of the Ottomans after the fall of Timisoara. The mix of Christian and Muslim names in the registers is quite revealing – an 'Ali from Bosnia' next to a 'Dimitri Diragas', a 'Murad Abdullah' next to a 'Nikola Manoylo' – and suggests that soldiers from both faiths fought quite closely together, in very small companies (rarely more than a dozen were found in an Ottoman *oda*).[25] Slav names such as Vuk, Petri and Lazar abound, and can be found in the same small companies as Muslims – even though, it should be said, the general tendency seems to have been to have Muslim soldiers in their own companies, and Christians together with new Muslim converts.

We know who the fresh converts to Islam are in the registers, because they are usually called 'Abdullah' or 'son of Abdullah'. Ottoman clerks were reluctant to write down the Christian names of converts' families in their registers, so they simply wrote 'son of Abdullah'. Their number is enormous – practically over a *quarter* of the so-called 'Muslim' soldiers listed were recent converts, probably from Bosnian or Serb Christian families. Although we regularly use the word 'Turkish' to describe these armies stationed in Hungary, the number of actual ethnic Turks in these garrisons is very low, perhaps as little as 5 per cent. As the historian Dimitrov puts it, Ottoman rule in Hungary was established mainly through Balkan and Bosnian Christians, Islamised Christians and the immediate descendants of these newly converted Muslims.[26]

Certainly, different kinds of Christians served in the Ottoman armies at a variety of different levels, and in a variety of different ways. The Ottoman *voynuks* – one of the largest military formations within the Ottoman Empire – almost completely consisted of Bulgarian serfs. Some Christians worked as artillerymen (*topcilar*) or with the heavy cannons (*humbaracilar*). Most Christians could be found fighting as unattached soldiers (*martolos*) alongside the official regiments of the sultan, as soldiers in castles or in the Ottoman fleet on the Danube. Thousands of Christians also served as raiders (*akincilar*), troops recruited mostly from the northern Balkans who carried out slash-and-burn raids on pre-selected areas before a campaign.[27] The greater part of the backup for an Ottoman army – the Ordnance corps who supplied the gunpowder, provisions, repairs, etc. – were mostly local Christians: carpenters, armourers, smiths. The shipbuilders of Pest, for example, were almost exclusively Christian. Finally, there were the least-privileged 'helpers' of the Ottomans, the *cerehor* or common labourers, an enormous sub-group of usually poor Christian peasants who assisted in the construction or transportation of the army's infrastructure.

Today's international trade in arms and weapons technology, the reader may be depressed to learn, also had its mirror image in the Ottoman sixteenth and seventeenth centuries. A surge in the development of military technology was taking place in the Ottoman Empire, most of it driven by both Western and Ottoman Christians. Foreign military experts, particularly those with artillery expertise, were regularly employed or, in some cases, captured. During the siege of Belgrade (1456), for example, many of the cannons were operated by Germans, Italians or Hungarians. Western travellers to Istanbul often remarked upon the striking number of Christians and Jews working in the foundries – in 1510, twenty of the eighty workers from one foundry were said to be of Christian or Jewish origin.[28] The work of the historian Ágoston reveals Istanbul to be a hive of technological innovation, where Venetian shipwrights, Persian blacksmiths, Jewish iron-workers, Dutch engineers and Armenian and Greek miners and sappers would all have rubbed shoulders with one another to provide teeth for the Ottoman war machine.[29]

The story of Lodovico Gritti

I have been trying to emphasise the complexity of what is viewed as the Muslim conquest of a Christian country – how the infamous and much-demonised armies of the 'Terrible Turk' were actually a fused coalition of extremely diverse Muslim and Christian groups, a compact and impressive amalgamation of very different religious identities, only superficially 'Islamic'. If there is a single story which illustrates this complexity more than any other, it is the tale of Sultan Suleiman's right-hand man and negotiator, the Italian Lodovico Gritti.

Gritti's story – and the last four weeks leading up to his violent death – says a great deal about the complicated developments within the Ottoman conquest of Hungary, and the volatile, unpredictable relations between the powers and various ethnic/social groups involved. Although Gritti was a merchant, his father was none other than the Doge of Venice, and had lived for twenty years in Istanbul as a diplomat; as a result, Gritti had grown up in the Ottoman capital, speaking Turkish and Greek as fluently as Italian. Gritti was both a merchant and a socialite: he pursued the life of a Turkish nobleman in Istanbul, dressing in silk like an Ottoman courtier and giving enormous dinners for European and Turkish dignitaries in his lavish house (one guest-list from 1524 records a banquet given for three hundred Christians and Turks). Clearly a born networker, Gritti used his pseudo-aristocratic standing in Istanbul to generate enormous revenues for himself as a merchant, striking up a close friendship with the Grand Vizier Ibrahim Pasha – so much so that, when the Ottomans captured three Venetian galleons in 1533, Ibrahim gave them to his friend Gritti (complete with the prisoners-of-war) as a gift from the sultan.[30]

At this point, we should interject a note of caution: for all Gritti's cosmopolitanism and multi-faceted identity, we should be wary of elevating him to some idealistic status of free-spirit and universal soul, conversing with Christian and Turk alike, a brother to all mankind. Gritti was greedy, cruel and egoistic. Although his friendship with the grand vizier was probably genuine, his loyalty to the Ottomans was not – when the Habsburg envoy met him at the sultan's court in 1534, Gritti took him to one side and secretly shared with the amazed diplomat a wild, fantastic plan to unite the European powers and re-capture Istanbul from the Turks.[31]

In a way, the Venetian's success as a social climber in the upper echelons of Turkish society also brought about the circumstances of his eventual death. Gritti achieved such a position of respect within the Ottoman court that, in negotiations with the Hungarians and the Habsburgs, the sultan and the grand vizier began telling both parties that they would send Gritti into Hungary on their behalf to draw up the frontiers of all three parties' territories.[32] Gritti, who was reluctant to leave Istanbul, did not relish the idea of leaving behind his money-making enterprises in the capital to embark upon a diplomatic mission in extremely hostile circumstances. The Hungarian territories were a low-level battleground, replete with skirmishes, abductions and roving mini-armies. As it was, many figures around Suleiman the Magnificent were already jealous of the Italian's financial success and his intimacy with both the sultan and the vizier. One Ottoman noble allegedly told Gritti before he left, in no uncertain terms, that if anything were to happen to him in the Balkans, he would not come running to help him. Another – the chief interpreter at the sultan's court – asked an Austrian diplomat in disgust why no Hungarian had been found 'to do away with that son-of-a-bitch'.[33]

And so, in July 1534, Gritti set out north as the official emissary of the sultan, an Italian invested with the incredible powers of dealing with the Austrian and Hungarian kings – Ferdinand and Janos – on the sultan's behalf. His destination was the distant town of Medgyes, where King Janos was supposed to meet him. With him went an army of around two thousand Ottoman cavalry and infantry. Unaware of the dangers which were waiting in store for him, Gritti also took his twelve-year-old son along. He imagined he would be returning to his mini-palace in Istanbul within six months, at the very latest. He had no idea he would never see the city again.

His first stop – at the town of Tirgovişte (now in present-day Romania), to visit a particularly unpleasant *voivode* or Ottoman vassal – immediately plunged him into the intricate web of tensions and power-struggles of the Ottoman Balkans. The sultan had ordered the *voivode* to lend Gritti a thousand Romanian mercenaries. As Gritti approached the city, seventy-five local rebels – enemies of the *voivode* – joined his army and asked him to help them overthrow the local ruler. When they were quickly re-captured, Gritti had to watch on as the *voivode* cut off the ears and noses of all seventy-five and then had their eyes gouged out, before finally executing them. Once he obtained his extra men, Gritti moved quickly on.[34]

The next stop was another Romanian town, Braşov. Here we should dwell a moment on the army which Gritti took with him into the town, as it offers an illuminating insight into the nature of most military conflict in this period. First of all, there were two thousand Ottoman cavalry, mainly Turkish and Greek. Next came the thousand or so Wallachian (Romanian) horsemen the *voivode* had lent (the Romanians, as Greek Orthodox subjects, had little love for their Catholic Hungarian neighbours, who did not even consider them as a minority in Transylvania). Finally, a contingent of about a thousand Hungarian soldiers which had joined them on the way, led by Gritti's eldest son, Antonio. An army, in other words, of Turks, Greeks, Romanians and Hungarians, led by Italians on behalf of the sultan. Some Jewish merchants also accompanied them.

When Gritti reached Braşov, he made a clumsy and ultimately fatal mistake. Among the moderately sympathetic elements who received him in the town was a sworn enemy, the Bishop of Várad, a Hungarian bishop who also happened to be a soldier and a general, and whose anti-Ottoman sentiments Gritti was fully aware of. If we are to believe the accounts, Gritti had the poor bishop stabbed and decapitated barely one week after arriving in Braşov; even worse, the assassins brought the bishop's head to Gritti just as he was in conversation with two of the bishop's former colleagues, Maylád and Kun. A strange moment must have passed as the two men absorbed, in shocked silence, the sight of the severed head of their old friend. Gritti immediately claimed he had nothing to do with the crime and vowed to find the murderer. The bishop's colleagues, terrified, politely took

their leave of Gritti and fled the camp as quickly as they could, fearful
of the same fate.[35]

The Venetian, it was said, had in his possession a whole shopping-
list of people he wanted to do away with. And yet Gritti's cruelty
here ultimately rebounded on him. The murder of the fiercely
patriotic bishop, instead of frightening the Hungarians, emboldened
them to remove the Italian as quickly as possible. When his army
moved on to their final destination, Medgyes (today a town in the
exact middle of Romania), they found themselves locked outside
by the frightened townspeople. Neither of the kings Gritti was
supposed to negotiate with were anywhere to be seen. After much
cajoling, including a charming threat from Gritti's Hungarian
henchmen to blow up the city's walls, the reluctant magistrates of
the town agreed to let the army enter, and emptied dozens of houses
to provide shelter for the troops.

The situation was quickly growing chaotic, as no sooner were Gritti's
troops inside, than a force of Transylvanian rebels (Hungarians,
German-speaking Saxons as well as Széklers) magically appeared
outside to besiege the town. There were thousands of them. Among
the troops could be found some of the *voivode*'s soldiers, who had
decided to change sides in the meantime. Gritti wrote off letter after
letter to King Janos, asking him to come and provide assistance. The
Hungarian king was well aware of the events as they developed – he
pretended to march as far as Várad, to show Suleiman the Magnificent
he had tried to help his emissary. Although he had received every one
of Gritti's letters, he chose not to reply, reporting instead to the sultan
that Gritti had tried to take hold of power for himself in Hungary,
and was betraying the sultan with his own designs. Medgyes, in the
words of one historian, was a mousetrap – and Gritti, the sultan's
emissary, was the mouse.[36]

To make matters worse, during the siege Gritti fell seriously ill with
colic, and could not leave his bed as the surrounding army began to
bombard the walls of the town. His Hungarian auxiliaries were
desperate: 'What shall we do?' asked one of them. 'What shall we do?'
roared Gritti. 'Do what you have promised and for what you have
been given so much treasure. "What shall we do?"! Keep fighting!
You're asking me what to do?'[37]

Gritti's Hungarians were clearly uneasy about the situation – trapped
in a Hungarian town alongside Turkish, Greek and Romanian
mercenaries, besieged by a large army of their own compatriots. When

the Transylvanians finally stormed the city walls, it was because they had done a deal with the Hungarian soldiers guarding the gates. 'Hungarians, do not fear, no harm will befall you!' they cried to the townspeople as they rushed inside, attacking only the Turkish and Greek soldiers they found, as well as the unfortunate Romanian mercenaries who had not already fled. Gritti and his sons tried to ride out of the city with a small escort of Turks and Italians, but eventually fell into the hands of the Hungarian besiegers, who handed them over to Maylád and Kun – the two men Gritti had been talking with when the head of the bishop arrived in a bag. The soldiers who brought Gritti shouted angrily: 'Let's just kill him, kill this Turk'.[38] Gritti begged for a quick, painless death, and by bribing his executioner with a diamond brooch hidden in his boot received it – his head was lopped off by the side of the road. The Hungarian who had killed the bishop for Gritti was less mercifully dispensed with: he was, we are told, 'beaten to death while sitting, like a dog'.[39] The Greek and Jewish merchants who had travelled with Gritti were relieved of the burden of their wealth, while out of the two thousand Ottoman troops who marched into Medgyes, barely two hundred made it back to Istanbul alive.

The murder of Gritti at Medgyes is just one small moment in the tumultuous history of Hungary as it moved through that grey, violent, sixteenth/seventeenth-century no-man's-land between Ottoman and Habsburg domination. It tells us, however, three things: first of all, how little use terms such as 'Muslim' and 'Christian' are to describe the almost hopelessly complex web of shifting power-relations, feudal alliances, ethnic sympathies and historical grudges that moved not just among the various peoples of Hungary, but also within the court and power-apparatus of Istanbul. Secondly, how scheming the various parties could be – and how the needs of the moment and the allure of realpolitik were quite capable of overturning an individual's sense of his own ethnic or religious identity. Thirdly, and perhaps most importantly, the Italian's story shows how easily non-Muslims such as Venetians, Greeks and Jews could be subsumed into functioning parts of the Ottoman project: for non-Ottoman outsiders, naturally, there was little difference between a Turk and a Greek – both were travelling under the standard of the sultan.

The division of Hungary (or,
how the Turks helped the Reformation)

Personal feuds, ethnic differences, class struggles . . . all of this seems convoluted enough; unfortunately, we have yet to introduce another complication into the Hungarian context – that of denominational strife. In a word, the Reformation.

In the years after the death of Gritti, Hungary's fate was to slide quite literally in three directions. There was a failed attempt by the Habsburg King Ferdinand to take advantage of King Janos' death in 1540 – Suleiman the Magnificent, in a supreme act of international childcare, swept in to claim the dead monarch's infant son as the true successor . . . and himself as its true guardian. What followed was effectively the tripartite division of Hungary: the most western third retained its Habsburg lords, and belonged to Vienna. The eastern third – essentially the realm of Transylvania – became an autonomous principality, with its Ottoman masters applying a more-or-less laissez-faire policy to its own internal affairs. The middle chunk of Hungary, however, became part of the Ottoman Empire itself. A golden crescent was planted on top of the city of Buda which would only be knocked off a hundred and fifty years later.

What had Hungary's division into three sectors – Habsburg, Ottoman, Hungarian – to do with the Reformation? Turkish antipathy towards the Habsburg-friendly Roman Catholic Church, particularly throughout the 1550s and '60s, enabled the newly established faith of the Protestants in Hungary to breathe and grow. In fact, the Ottomans helped the Hungarian Protestants so much that some historians interpret the Turkish victory of the battle of Mohács as a phase of the Reformation.[40] By 1540, the shock-waves of Luther's Wittenberg declarations were rippling out into every corner of Europe. In Hungary, and its unique political situation, Protestant and Calvinist missionaries found in the Ottomans an unexpected protection against the defensive might of the Catholic Counter-Reformation. A rapid rise of Protestants – and a plummeting number of Catholics – took place in most of the Hungarian territories under Ottoman control. In some Turkish areas, the quota of Catholic priests fell by 70 per cent.[41] To put it bluntly, the Ottomans and the Protestants both arrived in Hungary at around the same time – a fact both parties appear to have enjoyed to their mutual advantage.

The main factor in this flight of Catholics from Turkish-controlled areas does not appear to have been any physical oppression of Hungarian Catholics, but rather a consistent legalistic prejudice against them on the part of the Ottoman authorities. When Protestants and Catholics argued in Ottoman Hungary, they usually took their problems to be resolved before the *kadi* or Turkish judge. What we see, especially in the period between 1540 and 1560, is a repeated Ottoman sympathy for Protestant complaints over Catholic ones, and a clear bias when it came to protecting Protestant communities over Catholic congregations.

The Protestants were delighted. 'The Good Lord has protected us miraculously through the Sultan and the Turkish nobles!' wrote one pastor in 1542.[42] Everywhere else, Lutherans and Calvinists were being persecuted and imprisoned, while under the Turks, they were not merely allowed to preach, they were protected, and in some areas (of high Catholic concentration) even actively encouraged. The Hungarian town of Debrecen experienced so many Protestant conversions that it quickly became known as 'the Calvinist Rome'. The great Reformer Melanchthon (Luther's right-hand man) received such positive news about developments that he even considered visiting Hungary to see for himself.[43] Abroad, 'Turkish tolerance' quickly became a classic propaganda instrument in Protestant criticisms of Catholic oppression. One German writer, in 1550, hoped the Christian monarchs of the free countries 'would shame themselves, when they hear how the Turks tolerate and protect the true servants of Christ'.[44] This idea that Christians should feel ashamed at the superior religious tolerance of their Turkish neighbours became a standard and familiar refrain. As one 1676 English pamphleteer put it, the Turk was 'the Common Enemy' of Christians, and yet 'to our endless shame, he lets Christians live under him with more ease and freedom than Christians do'.[45]

Why were the Ottoman authorities so tolerant, and even hospitable, towards the aggressively missionary-minded Protestants? Let's start with the least cynical reasons first. To begin with, it was fairly standard practice within the Ottoman Empire to preserve local laws for the local communities – Ottoman shari'a law, in any case, had to respect the status of the Christian and the Jew (the *rum* or *gavur* and the *yahudi*). This meant that, in many cases, the Bible was seen as a legal code to be used in all Christian disputes – in towns such as Mohács and Tolna, the pasha declared that any Christian who contradicted the Bible would have their tongue cut out.[46] So the idea of 'Turks protecting Protestants' was only amazing to those Europeans who had no knowledge of Ottoman legal practice.

Secondly, there was certainly a reserved fascination and tacit sympathy on the part of Ottoman Muslims for these new Christians called 'Protestants'. The Calvinist hatred of icons and pomp would have found some resonance with Turkish Muslim observers – Islam, we will recall, also prohibits representation, and features a central belief in predestination which some theologians would consider 'Calvinist'. In the Hungarian town of Szeged in 1545, we are told, the pasha regularly attended Protestant services and visited schools. The same pasha also appears, in local disputes, to have sided with the evangelicals against the Franciscans. Curiosity was doubtless a factor – Muslims tended to see Protestants as followers of a new religion. There were frequent reports of groups of Turkish Muslims who would silently file into Protestant churches and observe proceedings until the communion host was handed out – at which point they silently crept outside again.[47]

For all such curiosity, conversions on either side were rare, although they did take place. We know of one Turkish Muslim who converted to the Protestant faith and studied theology in Debrecen, before finally becoming a pastor in Szepsi around 1563. Going in the other direction, there was the famous case of the German Adam Neuser, an anti-trinitarian Protestant from Heidelberg who, after various diplomatic adventures, moved from being a Transylvanian church pastor to finally converting to Islam at the sultan's court in Istanbul. There was even a belief, among many Protestants inside and outside Hungary, that the developments which were taking place in areas such as Transylvania would be the beginning of a gradual 'Christianisation' of the Ottoman Empire, as the seeds of the Protestant faith made their way downwards through the Balkans, into Constantinople – converting the sultan – and then out through the Muslim world.[48]

However, one of the most compelling reasons why the Ottomans tolerated, even encouraged, Protestants in Ottoman Hungary was the same reason why the United States, in the 1970s and '80s, financed American evangelical missionary activity in Latin American countries – to dissolve political solidarity. Catholics, with their Rome-centred faith forever looking West, were untrustworthy Ottoman subjects. If the conversation in 1541 between a Protestant missionary and the Pasha of Buda is anything to go by, it seems the Ottoman-friendly substance of the Protestants cannot be overlooked as being helpful to the sultan's control of a newly conquered (and predominantly Catholic) country. The pasha, having never met a Protestant before, asks him what the main principle of his new religion is. The missionary replies (displaying a genius for tact) 'to remain obedient to worldly-temporal authority and to discourage the people from rebellion and uprising'.[49] The Pasha, not surprisingly, is delighted to hear this, and sends the missionary away with a blessing, reminding him to pray daily and not to keep company with Catholics.

We should not paint too rosy a picture of Protestant life under the Ottomans – in the town of Tolna, one writer tells us he didn't know of any Protestant minister who had not been manhandled by Turkish soldiers.[50] The Ottoman strategy of conquest-through-cultural-tolerance, as well, does force us to view the religious freedoms they offered with a more cynical gaze. Although religious freedom in Transylvania continued until re-conquest by the Habsburgs in 1689, the special favouritism shown towards Protestants over Catholics only really enjoyed a period of time leading up to the 1560s. After this, the judgements of the *kadi* had more to do with moods and bribes than foreign policy from the sultan. Nevertheless, when we see some of the things the Habsburgs did to Hungarian Protestants, it is not too difficult to understand the energy with which the latter took the Ottomans' side. In 1674, when seven hundred Protestant ministers are dragged in chains towards a court in Pressburg, the Catholic bishop tells them: 'We have drawn up a rope for your necks here, so that when we finally place it over your heads, the evangelical's religion will never walk again'.[51] Given the behaviour of such 'Christians', it is hardly surprising Protestants developed a multicultural pragmatism so quickly – next to Habsburg absolutism, the cleverer sensitivities of the Ottomans must have seemed like Paradise.

Life in Hungary under the Ottomans

So what was life like for everyday Hungarians living under Ottoman rule? How far did Muslims and Christians – Orthodox, Protestants, Catholics – live and share a common culture in the *pax ottomanica* of sixteenth/seventeenth-century Hungary? The Ottoman period has always been a sensitive and controversial subject for Hungarian historians, with striking disagreements on exactly what effect Turkish domination had on the region. The initial view – that of complete catastrophe, with an absolute rejection of Ottoman culture on every level, accompanied by a conviction that the Turks were responsible for Hungary's deforestation, economic stagnation and massive population loss during the period 1526–1683 – began to be contested in the late nineteenth century, as a generation of nationalist Hungarian historians (the so-called 'Turkophile' school), resentful of Austrian rule, began to re-examine the Ottoman legacy. Subsequent scholarship has begun to show that, contrary to the previous demonising of the Ottoman centuries, no massive population loss actually took place, that Turks were not solely responsible for the region's large-scale deforestation, and that Hungary had already been in a phase of economic and political decline well before Suleiman ever set foot in the country.[52]

Most significantly, the picture of absolute non-cooperation between Hungarians and Turks has, thanks to the research of several historians, significantly changed. This last sentence should not be misunderstood: the Ottoman period has not been transformed into some previously undiscovered Eden of mutual respect and cultural tolerance. However, it is becoming clear that there was certainly a level of co-existence between Hungarian Christians and Ottoman Muslims in this period which was not previously recognised. It is most definitely a lower level of cultural exchange than we find elsewhere in the Ottoman Balkans. Ottoman Hungary did not really offer, as in Bosnia, towns and cities where mosques, synagogues and churches were hopelessly, wonderfully mixed together on the same streets; and we will seldom come across the kinds of stories we can find in Macedonia – of Christians who knew their Muslim neighbours so well that a Christian merchant could imitate an imam, his language and gestures, so that even other Muslims were taken in by the trick.[53]

The practical needs of daily life were shared by both faiths. As the scholar Fekete tells us, Muslims and Christians in Budapest had shops next to one another; Turkish butchers of mutton would have sold their meat next to Christian butchers of pork. There were usually two different kinds of bakery, confectionery and barber – a Turkish and a Hungarian one. Hungarian taverns sold their alcohol alongside Turkish sellers of *boza* or fermented grape juice. Both kinds of bread, both Turkish and Magyar, were consumed by the local population. With the Ottoman conquest, it was not simply new foodstuffs that were brought in, but also new products and clothes. That they were worn by both Christians and Muslims is clear from the fact that many Turkish words – such as those for 'slipper' (*papucs*) or 'boot' (*csizma*) – passed into modern Hungarian.[54] Turkish craftsmen abounded – not just carpenters and shoemakers, but also many of the more skilled trades. The clock of the city of Buda, built into the spire of a converted church-mosque, was fashioned by Muslims, and operated in 1638 by a certain Hüseyin *Usta* (Master Hüseyin).[55]

Most of the so-called 'Turks' (*török*) in Hungary at this time, we should recall, would actually have been Bosnian Muslims, and the Ottoman conquest would have meant a massive change in the administration and infrastructure of the country, as the ruling social class was replaced, practically overnight, with an entirely new elite – Bosnians, Albanians and Greek Orthodox Serbs.[56] After the Ottoman conquest, the majority of Buda's churches were almost immediately converted into mosques, transforming it into the first 'Oriental' city a Western traveller would see coming from Europe. The first impression which greeted a traveller from the North would be a skyline filled with church spires and minarets – it was a vista which featured in many travel accounts, and for most Europeans would have been the first Ottoman city they had ever seen. Although many Ottoman buildings have not remained, it was the famous Sokollu Pasha who was responsible for one of the city's largest building programmes, which left Budapest over thirty public buildings – four great mosques, six (normal) mosques, two schools and over sixteen public baths.[57] The city also had two Jewish synagogues, it seems, one Spanish and one Polish, whose communities did not have much to do with one another – their respective *mahalle* or districts were in different parts of the city. The Greek Orthodox who came with the Ottomans also had their own church and diocese in Buda, and were largely looked upon by the Hungarians as an extension of the Ottoman hierarchy.

A reciprocal influence in the realm of Hungarian literature and the arts took place between Muslims and Christians; although quite meagre in comparison with the Golden Age of Muslim Spain, it was certainly far from negligible. Probably the finest Hungarian poet of the sixteenth century, Bálint Balassi, was an accomplished imitator of divan poetry, and appears to have translated a number of Turkish poems into Hungarian.[58] From the other side, there were a small number of Turkish writers and poets interested in Hungarian culture – most notably the great Turkish historian Ibrahim Pechevi (d. 1650), whose extraordinary curiosity and open-mindedness led him outside the confines of his own culture to investigate Hungarian historians such as Gáspár Heltai (Pechevi, it has to be said, was one of the few Turkish writers who was willing to delve into the sources of the 'infidel' as well as the Muslims).[59] We also have a number of Turkish ghazals and lyrics declaring their love of Buda and their adoration of the city, which suggests it did not take long for Ottoman poets to see the newly conquered town as their own.

The Fifteen Years' War (1591–1606) and after

And so, while England was warding off Spanish fleets, hiding its priests in washing cupboards and accustoming itself to a new queen, the three mini-states of Hungary on the other side of Europe – Habsburg and Ottoman Hungary, as well as the semi-independent state of Transylvania – moved through a difficult period of barely concealed war. A long line of fortresses and castles ran along the Ottoman-Habsburg frontier, a porous and disputed border which experienced a constant level of small-scale military skirmish. It was a strange period, a Balkan free-for-all, where serfs, Catholics, Ottomans, Protestants, nobles, Habsburgs and even foreign (Dutch and French) mercenaries struggled with one another over an expanse of unclear and shifting territories. The Germans even had a word for this so-called period of peace – the *Kleinkrieg* or 'little war'. The fact that the Habsburg emperor could deliver the annual tribute to the Turks every year, while simultaneously keeping the level of hostilites going, serves to show how unwilling both sides were to enter into a full-scale military conflict.

And yet a full-scale war is what eventually took place. In 1591 a Turkish offensive on the Croatian stretch of the Ottoman-Habsburg border provoked what became known as the 'Fifteen Years' War'.[60] For our own story of Muslim-Christian alliances, the war offers a number of interesting points. Most superficially (and also most spectacularly), there is the unusual episode of an entire regiment of French soldiers who deserted the Habsburg side they had been sent to support and took up arms with the Ottomans. In the middle of the war (1597), in the castle of Papa on the Hungarian-Croatian border, a fight had broken out between a regiment of 1,500 French troops and a much smaller number of their Austrian fellow-combatants. The French troops, who had not been paid for many months, massacred the smaller Habsburg contingent and then, upon learning that a larger Habsburg force was approaching to 'discipline' them, made an offer to the Ottomans to come over to the other side and fight for the Turks.[61] The Ottomans quickly welcomed them, not merely for propaganda value but also for their military skill – the majority of the Frenchmen were experienced musketeers, and immediately distinguished themselves in the Ottoman siege of Kanije (1600) and in the Turkish defence of Istolni Belgrad (1601). If we are to believe the sources, some of the renegades even converted to Islam, with one of the French captains eventually becoming an Ottoman administrator in the district of Semendre. They were extremely well treated – one could even say pampered – by their new employers: in the first year alone of their service, the sultan's treasury spent over twelve million akce on their salaries and upkeep. Whether they were worth their special treatment remains debatable – although some of them returned home to France after the war, others remained in employment, apparently causing the French ambassador no end of problems with their unruly behaviour.[62]

A more substantial aspect of the Fifteen Years War, and the period leading up to it, was the way it revealed an increasing willingness on the part of the anti-Habsburg Hungarians to look on the Ottomans as a potential ally in their struggles against Vienna. The infamous alliance of Imre Thököly with the grand vizier in their march on Vienna, as endless historians point out, was no eccentric coalition of the impious (to use the Vatican's phrase) but the last in a very long series of collaborations. Three precedents can be found for Thököly before and around the time of the Fifteen Years War – all of them, usefully, beginning with the letter 'B': Báthory, Bocskay, Bethlen.

Báthory – not just a Transylvanian prince but also a future king of Poland – fought against a Habsburg-supported rival at the battle of Kerelöszentpál in 1575. The Ottomans were extraordinarily eager to help him, offering him all the troops he could wish for against Vienna's candidate. The pashas of Temsvar and Buda were ready to rush to his aid, the sultan promised him; the grand vizier even told Báthory before the battle began that, if he didn't feel his forces were strong enough, he should remain within his fortress until the Ottoman/ Wallachian reinforcements arrived. The Turkish participation in this battle, interestingly, was also downplayed: out of an estimated army of four thousand soldiers, it was said, Báthory only recruited two hundred Ottoman cavalry to help him. We now know this claim to be complete fiction: the historian Fodor, from other sources, has shown how somewhere between 1,000 and 1,500 Ottoman cavalry and infantry were present at Báthory's 'Hungarian' victory. Mingled in with the realpolitik, some personal factors were also involved here: the leader of the Ottoman auxiliaries was a Muslim called Receb Bey, a man who appears to have been on unusually good terms with Báthory. Báthory had asked the sultan to promote his Muslim friend to the governorship of a nearby province, and had also provided a recommendation for one of his chief officers. All compelling testament to the truth that cronyism, in the purity of its essence, knows no sectarian or ideological bounds.[63]

Bocskay was an even stranger case of collaboration, having been a sworn Protestant ally of the Holy Roman emperor (the Habsburg King Rudolf II, mad as a hare) until his volte-face in 1599. The increasingly anti-Protestant policies of Vienna eventually catapulted him into the leadership of one of the most widespread anti-Habsburg insurrections of the period; after a successful campaign of ambushes against imperial (Austrian) troops in 1604, a whole spate of attacks took place against Habsburg outposts all over western Hungary. They were attacks which enjoyed full support from all levels of society – even serfs and villagers joined in, clubbing soldiers with sticks and breaking up supply-lines.[64] The vigour of the uprising was hardly surprising – the pathologically brutal behaviour of the Austrian General Basta, who murdered, burned and tortured his way through most of northern Hungary, left memories of Habsburg atrocities that would endure for decades to come. The Ottomans, pleased to see their former enemy so successful against the Habsburgs, initially gave indirect support to Bocskay's efforts, and then later official recognition (in 1605, Sultan Ahmed I gave him, as Prince of Transylvania, a crown made in Persia). The support is all the more ironic, given that Bocskay had driven the armies of Grand Vizier Sinan back across the Danube ten years earlier.[65]

Bocskay's gesture – that of a Hungarian prince who changed from a Habsburg to an Ottoman saddle in mid-stream – was not the first of its kind, and certainly would not be the last. Common political and material needs clearly dictated how 'unbelieving' an unbeliever was; in struggling against a hated enemy, the temptation to enlist the aid of the ever-present Ottomans, along with their enormous resources of cannon and manpower, must have been irresistible. For Bocskay, this all turned into a Christian solidarity – but an anti-*Catholic* version, not an anti-Turkish one. One local poem, written by a grateful Protestant pastor, thanked Bocskay for liberating them from 'the neighbour-beating, country-wasting, cruel henchman' (i.e. the Habsburgs) and prayed that 'God, through your hand . . . may send the skullcapped, chanting priests back to Rome!'[66] Ecumenical harmony was hardly in full swing.

Our final 'B' stands for Bethlen. It is a comment on the instability of Hungarian politics that Bocskay had the rare misfortune to be poisoned by his own chancellor. The man who eventually followed him, in 1613, was Gábor Bethlen, a Calvinist who managed to walk a skilful path between Vienna and Istanbul, deftly using one to mollify the other. His career as monarch – essentially a vassal imposed upon the Hungarians by Ahmed I – had an embarrassing start, insofar as one of the conditions for Turkish support was the return of a fortress in Lipova. Bethlen actually had to besiege his own castle, defended by his own soldiers, in order to be able to hand it over to the Turks – after which he was known as 'Gábor the Mussulman'.[67] However, another Transylvanian prince was to follow who would receive this notorious title not merely in Hungary, but throughout all of Europe: let us finally turn to Imre Thököly.

Quitting cross for crescent: Imre Thököly (1657–1705) and the Vienna campaign

Although we are about to relate the story of how a Hungarian prince (Thököly in Hungarian, although often called 'Teckely' or 'Teckeli' in English) struck an alliance with the Turkish sultan to attack the Austrian empire together, we shall begin on a Scottish note – an angry poem written in Edinburgh in 1685, two years after the failed siege of Vienna:

> Base Apostate Rebel, Count Teckely by Name,
> All Christendom's scandal, the Protestants' shame;
> To find his imperial Landlord new work
> Divorced all Religion, strikes match with the Turk;
>
> Quits Cross for a Crescent, the Sun for the Moon,
> The Truth for a Turban; takes Mecca for Rome.
> Pawns his Grace and his God, and each glorious thing
> For the Nickname and noise of a Titular King.[68]

The poem is worth mentioning because it gives an idea of how famous (or infamous) Thököly was. In the cities of Edinburgh, Warsaw, Amsterdam and Paris, Thököly's name was known as the ally of the Turk. What many people saw as Thököly's act of 'betrayal' was reported on widely in Poland, France, England and Germany; intellectuals such as Leibniz, Swift and Daniel Defoe (author of *Robinson Crusoe*) all took an interest in him. Caricatures of the Protestant prince dressed in Turkish costume, with a devil whispering in his ear – or in one case, even with the face of Oliver Cromwell – appeared all over Europe.[69] In England there was a group of Whig politicians who, as Protestant admirers of the Hungarian, were known as 'Teckelites' for a time.

Even the most sympathetic reports – those coming from writers who were aware of how much the Habsburgs had abused their Hungarian subjects – basically depicted a Christian rebel who had, so to speak, put his money on the wrong horse. And yet few commentators asked themselves how it came to pass that a devout Protestant such as Thököly, and tens of thousands of his equally devout followers, could accompany Turkish and Tatar troops as far as Bratislava and the Polish border, under the Ottoman banner of the standard of Islam.

A knowledge of Thököly's childhood, and the events which took place during it, would have helped. Thököly's family was rich and Protestant; they came from the very far north of the country (from the now Slovakian town of Kezmarok), barely fifty miles from the Polish border – the very region Thököly would return to, decades later, with a Turkish army behind him.

Although wealthy and privileged, Thököly's childhood was definitely troubled. His father was a leading conspirator against the Habsburg regime they were living under, and in 1670 the thirteen-year-old boy saw him killed by imperial troops on the walls of his castle in Orava. The boy fled south to stay with his relatives in the Turkish-controlled, relatively safer state of Transylvania. Here he would grow up, in an Ottoman *dar-el-sulh* or 'land of peace' (basically a state the Ottomans chose to oppress only economically, not militarily), mingling with other refugees and nurturing a fervent anti-Habsburg nationalism against the murderers of his father.

The 1670s were particularly oppressive times for Hungarian dissenters – especially Protestants. A small group of politicians and administrators, which would become known thereafter as the Wesselenyi

Conspiracy, had been planning to re-take their land from the Austrians for several years, with secret help from a collection of foreign powers – Turkey, France, Poland and Venice. The conspiracy, it has to be said, had some slightly ludicrous elements in it; the collaboration of the Habsburg's own archchancellor, an alleged attempt on the emperor's life in the form of a poisoned tart, and a distinctly unprofessional level of secrecy – a Turkish interpreter blabbed the whole thing to the Austrians at the Viennese court so that, by the end, it seems the only people who didn't know the conspiracy had been uncovered were the conspirators.[70] Thököly's father had been involved in this plot, whose discovery prompted an oppressive backlash of legendary proportions.

To begin with, practically all of the participants were executed after a series of unconvincing show trials – the exception being Prince Rákóczi, whose Catholic mother intervened and, promising the conversion of her son, managed to save him from the gallows. The Hungarian constitution (what little of it there was) was immediately suspended; Lutheran and Calvinist pastors everywhere were arrested and imprisoned, or even sent to work as slaves in galleys. Books were burned, churches closed, Protestants from all classes (both aristocrats and serfs) were dragged into Catholic chapels and forced, with their arms bound to their sides, to take the Catholic host. Unscrupulous German officials took full advantage of the crisis to 'confiscate' enormous amounts of Hungarian money and property (a tactic, it should be said, also employed by Protestants when the Reform was sweeping through Hungary). Hungarian Catholics complained bitterly about the hypocritical use of 'religion' to justify what was, for them, essentially a tightening of colonial rule.[71]

To be fair to the Habsburgs, we know from court records in Vienna that there were elements within the emperor's hierarchy who were arguing for a more lenient treatment of the 'Magyars'. The Habsburgs were not stupid – many of them were well aware the new absolutism would only work against them in the long run. Unfortunately, the Habsburg doves in this case were less influential than the hawks in turning Emperor Leopold's ear. Greed appears to have been an oft-recurring motivation: the temptation to appropriate a noble's palace or a pastor's church in the course of a time of 'crisis' or 'threat' was simply too irresistible.[72] There is little doubt that, if Habsburg rule in Upper Hungary had been more interested in justice than control, the Turkish-Hungarian army would not have been able to sweep through it so quickly on its way north, annexing one town after another with little resistance.

Events abroad: Louis XIV's Turkish alliance

What was happening outside the Balkans? Like Thököly, the French King Louis XIV was also the subject of a 'media war' in the same period. Although Franco-Turkish alliances were hardly a new phenomenon – the Habsburg annihilation of Francis I's forces at the battle of Pavia (1525) had sent the French king running to Suleiman the Magnificent for help against Charles V – Louis XIV became the subject of many venomous satires and polemics, both in France and outside, for his support of the Ottomans against a Christian European state. In particular, his decision to attack Strasbourg, in the Habsburg West, just as the armies of Kara Mustafa were laying siege to Vienna symbolised for many an especially nasty example of military opportunism. One tract considered the French monarch 'a Christian Turk and as great an enemy to Europa as the Mahometan one', while a 1683 pamphlet featured the French secretary of state telling the Prophet Mohammed how excellently the French and the Turks understood one another.[73] Inside France, however, a climate of Turcophilia certainly seemed to prevail in some areas of society – when an aristocrat and socialite such as Madame de Sévigné can write to her daughter of 'our friend the Turk', it seems clear that even for French Catholics, the choice between the rising power of an Austrian neighbour and the more distant rumblings of their Ottoman enemy was no longer a question of religion.[74]

Louis XIV's support of the Ottomans was as close to pure, undistilled *realpolitik* as any other alliance to be found in this book. As late as 1664, French troops helped the Habsburgs defeat an Ottoman army – composed largely of Christian and Romanian vassals as well as Turkish troops – at St Gotthard, a 'Christian' battle organised by the Pope in which the Habsburg emperor himself had said French help was not welcome.[75] Louis XIV had sent French troops to help his hated enemy against the Ottomans mainly to have a foothold in German affairs, not out of any sympathy for Habsburg territory (indeed, the very general who won the battle would, eight years later, be leading armies against France itself on the river Rhine). Louis secretly promised, but did not deliver, an army of 1,500 men to assist Hungarian rebels in 1666; in the Wesselenyi Conspiracy France was a major component, until the plot was discovered – at which point, to save his own ambassador's neck, Louis congratulated the Habsburg emperor at having foiled the dastardly and malicious plans made against him.

Not surprisingly, France only officially began to support the Ottomans after the Austro-French war broke out in 1673 – after which point it threw itself into the affair with unbridled passion, promising benevolent neutrality to any Hungarian-Ottoman attacks on the Habsburg border, financing Hungarian insurrectionists, even using its ambassadors in Berlin to dissuade the Prussians from coming to Vienna's assistance as the grand vizier's army drew nearer. This long-standing French antipathy towards the Austro-Habsburgs didn't go away in a hurry – even into the 1700s, as Hungary was involved in its independence wars against Vienna, French diplomats in Istanbul were busy trying to persuade the Ottomans to launch another attack on Austria.[76]

Poland here is also worth a mention. Its armies – as we shall see – effectively saved Vienna from the Ottoman besiegers at the very last moment, as the Polish King Jan Sobieski stormed the Turkish camp and drove them from the Kahlenberg. And yet, the history of Poland's relations with the Ottoman Empire was far from hostile. No other foreign state sent as many envoys to Istanbul as Poland.[77] Some common military campaigns had even taken place between the Poles and the Turks – in the 1560s there were serious attempts to set up a Polish-Ottoman coalition against Moscow, while in the 1630s a Polish-Ottoman force was sent out against the Cossacks.[78] Antagonistic feelings between Poland and the Habsburgs had often led to a sympathy with some Ottoman strategies – the Ottoman vassal states of Moldovia and Wallachia (today in Romania) were looked on by the Poles as buffer states against Habsburg expansion. Like France, Poland was mistrusting towards its aggressive Habsburg neighbour; unlike France, it eventually opted to help it at the last minute – for a carefully agreed price.

Thököly's rise to power

And so, in the slow build-up to the siege of Vienna, we see a gradual coming together of different forces: a rising tension between the ascendant Habsburg power and its neighbours – Poland and France on either side, and the German states to the north; a pragmatic willingness, on the part of France, to help its enemy's enemies, up to the very edge of Europe and beyond; a growing dissatisfaction on the part of the northern Protestant states with the Habsburg's treatment of its non-Catholics; friction in Hungary between nobles, soldiers and serfs; and the beginnings of a whole series of new insurrections in the Hungarian territories, fomenting a mood of revolution the Ottoman court would ultimately decide to make the most of in its own designs on central Europe. This near-chemical mixture of disgruntled Protestants, humiliated peasants, ambitious viziers, insensitive kaisers, greedy nobles and meddling cardinals provided the basic elements for a reaction which would bring one of the largest Ottoman armies ever seen (over 120,000 men) into the very middle of Europe.

For a certain time, Thököly played a central part in this reaction. His fate was to be a melancholy one, and it is difficult not to view the early, enthusiastic, explosive years of his life with some degree of wistful irony – everything went right for Thököly up to the year 1683, and practically everything went wrong after it. Young, charismatic, full of confidence and patriotic fervour, he cast a spell over his contemporaries which perhaps blinded them to his faults – a lack of political foresight and a less-than-impressive grasp of military planning. That he was gifted is beyond doubt; by the age of twenty-three, we find him appointed general of the Kurutzen and already forming a reputation for himself as a rebel leader.

The Kurutzen (in Hungarian *Kurucsok*, literally 'cross' or 'crusader') were tough, often unruly Hungarian fighters, sometimes former outlaws, sometimes former soldiers, who became one of Thököly's most valuable assets in the struggles which followed. Responsible for storming, raiding and plundering villages and small towns in Habsburg territories, sometimes in collaboration with Turks or Tatars (so much so they were sometimes called not Kurutzen but 'Kruzitürken'[79]), Thököly somehow managed to exact an extraordinary level of loyalty and obedience from them; it was a key factor in his emergence as the outstanding leader of the rebel movement. In Turkish Thököly was even known as *Kurus Bey* or 'the Prince of the Kurutzen'. Both Paris and Istanbul recognised him as the only candidate for a future Hungarian king.

In 1678, five years before the final assault on Vienna, Thököly declared open war on the Habsburgs, and moved with his army of Kurutzen – and an Ottoman blessing – through the mountains of Austrian-controlled Upper Hungary (today's Slovakia), capturing town after town with remarkable success. By 1681, the larger part of the region was under his control. With ten thousand Kurutzen and now an Ottoman army belonging to the Pasha of Oradea on his side, he was able to force the Habsburg emperor into an armistice.[80] The following year, to conclude this astonishing rise to power, he was crowned King of Upper Hungary by the Pasha of Buda, and married – at the age of twenty-five – the love of his life, Ilona Zrínyi, a woman thirteen years his senior. The gods were clearly smiling on Imre Thököly.

There is a debate among historians about who first had the idea to try to take Vienna; popular opinion at the time widely blamed Louis XIV for inciting the Turks to march into Europe. Others have insisted it was the grand vizier – Kara Mustafa – who persuaded the sultan to lay siege to the 'Golden Apple', the mythical European city whose fall to Islam would bring about the end of the age. Many people, however, have claimed it was Imre Thököly who, in conversation with Kara Mustafa, first gave him the idea of capturing the imperial capital. The historian Köpeczi takes this view, partly because Thököly wanted the vast army of the Ottoman advance to move on as quickly as possible through Hungary, and partly because an Ottoman presence in Vienna would have strengthened his own position in Hungary.

Thököly had problems because his own nobles were not wildly happy about his close liaison with the Ottoman court. Eager to protect their own social status and perturbed at the growing intimacy with which Thököly was consorting with the pashas, they demanded to know exactly what kind of documents the 'Kurutzen Prince' had signed with the sultan. Thököly refused, at first diplomatically ('It is just not done, to make such documents available before they have even been ratified,' he told them). The nobles insisted that if they did not see the documents, they would withdraw their support. 'So God help me,' Thököly raged, 'if you do not join me, you'll pay for it not just with your gold and property, but with your lives.'[81]

Was Thököly a Turcophile? Exactly how friendly was he to Kara Mustafa and the Ottomans he was in such close collaboration with? The allegation that the Hungarian-Turkish alliance was one based on a mixture of fear and opportunism certainly has some truth to it. Thököly quite simply saw the Ottomans as the only means of driving the Habsburgs out of his country – 'independence under the emblem of a crescent', as one historian has put it.[82] However, the murder of his father, the material assistance of the pashas in re-conquering towns such as Kassa, not to mention his own Protestant faith – which, against the background of Catholic Habsburg persecution, should not be underestimated – would also have played a part in his collaboration with the Ottoman side. It is difficult not to be struck by a visible sense of unity and resolve when reading the accounts of Thököly and his meetings with the grand vizier. When Kara Mustafa receives Thököly at the Hungarian town of Essek (now in Croatia), there are the usual official formalities: Thököly kisses the vizier's robe, exchanges gifts, etc. But it is the smaller details which stand out: the large number of pashas and dignitaries who ride out to greet Thököly as he arrives, the various Hungarian flags which are intermingled among Turkish ones in the procession of soldiers which goes by, or the way many of Thököly's officers are seen leading Turkish cavalry.[83] From the Ottoman side, it is also interesting to read – in Muslim reports of Thököly's part in the campaign – how derogatory, insulting remarks to Christians as 'unbelievers' (*gavurlar*) are found on the same page, sometimes in adjacent sentences, as highly respectful references to the 'Kurutzen prince' (*Kurus Beg*).[84] Quite clearly, there were two kinds of Christian for the Ottoman Muslim: the Christian who was against them (the *gavur* or infidel), and the Christian who was on their side – in which case, their allies' Christian faith simply faded out of view and ceased to be a matter of interest.

The siege of Vienna (1683) and its aftermath

On 3 May 1683, the Ottoman army which was to set forth for Vienna finally gathered in Belgrade. Its nationalities and races, as the historian Barker points out, were legion: apart from the Muslim contingent – Turks, Arabs and Kurds – there were Greeks, Armenians, Serbs, Bulgars, Romanians, Hungarians, Szeklers and a whole host of Western renegades. The actual size of the legendary army is hard to verify, although estimates seem to average somewhere between 100,000 and 120,000 men, including an estimated twelve thousand Moldovian/ Wallachian (Christian) auxiliaries.[85] Thököly's army lay much farther to the north, and would undertake a separate operation for most of the campaign, moving through Upper Hungary towards Bratislava in a joint advance with Turkish troops under the command of Kör Huseyin Pasha. If we are to accept the rough figure of 100,000 for the number of Kurutzen and other partisans Thököly had gathered to join him, then one fact becomes clear: well over half of the 'Turkish' army marching against the Habsburgs were Christians.[86]

In Vienna, understandably, the atmosphere was tense. The sultan's army – essentially the contents of two packed football stadiums, shuffling forwards from town to town – moved with the speed and efficiency the Ottomans were famous for.[87] By 14 June, they had reached the town of Essek. Emperor Leopold, listening to his advisors, fled the city by sneaking out of the walls in the middle of the night – an unpopular action he would never really live down (what we would probably term today a 'bad PR move'). As news arrived in Vienna of each Hungarian town which, due to poor relations with the Habsburgs, capitulated without resistance to the Turkish army, a mixture of anger and panic pervaded the capital. All along the way to Vienna, events told the same story: towns such as Keszo and Rábaköz quickly came to terms with the invading army – a process, as more than one Austrian commentator acknowledged, made easier by the level of Hungarian resentment towards the retreating imperial forces. At Keszo the locals refused to help the Habsburg army destroy their bridge as part of a defensive stratagem. One local noble wrote to Emperor Leopold telling him everyone in his district had gone over to Thököly and the Turks. Hungarian aristocrats loyal to Vienna were not spared: Sopron Protestants helped Thököly's partisans, for example, loot Count Esterhazy's palace as the army passed by.[88]

It is interesting to see how, even in 1683, people were more than willing to hold their superiors accountable for a flawed foreign policy. In Vienna, ordinary people expressed their anger at the Catholic church, whose treatment of the Magyar Protestants was widely held to have brought the Turkish army and Hungarian Calvinists upon them. On 5 July, a mob inside the city smashed the windows of Bishop Sinelli's house. It quickly became difficult for priests to walk outside on the streets, so frequently were they subject first to verbal abuse, and then actual physical violence. In the countryside around Vienna, things were even worse, with the clergy eventually having to disguise themselves in ordinary clothes to avoid assault.[89]

Peasants coerced into manning roadblocks outside Vienna were particularly unhappy and non-cooperative. For many years they had been forced to pay a *Türckensteuer* or Turk-Tax, whose purpose was to defend them precisely against the threat which was now here. The warning system of fires had failed and the aristocrats who should have been leading them, including the emperor himself, had all fled. Not surprisingly, corruption abounded, as serfs and labourers exacted bribes for passing through the roadblocks they were supervising. Priests, in particular, were often forced to pay for the use of such roads, frequently being cursed and abused as they passed through.[90]

Although, from the point of view of this book, the Vienna Campaign of 1683 was one of the largest single Muslim-Christian military collaborations in the history of Europe, co-operation between the different faiths was not always harmonious, despite having a common enemy. Thököly and the pasha with whom he was advancing on Bratislava, Kör Huseyin, do not appear to have enjoyed the highest regard for one another (at one point the grand vizier had to step in publicly and force the two to make peace). The operation was an important one – six thousand Turkish troops, alongside fifteen thousand of Thököly's soldiers, were involved in the attempt to take the small Slovakian city. Thököly seems to have negotiated the peaceful surrender of the town with the (largely Protestant) administration, and the resulting reluctance to enter into combat appears to have caused disagreement on tactics between the Hungarian and Ottoman officers. In fact, if we are to believe one (extremely hostile) Muslim account of Thököly's collaboration, the Kurutzen Prince was worried on more than one occasion that his Christian soldiers, fighting their

1683 engraving of Soldiers paying homage to Thököly and Grand Vizier Ibrahim

co-religionists, would go over to the other side. There is also a moment where Thököly has to remind his fellow Ottoman officers that the local inhabitants are going to be future Ottoman subjects once the war is won – and therefore more valuable alive than killed.[91]

The end of the siege of Vienna is well known, and by now has passed into legend. The grand vizier's army lay camped outside the city for just under two months, mining and bombarding the outer walls, while the Pope finally managed to persuade the Polish King Sobieski to join a coalition to defend the city. Kara Mustafa had made the fatal mistake of leaving his siege-camp practically open to attack. On 12 September, seven weeks after the siege had begun – and as the Ottoman forces were on the verge of breaking through the city walls – a relieving army led by the Polish king arrived behind the besiegers and drove them out of their own camp, scattering them in a defeat which, for the Ottomans, turned into a rout southwards all the way back to Buda.

For the Ottomans, the failure of the siege was a defeat which would ultimately result in the loss of the Balkans. For Thököly, who had burned practically all of his Habsburg bridges to side with the Ottomans, it was the worst news he could have heard. He would fight a further three battles for the Turks in a struggle to win back Hungary from Habsburg rule – Zernest (1690), Slankamen (1691) and Zenta (1697). Although he fought bravely and with distinction, leading the Turkish horse alongside his own smaller number of still-loyal Kurutzen against the imperial forces, all three conflicts were minor moments of resistance against the inevitable. The Austrians were back in Hungary to stay: Buda had already fallen in 1686 – Turks, apparently, were skinned and their skins used as medicines in apothecaries. The Jewish population of Buda also appears to have been drastically reduced with the Habsburg 'liberation'.[92] Catholic persecution of Protestants intensified – Cardinal Kollonich's *Einrichtungswerk* project of 1689 was largely a scheme for the colonisation and assimilation of Hungary into the Habsburg Empire. In other words, Hungary had slipped from one master into the hands of another, with little cause for rejoicing among everyday Hungarians. Platitudes from Western historians about how 'Christendom was saved' tend to overlook this renewed subjection of the Hungarian people necessary in order to enjoy such a moment of European self-congratulation.

As for Thököly, his was the melancholy lot of exile. First to Istanbul, with his wife, where living as an exiled monarch-of-sorts, he still entertained the faint hope of a return to his homeland. They lived in the European quarter of Galata, with a small yet reliable retinue of servants. As Ottoman influence in the Balkans decreased, however, so did his chances, and in 1701 the influence of Vienna's powerful lobbies in the sultan's court forced him to be moved even further out, to a small provincial town called Izmit (today an hour's drive outside Istanbul). It is strange to think of the former Hungarian prince and his glamorous wife, the correspondent of Leopold I and Louis XIV, once the proprietor of thousands of square miles of Hungarian estate, ending their days in a Turkish village where (if reports are to be believed) they even tended a small garden and relied on Hungarian visitors to give them news of developments at home. Thököly's wife died in 1703 and, after a further two years of living alone, the would-be prince followed her in 1705. He was forty-eight years old.

In the end, it is difficult for us – whether as human beings or as historians – to live with truths that are simply too uncomfortable. Nobody wants a series of facts, or a narrative, which constantly makes us doubt our own goodness. The hundred and fifty years of Ottoman-Habsburg conflict was a disaster for Hungary – no one can deny this. Nor can anyone deny the extraordinary amount of misery inflicted upon ordinary people during this period – the burnings, rapes, murders, torture and breathtaking levels of cruelty (the flaying-alive of prisoners, for example, practised by both sides).

What can and should be questioned, however, is how far one of the most traumatic events of the seventeenth century can be understood using words like 'Muslim' and 'Christian', or even 'European' and 'Turk'. The Habsburgs – and, even today, the Western historians who are sympathetic to them – used these words because they had a certain function. In constantly talking about the Terrible Turk, they were able to remove some of the more uncomfortable factors from the discussion: their own ruthless exploitation of the poor, the unjust treatment of other denominations, the unscrupulous appropriation and control of another country's resources. The Ottomans, too, played a similar game: the ridiculousness of an 'army of Islam' which relied upon the collaboration of enormous numbers of 'infidels' was an absurdity seldom acknowledged except by the most radical 'ulema. Perhaps the lesson in all of this is that the decision to give up words such as 'Islam' and 'Christendom', 'infidel' and 'Turk' requires a certain courage, a willingness to open up oneself and one's society to unreserved criticism. In many ways, the myth of a Christian Europe, attacked by an army of Islam, persists because we have not yet found this courage.

Sources

G. Ágoston, *Guns for the Sultan: Military Power and the Weapons Industry in the Ottoman Empire* (Cambridge University Press, 2005).

L.M. Alföldi, 'The Battle of Mohács', in J.M. Bak and B.K. Király (eds), *From Hunyadi to Rákóczi: War and Society in Late Medieval and Early Modern Hungary* (Brooklyn College Press, 1982).

Ian Almond, 'Leibniz, Historicism and the Plague of Islam', *Eighteenth Century Studies* 39:4 (2006).

T.M. Barker, *Double Eagle and Crescent: Vienna's Second Turkish Siege and its Historical Setting* (SUNY, 1967).

L. Benczédi, 'The Warrior Estate', in Bak and Király (eds), *From Hunyadi to Rákóczi.*

Nora Berend, *At the Gate of Christendom: Jews, Muslims and Pagans in Medieval Hungary 1000–1300* (Cambridge University Press, 2001).

M. Bucsay, *Der Protestantismus im Ungarn 1521–1978* (Bohlau, 1977).

L. Fekete, *Buda and Pest under Turkish Rule* (Budapest, 1976).

C. Finkel, *The Administration of Warfare: the Ottoman Military Campaigns in Hungary, 1593–1606* (Vienna, 1988).

P. Fodor, *In Quest of the Golden Apple: Imperial Ideology, Politics and Military Administration of the Ottoman Empire* (Isis Press, 2000).

—'Volunteers in the 16th century Ottoman Army', in Géza David and Pál Fodor (eds), *Ottomans, Hungarians and Habsburgs in Central Europe* (Leiden, 2000).

Géza David and Pál Fodor, 'Hungarian Studies in Ottoman History', in F. Adanir and S. Farooqhi (eds), *The Ottomans and the Balkans: A Discussion of Historiography* (Leiden, 2002).

H. Inalcik, *Studies in Ottoman Social and Economic History* (Variorum, 1985).

M. Köbach, 'Der Literarische Widerhall des Verlustes von Ofen 1686', in B. Köpeczi and A. Tarnai (eds), *Laurus Austriaca-Hungarica: Literarische Gattungen und Politik in der 2te Hälfte des 17. Jahrhunderts* (Budapest, 1988), pp.225–48.

D. Kolodziejczyk, *Ottoman-Polish Diplomatic Relations (15th–18th centuries)* (Leiden, 2000).

B. Köpeczi, *Staatsräson und Christliche Solidarität: Die Ungarischen Aufstände und Europa in der zweiten Hälfte des 17. Jahrhunderts* (Vienna, 1983).

—*Hongrois et Français: De Louis XIV à la Revolution Française* (Corvina Kiadó, 1983).

—'The Hungarian Wars of Independence', in Bak and Király (eds), *From Hunyadi to Rákóczi.*

R.F. Kreutel and K. Teply (eds), *Kara Mustafa Vor Wien: 1683 aus der Sicht türkischer Quellen* (Verlag Styria, 1982).

Jean Leclerc, *Histoire d'Emeric Comte de Tekeli, ou memoirs pour servir à sa vie* (Cologne, 1693 – copy located in Staatsbibliothek Berlin Unter den Linden).

L. Makkai, 'Bocksai's insurrectionary army', in Bak and Király (eds) *From Hunyadi to Rákóczi.*

B. McGowan, 'Matija Mažuranic's *Look at Bosnia*', in *Journal of Turkish Studies* 8:1984.

Miklós Molnár, *A Concise History of Hungary* (trans. A. Magyar – Cambridge University Press, 2001).

Rhoades Murphey, *Ottoman Warfare 1500–1700* (Rutgers University Press, 1999).

Muslime und Christen: Das Osmanische Reich im Europa, K. Hegyi and V. Zimányi (eds), (Budapest: Corvina, 1988).

Ottoman Garrisons on the Middle Danube, A. Velkov and E. Radushev (Budapest, 1995) with an introduction by S. Dimitrov.

Amir Pašić, 'Islamic Art and Architecture of Bosnia and Herzegovina', in R.M.Z. Keilani and S. Todorova (eds), *Proceedings of the International Symposium on Islamic Civilisation in the Balkans* (Istanbul, 2002).

F. Posch, *Flammende Grenzen: Die Steiermark in den Kuruzzstürmen* (Verlag Styria, 1986).

J. Strauss, 'Ottoman Rule Experienced and Remembered', in Adanir and Farooqhi (eds), *The Ottomans and the Balkans.*

F. Szakály, *Lodovico Gritti in Hungary 1529–1534* (Budapest, 1995).

—'Das Bauerntum und die Kämpfe gegen die Türken', in G. Heckenast (ed.), *Aus der Geschichte der Ostmitteleuropaischen Bauernbewegungen im 16te und 17te Jahrhunderten* (Budapest, 1977).

—'Türkenherrschaft und Reformation im Ungarn um die Mitte des 16te Jahrhunderts', in *Etudes Historiques Hongroises* II:1985.

A. Várkonyi, 'Rákóczi's War of Independence' in Bak and Király (eds), *From Hunyadi to Rákóczi.*

—'The Principatus Transylvaniae', in *Etudes Historiques Hongroises* (1985), vol. 2.

—*Europica Varietas – Hungarica Varietas 1526–1762* (Budapest, 2000).

D.M. Vaughan, *Europe and the Turk: A Pattern of Alliances 1350–1700* (Liverpool, 1954).

K. Wawrzyniak, *Ottoman-Polish Relations in the Sixteenth Century* (Unpublished MA thesis, Bilgi University, 2003).

Chapter Five

THE CRIMEAN WAR (1853–6): MUSLIMS ON ALL SIDES

Our final chapter takes us another step eastwards – and another 150 years onwards – to the Ukrainian coast of the Crimea, in the middle of the nineteenth century. The Crimean War, a war which actually stretched all around the Black Sea from Bulgaria to the borders of Georgia and northeastern Turkey, has been called the first truly modern war. There are a number of reasons for this: it was the first war to make use of the telegraph and the war photographer, and was also the first conflict to be covered on a day-to-day basis in the popular press; it bore witness to the first naval minefield and the first battle involving steamships; most significantly, for our own investigations, it was the first major conflict of a truly global stature in terms of the different nationalities of its combatants. Soldiers in the Crimean War were not simply British, Turkish, French and Russian; they came from as far afield as India and Tunisia, Ireland and the United States, Syria, Finland and Mongolia.

The Crimean War was, first and foremost, a clash not of civilisations but of imperial projects. An alliance of France, Britain and later Italian Sardinia, joined forces to save the Ottoman Empire from the threat of Russian invasion. The result was a series of battles, over the next three years, in which Muslim regiments could be found fighting in all the armies involved: Tatar divisions in the Russian Army, Arab regiments of Algerian soldiers in the French force and irregular 'Bashibozouks' working with the British. At the same time, the Ottoman armies fighting alongside the French and British also featured significant numbers of Christian officers and soldiers – Polish Cossacks and Romanian militia, Ottoman Greeks and Armenians in the navy and the medical service, and a large number of European officers who (under Turkish names) led Ottoman troops against the Russians on the very edges of the Ottoman Empire.

In this final chapter, I will look at these moments of cross-faith collaboration and ask a number of questions: exactly how mixed were followers of the two religions in the Ottoman/Allied and Russian armies? what did Christian and Muslim troops think of one another as they fought next to each other on the battlefields of the Crimea? when it came to the question of Christian soldiers in Muslim armies, as well as Muslim soldiers in Christian ones, how aware were they of their own faith? and did they see any contradiction in what they were doing?

How did the Crimean War begin?

There were specific events which led to the eventual outbreak of hostilities between Russia and the Allies: the refusal of the Ottoman government to hand some Hungarian political refugees back to the Russians; quarrels about the specific sovereignty of Christian subjects in the Ottoman Empire; an argument over who should have the keys to the Bethlehem cathedral in the Holy Land; or even what kind of star should be put above the site of Christ's birth (Catholic or Orthodox?).[1] However, these slightly trivial disputes were not causes, but symptoms of a much deeper set of tensions. In order to understand how such a variety of different interests (British generals, Ottoman pashas, Kurdish peasants, Polish revolutionaries) could combine against the imperial armies of Tsar Nicholas I, we have to bear in mind the immense resentment and anxiety caused by Russian expansionism.

By 1852, a general fear pervaded Ottoman and Western European circles that the tsar wanted to turn the Black Sea into a 'Russian lake'. Some of the speculations (as we still find today) concerning Russia's intentions were prejudiced and hysterical; although the British Secretary of State firmly believed 'the Russian hordes were about to pour into Turkey from every side', Nicholas I never quite declared an intention to extend the borders of the Russian Empire to the Holy Land or the edges of Saudi Arabia, although he did suggest a plan to carve up the Ottoman Empire into various swallowable pieces – the Russians would get Romania and Bulgaria, Britain would get Egypt, Austria would have a slice of northern Greece, while the French would get Crete. Istanbul – a city the Russians referred to as Tsargrad – would become an international port, administered by a Russian garrison.[2]

ԱՐՏԻՆ ՇԱՀՄԻՐԵԱՆ
ՎԱՃԱՌԱՏՈՒՆ ԵՐԿԱԹԵՂԻՆԵԱՑ
Կալաթա, Մահմուտիէ Ճատտէ Թիւ 80
Կ. ՊՈԼԻՍ

ΑΡΤΗΝ ΣΑΧΜΗΡΙΑΝ
ΚΑΤΑΣΤΗΜΑ
ΣΙΔΗΡΙΚΩΝ, ΜΑΧΑΙΡΙΚΩΝ, ΜΗΧΑΝΩΝ
Γαλατά, Μαχμουδιέ Δζαδδεσι Αρ. 80
Κωνσταντινούπολις

ARTIN CHAHMIRIAN
QUINCAILLERIE & FERRONNERIE
Galata Rue Mahmoudie No. 80

Constantinople, le 21 Juin 1927

M   pour Hopal baloukli Doit

pour le fournitures suivantes:

Everyday life in cosmopolitan Istanbul – a bill written in Turkish, French, Greek and Armenian

The weakened state of the Ottoman Empire – which was widely (and erroneously) perceived to be on the edge of implosion – encouraged these plans to some extent. In contrast to the dynamic and aggressive power we saw in Chapters Three and Four, the Ottoman Empire by 1852 was more bullied than bullying, a fading version of what it once had been. Although a number of arrogant Western cliches attached themselves to and exaggerated this reality – the most famous one being Turkey as the 'sick man of Europe' – the Ottoman Empire was certainly not what it had been, despite having modernised its army in the 1820s. The awesome Sultanate which had once terrified Western envoys with its solemnity and grandeur was not even consulted in the writing of the infamous 'Vienna Note' of 1853 – a proposal which directly concerned them. The fact that over half of the Muslim empire's thirty million subjects were Christian (Greek and Armenian) made the prospect of its demise even more attractive to the tsar.

Russia's relations with both Ottoman Turkey and the European powers had not always been so hostile; as late as 1845, the Russian Tsar Nicholas I had visited England, and had even awarded the Gold Cup that year at Ascot. Aristocratic affinities between Russia and the royal families of Western Europe were manifold, primarily because of Nicholas' German wife, Princess Charlotte of Prussia. Even as far as the Ottomans were concerned, the picture was not one of enduring, unbroken hatred. Quite the contrary – barely twenty years earlier, the Russians had joined a military alliance with the Ottomans against the Egyptian army of Mehmet Ali Pasha. In 1833 the tsar had sent a squadron of troops, under the command of Admiral Lazarev, to help the Turkish forces defeat their Egyptian enemy (barely a decade later, the Egyptians would be helping the Turks attack the Russians).

Empire – and imperial pride – played a dominant role in the outcome of events. Both the British and the French looked on Russia as an imperial rival; the lightning expansion of the tsar's kingdom into Kazakhstan and Turkestan, bringing Russian colonies to the very borders of China, was increasingly seen as a threat to British influence in central and south Asia. More importantly, the idea of a collapsed Ottoman Empire giving way to Russian occupation – bringing the tsar's influence to the very shores of the Mediterranean – was a scenario both the French and the British found extremely unpalatable. This fear of a *pax slavica*, extending from Moscow to Cairo, from St Petersburg to Persia, was what brought about the historically unlikely alliance of France, England and the Ottoman Empire.

The large number of Poles, Hungarians and Romanians (called 'Wallachians') fighting for the Ottoman armies was also a consequence of Russian occupation or influence over these territories; as we shall see, the Polish and Romanian regiments fighting in the Ottoman army – as well as the Hungarian officers who were to lead Turkish troops not just in the Balkans but also in the Caucasus – were often revolutionary exiles, pragmatically supporting an Ottoman cause (as Thököly had in the last chapter) to free their lands from tsarist influence.

As Britain moved nearer to war, through the repeated breakdowns in diplomacy between the tsar and the European powers, popular British opinion in the press increasingly began to call for action. Today, it is difficult not to read the newspaper coverage without some degree of surprise. The usually demonised image of the Turk suddenly took on the role of saintly victim, as the evil Russian barbarian lustily threatened to ravage her. In the months during the countdown to the official declaration of war, the British newspapers seemed to find a remarkable solidarity in their support of the Ottomans – and their hatred of the tsar: 'Why should we not sustain our old and faithful ally', asked *The Observer*, 'whose conduct is so just under so much unjust aggression?' Most newspapers agreed. *The Daily News* insisted: 'France and England [should] save an ancient and peaceful ally from the robber lust of the Barbarian [Russia]'.[3] There was much talk of 'English honour' and 'English interests', and a general sense (in the press at least) that Britain was duty-bound to protect a vulnerable, less powerful country. As the historian Badem points out, pro-Ottoman meetings in support of defending Turkey were held in the public halls of many British towns up and down the country – Manchester, Southampton, Newcastle, Derby. In some quarters, there was even the suggestion (unusual for the xenophobic climate of British popular opinion) that Russia was less 'civilised' than Turkey, particularly in view of the latest Turkish reforms. One British lord wrote in *The Times*:

the Crescent means religious toleration, personal freedom, national independence, and social order; while the Cross (whether Greek or Roman) is misused as the banner of those who would establish religious intolerance, personal slavery, absolutism in governments, and a return to the middle ages in literature and society. . . . The contest is between civilisation and barbarism, right and wrong, progress and retrogression, liberty and tyranny.[4]

This unusually sympathetic view of Turkey and the Ottomans was certainly not shared by most of the generals in the British army, or by that many senior figures in the British government. The British Prime Minister Lord Aberdeen loathed Muslims in general ('These barbarians hate us all,' he remarked warmly to one colleague on the outbreak of the war, 'and would be delighted to take their chance of some advantage, by embroiling us with the other powers of Christendom'). When a much younger Gladstone tried to persuade the prime minister to support the war, he had to struggle tooth and nail to overcome the old man's firmly anti-Ottoman sentiments: 'He said how could he bring himself to fight for the Turks? I replied we were not fighting for the Turks, but we were warning Russia off the forbidden ground.' In the end, the threat of a Russian presence in the Mediterranean – along with the annual £8.5 million trade Great Britain enjoyed with Turkey – was enough to bring Lord Aberdeen over to the Turkish side.[5]

Throughout the first half of 1853, Russian naval manoeuvres and troop movements were beginning to make the negotiations being held in Istanbul look faintly farcical. The Russians had sent a prince – Prince Menshikov – to deal with the Ottoman and Allied delegates, but by the beginning of May it was becoming clear the path of war had already been embarked upon. Whether there had ever been any serious intention to negotiate at all is debatable – when Menshikov landed, he deliberately chose to offend the Ottomans by inspecting their troops in civilian clothes. The gradual build-up of Russian troops in Romania also gave the impression the tsar was about to launch a full-scale assault on the Balkans, in an attempt to capture Istanbul and gain control of the Europe-Asia straits of the Bosphorus. In response to Ottoman anxieties, the British and French moved a large portion of their fleets first to the eastern Mediterranean, and then closer still to the northwestern coast of Turkey.

What is interesting about the Crimean War is how a number of different parties, from all sides, would try to see the conflict as a religious one, despite overwhelming evidence to the contrary. As the Russian army moved into Romania, the tsar asked all believers to pray for the victory of cross over crescent, even though the opposing Ottoman army was full of Romanian and Polish militias (and even though the tsar had Muslim Tatars in his own regiments);[6] Greeks still living under Ottoman rule in Macedonia and Thessaly also saw the approach of a Russian occupation as a chance to obtain Christian liberation for themselves from their Muslim oppressors (their rebellions were crushed by the Ottomans with the help of British and French warships). Turkish soldiers charged into battle with cries of 'Allah Allah!' and 'Down with the infidels', even though they were fighting alongside infidels of a different nationality. At the Russian siege of the eastern Turkish town of Kars, local Muslims would support the Turkish troops with cries of 'Kill the infidel (*gavur*)', even though half of the town's population was Armenian.[7] The overwhelming desire to believe one was fighting for one's faith appears to have helped the believers filter out the presence of any 'infidels' on their own side – in the Crimean War, this is a phenomenon we will witness again and again.

The Allies made sure Istanbul was secure by basing over fifty thousand British and French soldiers just south of the metropolis, around Gallipoli and the Dardanelles (the very same straits which, sixty years later, British troops would be storming with a very different aim in mind). Hardly had the armies settled into their camps, than it was decided to move the larger part of the field operations north to Bulgaria, where the Russian army was threatening to advance. Varna was chosen as the town where, by the end of July 1854, over 130,000 Allied soldiers – Ottoman, French and British – would congregate. It was an enormous operation, whose magnitude was made even more impressive by the diversity of the nationalities involved, as the Ottoman and French armies contained a number of Tunisian and Algerian units. One French observer records the scene:

> It was a curious spectacle to look on, this assembly of troops ... drawn here from Europe, Asia and Africa, in defence of a common cause, and all on such good terms with one another!
>
> For here were men of the North – English, Irish and Scotch – with their fair complexions, blue eyes and showy costumes; the Frenchman, with his open and expressive countenance, his smiling and intelligent look [the author is French] ... the Turk, with his grave air and mien so full of dignity; the Algerian with his swarthy angular features; the Egyptian, with crisp hair, withered looks and gaudy dress; and finally, the inhabitant of Nubia [Sudan] with his thick lips and ebony skin ... crossing and intermingling with one another in the narrow streets of a Bulgarian town – who could have believed it?[8]

Racial stereotypes apart, the observer's view is somewhat idealistic – relations between the soldiers, as we shall see, were far from cordial. And yet there must have been something undeniably striking about the sight of so many soldiers and uniforms, so many different headdresses, capes, hoods and jackets, jostling about on the same street together. In many ways, the Bulgarian town of Varna was the calm before the storm – the last taste of peace the Allied troops would have before embarking for the horror of the Crimea.

Before moving on to the war itself, let us examine the various Muslim soldiers who fought in each army – and, of course, the Christians who were present in the Ottoman ranks.

Muslims in the British army – the 'Bashibozouks'

The Turkish word *başibozuk*, which literally meant 'broken head', was used to describe the large numbers of irregular soldiers and mercenaries who were brought into the Allied campaign from other places. In classical Ottoman times these had been mostly Christians, but by the time of the Crimean War were mostly Muslims, and came from a variety of different groups: Arabs (from Morocco to Iraq), Albanians, Kurds, Turks and Turkmen, Afghans, Persians and Indian Muslims. Like irregulars and mercenaries in any war, they were often difficult to control, and their name became a byword for looting, plunder and rape. Often they looked exotic, even ridiculous, to the regular soldiers, dressed in their individual costumes, sometimes even travelling in families (one eyewitness records seeing a Kurdish grandmother, at least seventy years of age, on horseback with a loaded pistol in either hand). Although their infamous reputation was partly deserved, activities such as looting, rape and plunder were by no means limited to the Bashibozouks; large numbers of French and British soldiers were punished, and sometimes even executed, for similar offences throughout the war.

The British officers sent to manage the Bashibozouks were mostly officers who had worked in the Indian army, a fact which says a great deal about the imperialistic attitude the British had towards them – effectively, they were recruited 'natives'. A number of the British officers spoke fluent Hindustani, and were clearly recruited on the basis of their experience with 'Orientals' (an Arab mentality, presumably, being no different from an Indian one). This may also have been because of the large number of Indian/Afghan soldiers in the Bashibozouks – one regiment, we are told, had over a hundred Hindustani speakers in it. The man in overall charge was a British general called Beatson, who administered the four thousand-strong force of Bashibozouks with the help of a large team of interpreters. The leader of this team was an officer who could speak nine languages – a necessity in an environment where Arabic, Turkish and Kurdish were everywhere to be heard. Beatson was also advised by an officer who had written a book on Mecca and Medina, an interesting comment on how a racist institution such as the British Empire was able to tackle the issue of cultural sensitivity when it was profitable to (we see this again in the siege of Kars – when Turkish soldiers caused problems by wanting to fast during Ramadan, British officers were able to point out a passage in the Koran which exempted warriors from doing so in times of conflict).[9]

There seems to have been some disagreement among the British officers as to how to manage such a varied army of tribesmen, renegades, mercenaries and adventurers. Some tried to be regimental and authoritarian; others compromising and pragmatic. One officer's account laments how some of the British officers became just as 'Oriental' as the Bashibozouks they had been asked to command – smoking water-pipes, sitting around in the tent all day, allowing all manner of 'mischief' to go unpunished. We have an interesting description of how a British commander would issue orders to his Bashibozouk subordinates. First of all, the various leaders (Arab, Kurd, Turkish) gathered together to sit in the commander's tent and smoke a water-pipe together. An interpreter was present to translate the commander's words into the several languages of the occupant. After some time of amiable banter, the commander – sitting cross-legged on the floor with the other Bashibozouks – repeated some words quite clearly, so that the translator could emphasise what he wanted to say: 'Tell them . . . in me they have an officer in whom they can confide . . . and I promise them that as long as I am at their head, irregular [independent] they are and irregular they shall be.' These words, apparently, were received very favourably by all the Bashibozouks present.

There were certainly problems, however. Fighting and quarrels, often leading to bloodshed, regularly broke out not just between the Bashibozouks and the Christian (French, British) soldiers, but also between the Bashibozouks and the regular Ottoman troops. In the

Dardanelles, after one of the Bashibozouks had shot a regular Turkish soldier, the local pasha wanted them all disarmed upon entering the town.[10] When an Albanian brigand was imprisoned for the rape of a local girl, nearly a hundred of his fellow fighters rode up to Beatson's tent and demanded his release. When Beatson finally gave in and freed the man, they left the camp together with him and abandoned the war. Such desertions were commonplace, although for many of the Bashibozouks who had come from farther afield – Iraq or Tunisia – simply packing up and going home was not an option.

Muslims in the French army – the Algerian regiments

Unlike the British, the French forces had Muslims serving as regular soldiers and officers within the French army itself. The presence of Muslims in the French army, however, was not so much a testament to the cosmopolitan spirit of the French, but rather to the success with which European imperialism could assimilate and incorporate non-Europeans into its war-machine. One word explains how thousands of Arab Muslims came to find themselves fighting the Russians under the banner of Napoleon III on the cold, distant plains of southern Ukraine: Algeria.

The French conquest of Algeria, the story goes, began in 1827, when the *Dey* of Algiers struck the French consul in the face with a fly swat. However trivial the anecdote, what followed over the next twenty years was a large-scale programme of military conquest and colonisation, involving the murder and extermination of thousands of native Algerians, both Arabs and Berbers. It is difficult to know how many thousands were murdered in this 'expansion'. The incorporation of Algeria into the Second French Empire involved the introduction of a non-Arab settler population which was, for the most part, not simply French but also Spanish, Italian and Maltese. The Europeans formed around 10 per cent of the Algerian population, enjoying privileges and a level of prosperity most non-European Algerians did not.

The story of the French conquest of Algeria is relevant to the Crimea for a number of reasons. First of all, many of the French generals in the Crimean campaign were either French Algerian, or had spent a large amount of time there. General Pélissier, the supreme commander of the French army in the Crimea, had personally directed many of the massacres in Algeria himself. General Bosquet, the commander of the Second Division, had also served in Algeria, and was highly proficient in Arabic.[11] A number of Arab or Arab-origin officers were in the Crimean expedition – General Yusuf was in charge of the French division of the Bashibozouks, for example (like the British, the French and the Ottomans each received four thousand Bashibozouks to use as their own irregular unit), and Major Abdelal led the Fourth Division of the Chasseurs d'Afrique.[12]

More importantly, a significant part of the French army fighting in the Crimea had evolved as a direct consequence of the Algerian colonial experience. A good quarter of the French soldiers in the Crimean War came directly from French Algeria – well over thirty-five thousand men. Although the majority of these 'Algerian' soldiers were European, a large number of Muslim Algerians were also recruited. Whole regiments and divisions of the army – such as the Chasseurs d'Afrique – had been founded in Algeria barely a decade or two earlier. In the beginning, these regiments were dominated by large contingents of Arabs and Berbers. When the Chasseurs d'Afrique was founded in Algeria in 1830, its troops were largely what the French termed *indigène* or 'native'.[13] By 1853, however, the majority of these troops had been replaced by French Algerian settlers. This did not mean that no Muslim Algerians took part in the war, but rather that many of them were formed into separate companies. The Crimean French Expedition had a number of Muslim-only regiments such as the Algerian Riflemen (*Tirailleurs Indigènes*) and the Algerian Light Infantry (*Chasseurs d'Indigènes*), regiments which were to find themselves in the very thick of the fighting. When one British journalist sees the Algerian Light Infantry running into the battle of Inkerman, he will call them the 'Arab sepoys of Algiers', and typically comment on their 'swarthy faces contrasting with their white turbans'.[14]

Some mention should also be made of the Zouaves, the French Algerian footsoldiers who were to become so famous in the public imagination during the Crimean War, principally for their bravery and willingness to take risks. The Zouaves were established as a 'native' company of soldiers almost immediately after the French taking of Algiers – in other words, a regiment made up solely of Arab/Berber troops – although after 1840 they were enlarged with a sizeable number of French Algerians, so that by the time they found themselves in the Crimea, only a tiny proportion of Muslim soldiers remained. Nevertheless, the Zouaves still looked like 'Muslim' soldiers – their costume retained what would be, for British and Russian eyes, an 'Oriental' appearance. They wore a kind of turban headdress and baggy trousers which often caused them to be mistaken for Muslims – on their march through Istanbul to Varna, one officer recounts, Turkish villagers came out onto the streets to watch the 'Muslim' army go by. During their stay in Istanbul, the Zouaves had no problems visiting mosques or holy shrines, for the local Turks thought they were Arabs, and allowed them in without any questions (a privilege not granted to French or British soldiers). Some Russians also shared this impression, as officers in the tsarist army occasionally referred to the Zouaves as 'Africans'.[15]

This impression must have been reinforced by the fact that many Zouaves, although for the most part European Algerians, spoke Arabic almost as well as they did French, and even mixed the two languages (as French Algerians commonly did). British soldiers engaged in drinking bouts with their Zouave comrades-in-arms, we are told, would be deluged by an incomprehensible flood of French and Arabic:

> *Englisch bono, Francis bono, Englisch et Francis semis amis, bibir soua soua, Crimea mackach bono, Arbia bono, chapard beseff*
> [The English are decent, the French are decent, the English and French are good friends, they drink together; the Crimea is an awful place, Africa is much better, full of money to be made].[16]

We should not read too much into this – although they spoke Arabic and looked like Muslims to many British observers, there must have been an awareness that they were not. The undoubted affection and high regard of the British soldiers for the Zouaves (their headdresses were distinctive on the field of battle and often brought up cheers of encouragement at their appearance) can hardly be said to have been replicated towards their fellow Turkish soldiers, who were gradually treated with increasing contempt as the war went on. Nevertheless, it is remarkable to see the extent to which Arabic was spoken in the French army on the Crimean battlefield. At the battle of Inkerman, General Bosquet rides up on horseback to the assembled lines of the Zouaves and Algerian battalions, and cries to them in Arabic: 'Come on, my brave Zouaves! Come on, my brave Chasseurs! Show yourselves to be sons of fire!' Even some of the recent French recruits in the Zouaves – coming from Paris and Marseilles – were quite 'Arabised', and sometimes referred to themselves as 'coming from the tribe of

Beni-Pantin or the Beni-Mouffetard' (Pantin and Mouffetard are two main streets in Paris).[17]

Muslims in the Russian army – Tatars and Turks

How did Muslims come to be fighting for the tsar? Given the recent escalation in conflicts over the past decade in Chechnya and Daghestan, the atrocities committed by Russian troops upon Muslims in the Caucasus (and the violent retaliations by Chechen separatists as a result), not to mention the Soviet Union's long struggle against the Taliban in the 1980s, the idea of Muslim fighters laying down their lives for the cause of 'Mother Russia' does sound unlikely to our modern ears, perhaps even surreal. And yet, by 1850, over thirty-seven thousand soldiers in the tsar's army were registered as being 'minority' (*inorodsty*) or non-Russian – and a good proportion of this 'minority' would have been Muslim.[18]

To understand this statistic a little better, we need to relocate the words 'Russia' and 'Islam' within a longer historical perspective, one which sees the two words not as opposites, but rather as two words which have attempted, over the past three hundred years, to 'live' with one another, or more accurately *within* one another. As we have just seen with the French in Algeria, Muslim regiments in the Russian armies were also a consequence of imperialism, of the expansion of the tsarist empire into eastern provinces such as Bashkiristan, Kazakhstan and Siberia. It was all part of an attempt to bring 'civilisation' – a word Russians understood to mean the language of Pushkin and the cross of the Orthodox church – to the 'uncivilised' steppes of central Asia and the bleak mountain landscapes of the Caucasus. There are dark episodes in this history – the expulsion of 300,000 Tatars from the Crimea in the eighteenth century (which Russia saw as a 'reclamation'), the shipping off of a further half-million Circassians into Ottoman Turkey, along with the wholesale destruction of Tatar architecture in a number of Crimean cities; on the other hand, there are also some interesting periods of co-operation – beginning with Empress Catherine the Great's financing of mosque-building programmes (instead of mosque-burning programmes), the establishment of an Islamic printing press at Kazan University, the appointment of a state head of Islam (a *mufti*) to dialogue between the Russian monarchs and the millions of Russian Muslims who had become their subjects.

When one bears this longer history in mind, it is not that surprising to learn that Muslim soldiers have *always* been fighting in Russian armies. Their leaders swore an oath to the tsar – on a Koran kept specially for this purpose in the Kremlin[19] – participating in a process which really goes back as far as the fifteenth century: in 1477, Kasimov Tatars were in the armies of Ivan III, and Siberian Tatars helped the Russians sack the Mongol Golden Horde in 1481. These same Tatars were also to be found in the armies of Ivan the Terrible (1530–84). Peter the Great had Kalmyk and Bashkiri Muslims in his armies – not merely in the Persian campaigns, but even in battles as far north as those against Sweden. Muslim troops served alongside Russian regiments in the Seven Years War (1756–63), while in the Russian campaign against the French forces of Napoleon Bonaparte, Bashkiri Muslim troops were to be found – on their way to the battle of Leipzig (1813) they stopped off in the German town of Weimar, where the poet Goethe had the local Protestant school turned into a temporary mosque for the Muslim soldiers, inviting some of the Muslim officers into his house for tea and cake.[20]

In the Crimean War, Muslims would officially fight in regiments such as the Tatar Uhlan Regiment and the Crimean Tatar Guard, the latter fighting under the leadership of General Ryzhov, and working in close co-operation with the 53rd Don Cossack Regiment and the Ural Cossacks. All of these regiments were to see action at the battle of Balaklava. Tatars also held some quite trusted positions – the staff of the Supreme Commander of the Russian Army, Prince Menshikov, was composed of many Tatar horsemen.[21] Moreover, on the eastern side of the Crimean War – the string of skirmishes and battles between the Russians and Turks in eastern Turkey – thousands of Azerbaijan Turks assisted Russians and Armenians against the Ottoman armies.

How willingly did Muslims fight for tsarist Russia – and what did the Russians think of them? For many it was a matter of conscription, not choice. In 1722 the Cheremisov Tatars were first called up for service, and in 1737 the Bashkiris also began to be drafted into the military.[22] As the historian Crews points out, some documents do seem to suggest that the Bashkiri regiments were grateful for the various honours and medals they were awarded for their service against the Swedes.[23] It is also true that the sons of Tatar nobles had the automatic right to serve as officers in the Russian regiments. However, there are frequent stories of Tatar soldiers deserting (in one case, all the way to Austria[24]), and given the history of ethnic cleansing tsarist Russia had inflicted upon its Tatar populations, one should be wary of assuming too much benign co-operation. As for what Russians thought of the Muslims in their army – a rising anxiety was becoming evident concerning the recruitment of local Muslims in the Eurasian regiments, particularly in strife-torn Chechnya and Daghestan (an issue, ironically, still very much in debate today – at the time of writing, over 15 per cent of the modern Russian Army espouses the Islamic faith). Nevertheless, nineteenth-century Russian writers were still able to slander the Jewish soldiers in their army, but write sympathetically about the Muslim troops in the mountain regiments – in one case even praising the regiment's mullah, who also served as the army doctor. When the Russian field marshal can proudly tell the tsar how 'our Muslims and line troops have always beaten the Turkish cavalry and the Kurds', it is difficult to see this remark – *our Muslims* – as indicating a strange, alien body of mercenaries.[25]

Christian soldiers in the Ottoman armies – Westerners, Poles, Armenians and Greeks

The Christian soldiers in the Ottoman army during the Crimean War can be put into three categories: Christian Ottoman subjects (Greeks and Armenians); Eastern European troops and regiments with a common resistance to Russian rule (Poles, Hungarians, Romanians); and a large number of foreign officers brought in (under Turkish names) to lead and organise the Ottoman troops.

By 1852, the Ottoman army was largely a Muslim army; in stark contrast to the previous chapters, where a predominant number of Greeks and other Balkan groups were seen to be fighting for the sultan on the battlefield, the Ottoman army by the middle of the nineteenth century had sifted out most of the Christians from its ranks. Its soldiers charged into battle crying 'Allah, Allah', called themselves (at least until 1841) the Victorious Army of Muhammad, and regularly observed religious festivals and duties together. The polyglot nature of the Ottoman army we have stressed in earlier chapters was largely (though not completely) gone by the nineteenth century. The only places where it persevered were in the navy and in the Ottoman army medical services (many army doctors were either Christian or Jewish). Although by 1845 the majority of the craftsmen in the navy workshop were still Greek or Armenian, over 90 per cent of the sailors were Muslim. A century earlier, it would barely have been half.[26]

One reason for this was the growth of national identity, which made Ottoman authorities gradually suspicious of employing *zimmi* or non-Muslims in the ranks. Christians made up just under half of the population of the Ottoman Empire. Throughout this book, I have been stressing how people in the eleventh or sixteenth centuries did not think of themselves as 'Italian' or 'Greek', but as belonging to a particular city-state or faith. In the nineteenth century, the century of the modern nation-state, all this was to change. The War of Greek Independence (1821–32) caused Greek sailors to be removed from the Ottoman navy (replacing them largely with Armenian ones).[27] Similar tensions could be found in the east of Turkey, where large Armenian populations began to be viewed as possible sites of rebellion, provoked and organised by outside foreign powers such as Russia (as far as the nineteenth century is concerned, these tensions would culminate in the massacres of the 1890s, in which at least 100,000 Armenians lost their lives). In Istanbul, conservative mullahs could declare with regard to military conscription, 'We don't want help from anyone who isn't of our faith' and 'We don't need help from idolaters'.[28]

The situation in the 1850s, however, is difficult to gauge. In some places Christians rebelled against conscription, so the Ottoman authorities were forced to hand the responsibility for recruitment over to the patriarch. In other towns, such as Smyrna/Izmir, significant numbers of Ottoman Greeks and Armenians actually volunteered patriotically to join the war effort.[29] Although it is clear many Armenians were looking for some form of independence from the Ottomans – and although the Russians did see Armenians as a kind of 'fifth column' – this should not distract us from the shared culture of Ottoman Turks and Armenians. In today's heated and controversial debates concerning the 'Armenian genocide', this co-existence is largely forgotten. In a town such as Sivas, in northeastern Turkey, Turks and Armenians used the same grocers, lived next to one another's churches and mosques, looked after one another's children; if we consult the court records, we find no sectarianism – one Armenian and a Turk bring a case against another Armenian, or two Armenians and a Turk prosecute another Turk. There is no doubt that Christian subjects enjoyed an inferior legal status in the Ottoman Empire, a situation it would be ridiculous to ignore. However, when the grand vizier can talk about the 'common homeland' (*vatan-i muşterek*) of Muslims and Christians, and when the Prince of Armenia can ask Turkish Armenians to 'defend to the last drop of your blood your country and the Sultan against the tyrant of the North [Russia]',[30] we clearly have to be wary about bringing modern prejudices about Armenians and Turks to the incredibly delicate and sophisticated multiculturalism of nineteenth-century Ottoman life.

Apart from Greeks and Armenians, Christian soldiers in the Ottoman army also emerged in the form of Polish, Ukrainian and Romanian contingents. Some of these decisions were somewhat last-minute in nature – when the Ottomans captured the town of Kalafat from the Russians in October 1853, so many Romanians (Wallachians) defected to the Turkish side that the Ottoman commanders even considered the possibility of setting up a Romanian regiment. Spontaneous defections, however, were not the only source of Christian military in the Ottoman army. In the 1830s and '40s, even with its highly religious title of the 'Victorious Army of Muhammad' (*Asakir-i Mansure-yi Muhammadiye*), there were cavalry regiments of Christian Cossacks to be found in the Ottoman divisions – complete with their own priests.[31] Just as every Russian Muslim regiment had its own mullah, every Cossack regiment in the Ottoman army had its own priest (the British army, it should be added, had just two priests for the thousands of Irish troops in its service – two priests, when Irishmen made up well over a third of the entire Crimean expedition[32]).

The advance of Russian imperialism – and the struggle of a whole variety of national and ethnic groups (Poles, Ukrainians, Cossacks, Romanians, Hungarians) to employ whatever means necessary to resist it – produced a number of nineteenth-century Thökölys. With regard to Polish and Ukrainian soldiers fighting for the Ottomans, probably the most interesting example is that of Michal Czajkowski and his regiment of 'Polish Cossacks'. Czajkowski's biography is simply bizarre: a Polish refugee who dreamed of establishing a Polish-Ukrainian Cossack state under the protection of the Ottomans, he led an exotic life of diplomacy, dancing between Polish princes exiled in France, grand viziers, Bulgarian nobles and even (in his anti-Russian fervour) establishing contact with the famous Chechen rebel Shamil (d. 1871). A Polish Catholic by birth, Czajkowski shocked many by suddenly converting to Islam at the age of forty-two – partly to avoid deportation, partly to facilitate a hasty divorce – and took the name of Mehmet Sadik (literally 'Mehmet the faithful'). Working for the next twenty years from Istanbul, Czajkowski established a 'Polish Cossack regiment' as an official part of the Ottoman army: it comprised over 1,400 men – mostly Poles, Ukrainians and Cossacks, but also with a smaller number of Bulgarians and deserters from the Russian army. The regiment played a decisive role in the first phase of the Crimean War, helping the Ottomans relieve the fortress of Silistria on the Danube and driving the Russians back north into Moldavia. Czajkowski's dream of an Ottoman-protected Cossack state, however, was never realised. In 1886, after three marriages, four children, several lovers and three changes of religion, he took his own life at the age of seventy-eight.[33]

A panoply of Western officers – Irish, Italian, English, Hungarian, even a couple of Americans and a Belgian baron – also served as Ottoman officers in the Turkish army, sometimes on behalf of their governments, sometimes on an independent basis. As Muslim soldiers in the Ottoman ranks were unhappy about fighting under the command of Christians, Western officers had to use Turkish names – an American officer by the name of Major Bonfanti was called 'Nevris Bey', while a Polish General Breanski went by the name of 'Sahin Pasha'. This gave the impression that they were Muslims, although in fact only a very small number actually converted to Islam. These 'European' officers did not always get on well with one another, and different groups of them formed friendships and loyalties with the different Ottoman officers they worked with. The situation must have been a curious one – some Turkish officers preferred the Poles over the English and Italians, and a number of complicated quarrels and factions appears to have developed during the course of the war. As we shall see, this created a number of problems as the conflict progressed.[34]

Two Battles – Balaklava and Kürekdere

What we understand by the 'Crimean War' was effectively a series of land-battles that took place first of all in Romania, and then for the most part along the Black Sea coast of southern Ukraine, on the Crimean peninsula. The scale of military operations was enormous, involving the movements of hundreds of thousands of troops; the battle of the Alma was the first major land-battle for the British army since Waterloo. Throughout the same period, on a smaller scale, a series of battles and skirmishes were taking place on the other side of the Black Sea, on the borders between Georgia, Eastern Turkey and the area we would today call Azerbaijan.

The first thing to be said about the Crimean War itself is that it was carnage. The enormous number of casualties – approximately a quarter of a million from either side – sprang mainly from disease, although military incompetence and the fatal combination of conventional field-tactics with increasingly lethal weapons technology naturally contributed to the horrifying number of deaths and seriously wounded. The journalist Russell, writing from the field, reported how some of the injuries 'were so hideously fantastic as to root one to the ground with a sort of dreadful fascination'; thousands of soldiers with no faces or legs, with split bones protruding out of their bodies like tent-sticks and limbs swollen to incredible sizes, were the result of the grapeshot, artillery fire and sabre-charging the conflict brought.[35]

It is difficult to read eyewitness accounts of the battles of the Crimea without wincing, whether at the savagery of the fighting or the breathtaking blunders which consigned thousands to their deaths: cavalry charges in fields bristling with artillery, bayonets plunged into faces, throats, groins, decisions which could have saved months of siege, conflict and infantry-life carelessly passed by. The infamous blunder of the Charge of the Light Brigade – a misunderstood order which sent six hundred British cavalry out into a valley lined on all sides with Russian cannon – was only the least in a whole array of omissions, bad decisions and unnecessary hesitations.

If the British, Russian and Ottoman armies shared anything, it was an officer class based more on croneyism and connections than any notion of talent or gift for leadership. There *were* talented officers in these armies – the Russian engineer Totleben probably did more than any other officer to keep the Allies out of Sevastopol, while the Ottoman Commander Omer Pasha gained wide respect for driving the tsarist army back from the Danube against all expectations, without any Allied help. All too often, however, officers with little ability found themselves in positions of power because of blood-relations or close friendships with influential figures. Late in the conflict, an entire division had to be created so that a favourite of Queen Victoria's, Lord Rokeby, might be given a divisional command before the war was over.[36] Similar stories could be told for the Russian and Turkish armies: some Russian officers were so detested by their troops that they were often shot in the back by their own men as soon as combat had begun.

In the Ottoman army, the extent of corruption, incompetence and croneyism was just as bad: Ottoman officers in the east of Turkey lived in palaces, served by their own mini-harems, while their soldiers

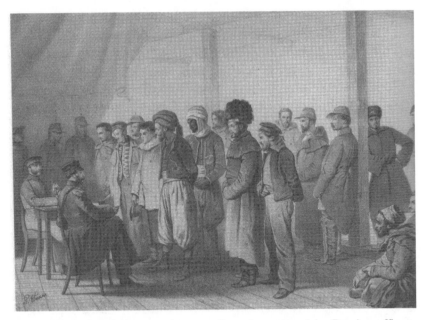

British, Turkish and French prisoners of war interrogated by Russian officers, Sevastopol

were crowded into tiny, overflowing barracks. Generals such as Ahmed Pasha helped themselves to the salaries of the privates and bought low-quality food for the army; commanders such as Zarif Pasha used astrological calculations to decide when to stage their attacks. Some of the Ottoman officers could not even read and write.[37] The French army, with its Republican background, did on the whole have a much more meritocratic view of things; there seems to be a consensus among the majority of historians that it was the best-prepared army on the Crimean battlefield, with the best-trained soldiers and most competent senior officers. The fact that they had sharpened their skills on the colonial battlefields of Algeria was of no little significance.

The commander of the British forces in the Crimea was a former secretary of the Duke of Wellington, Lord Raglan. Years of fighting the French in the Napoleonic Wars had ill-prepared him for collaboration with them when their armies finally found themselves alongside one another against the Russians. Reports say Raglan referred to the Russians as 'the French' on more than one occasion, mistaking the enemy for his ally. Raglan, who had been chosen primarily for his relationship with Wellington and not for any experience of commanding battalions (he had none), was a poor choice. Although a kind and sensitive man to his immediate staff, he was – as the historian Ponting shows in some detail – wholly out of his depth in the command of a military expedition. His blunders, from omitting to order special clothing and provisions for the British army in time for the winter to ignoring vital intelligence concerning imminent enemy attacks, made him an unpopular figure for many. Some British officers even ran away at the sight of his approach, in order to avoid having to salute him.[38]

The battle of Balaklava (25 October, 1854): Arabs and Turks in the 'Thin Red Line'

By October 1854, the British and French troops had been in the Black Sea region for just over six months. The surprise victory of the Ottoman army over the Russians on the Danube (the news, apparently, hit the British and French headquarters 'like a bomb'[39]) had largely removed the tsarist threat of an advance on Istanbul from the Balkans. The Allies had agreed to re-define their aim as the destruction of Russian sea power in the Crimea – which meant the capture of the truly formidable naval base of Sevastopol.

The battle of Balaklava took place a month into what would eventually be a year-long siege of Sevastopol, as French, British and Ottoman forces surrounded the town, bombarding it constantly with an increasing amount of artillery fire. Sevastopol is a town which has the unfortunate distinction of having been flattened twice in modern history. In 1855, however, the Allies were never completely able to cut off its supply lines to nearby Russian reinforcements. This fact – along with the brilliance of an engineering officer, Totleben, who was in charge of the Russian defences – would enable the Russians to keep hold of the base for over a year. A month into the siege, the Russian generals planned an assault on the Allied besiegers which, they hoped, would drive them into the sea. The plan was partly a result of the pressure of the tsar who, like his French counterpart, never missed an opportunity in Moscow to deliver expert advice and insightful tips to his generals in the field. After the humiliating landing of a French-British-Turkish army on Russian soil – the first French army in Russia since Napoleon forty years earlier – a crucial victory was needed to drive the invaders back across the water.

The battle of Balaklava is important not just because it provides British readers with two of the most famous aspects of the Crimean

War – the Charge of the Light Brigade and the phrase 'Thin Red Line'; it is also crucial because, partly in order to cover up for the blunders of the English officers, the Turkish troops involved were unjustly blamed for fleeing their posts and indirectly contributing to the disaster. It was an allegation which led to the widespread contempt and ill-treatment of Ottoman troops by Allied soldiers, many of whom regarded them as cowards and buffoons. As we shall see, the truth is actually quite the opposite.

The battle was essentially an attempt, by the Russians, to destroy the British base by sending fifteen thousand men and four thousand cavalry (including some Muslim Tatars) – a considerable body of men – over a defensive ridge of hills and then down into a valley which would eventually bring them surging into the port of Balaklava. The control of this port would have made life extremely difficult for the British divisions laying siege to Sevastopol.

Almost incredibly, even before the attack took place, Lord Raglan was informed about the Russian assault. The day before the attack, a Turkish spy working for the Ottoman army gave the British an accurate description of what was about to take place. Raglan, in a moment of what was to become characteristic ineptitude, failed to inform anyone a Russian attack was imminent, and made no attempt to fortify defences or recruit much-needed reinforcements for the assault which took place the next morning. As a result, the Russian forces took the line of defences largely by surprise when they attacked at six o'clock the following day.

The line of defences along the tops of the hills – called the Fedyukhin hills – were manned mostly by Ottoman troops, the majority of which were not Turkish, but Tunisian conscripts, poorly trained and underfed. It is not difficult to imagine their horror when, at the crack of dawn, uninformed by the British army and left defenceless by the Allied command, they saw thousands of Russian infantry making their way up the hillside towards them. British reports – including the *Times* journalist Russell as well as the nephew of Lord Raglan, Colonel Calthorpe – widely circulated the myth that the Turkish troops 'bolted' and ran down the other side of the hill. In actual fact, the Ottoman troops kept to their posts for nearly two hours, against odds of twenty-five men to one. It was a resistance which cost them 170 dead, practically a third of their outfit (a higher percentage, as one historian points out, than those who died later that morning in the Charge of the Light Brigade).[40]

The Arab/Turkish troops' stiff resistance, in many ways, prevented the battle of Balaklava from becoming the disaster it could so easily have been; it bought time for the British and French to collect themselves and come to the defence of the valley. It enabled the Allies to compensate for the utter absence of any preparation for the anticipated attack. Only after two hours did the Ottoman troops, unassisted and left to their own defences, begin to flee. As both Raglan and senior officers such as Cardigan only arrived at the battlefield as this was beginning to happen, towards eight o'clock, all they saw was a stream of Turkish uniforms fleeing the defences and running back to camp. Rather than calling into question the commander-in-chief's wisdom, competence and sense of preparation, the blame was predictably put on the Turks.

By nine o'clock, the entire range of defences along the Fedyukhin hills was taken over by the Russians. Raglan could only look on, from the opposite hillside, as a large body of Russian cavalry moved down the valley towards the route to Balaklava. A single line of just over a thousand Allied infantry, along with some artillery, lay between the route and the advancing Russian forces. Half of these infantry troops were British – the 93rd Highlanders, to be precise. This was the half which would later be immortalised in the *Times*' phrase 'the thin red line' (the journalist Russell actually used the phrase 'thin red streak'). The other half of the line, which British reports thereafter never even mentioned, was a battalion of Ottoman troops, made up largely of those Turkish/Arab soldiers who had just abandoned the hillside defences. In other words, half of that 'thin red line', probably one of the most famous military phrases in the English language, was Muslim. Together they drew up a line, Ottoman conscripts and Highlanders, first lying down in the grass, then standing to send off volley after volley of fire at the rapidly advancing Russian horse. To the Allies' relief, the Russian advance was stopped within a hundred yards and sent back with light casualties.

The events of the day were by no means over. Barely two hours later, towards eleven o'clock, a charge would begin which would soon acquire, in British national memory, fame and notoriety in equal degrees: the Charge of the Light Brigade. The story of a bungled order leading to a cavalry charge into the heart of a storm of cannon is so well-known we shall simply sketch out the details. Lord Raglan, who had already issued two confused orders that morning, despatched a message to the cavalry squadron of Lord Cardigan, gathered at the foot of the valley, ordering them to 'advance rapidly to the front'.[41] Although there is, to this day, still some confusion about exactly who was responsible for the suicidal charge, Raglan's vague and inept commands are generally given the greatest portion of the blame.

Matters were not helped by the fact that the despatch messenger was an officer, Nolan, who had written a book about cavalry tactics, and was almost fanatically convinced of the crucial importance of cavalry on the field of battle.[42] Although a junior officer, he was desperately eager to have the cavalry charge begin. When Nolan brought the message to the senior officer in charge, he could not believe what he was reading. The guns he was being ordered to attack were not even in sight, but at the other end of the valley. 'Attack, Sir! Attack what? What guns?' The junior officer Nolan, in a clear act of disrespect, gestured with a sweep of his arm to the general direction of the valley and said: '*There*, my Lord, is your enemy; *there* are your guns.'

And so the order was given. Approximately 670 men began to trot their horses along the beginning of the two-kilometre stretch which would lead them up to where the Russian cannons were positioned. It took around eight minutes for the British cavalry to cover the distance to the Russian guns. Almost immediately a rainstorm of shell and shrapnel started up as they grew nearer, turning into a torrent of explosions on all sides as the Light Brigade managed to reach the Russian cannons. During the last half of the charge, there would have been fire from all three directions, which ripped away whole chunks of men from the front and flanks of the Brigade. Nolan, the young and overenthusiastic advocate of cavalry, was ironically the very first to be killed. The Allied generals could do nothing but watch on in astonishment from the top of an adjacent hillside. 'It is magnificent, but it is not war' was the French commander Bosquet's famous comment (*C'est magnifique, mais c'est pas la guerre*).

The charge, all in all, lasted about twenty minutes from beginning to end. Out of the six hundred that rode 'into the valley of death', 118 were killed and about that same number again wounded. Although no Muslim took part in the charge, Muslims soldiers helped to lessen the rain of shrapnel and artillery-fire which poured down on the Brigade on their return back through the valley. French Algerian light horse – the Fourth Division of the Chasseurs d'Afrique, led by the Muslim officer Major Abdelal – swept over the Fedyukhin hills and knocked out the Russian guns there. This at least removed fire from one direction as the British cavalry rode – or perhaps more accurately, limped and staggered – back to their positions.[43]

That evening, a Russian general wrote a letter home to his wife:

> . . . by God's mercy I'm well. In memory of this day I send a Turkish watch which I bought from a corporal. Many Turks and English were killed by our Russian bayonets, and many English were pierced with lances of our Uhlans and Cossacks.[44]

In Britain, recriminations would slowly begin to multiply as the military authorities – and the British public – began to ask how such a cavalry charge, into a valley bristling with artillery, could ever have taken place. In the Crimea, however, one of the indirect consequences of the event was a souring of the already cool relations between Turkish and British troops. The widely circulated myth of the Turks' spontaneous flight led to some appalling treatment of Ottoman soldiers by their British and French comrades – beatings, abuse, floggings. The increasing dependence of the Turkish troops on the Allied forces for sustenance – partly because of Ottoman administrative incompetence, but also because the British wouldn't allow Ottoman ships to dock freely in their harbours – turned Ottoman troops, particularly the Tunisian conscripts, into a kind of slave-class, looked down upon by the British and the French. There was a mixture of imperialism and xenophobia in all of this – Lord Raglan did not want Turkish troops fighting in the same trenches as British ones because he felt they were too 'dirty' (it should be added, however, that such prejudices also applied within the British army – even in the middle of a full-pitched battle such as that of the Alma, men from the lower-class Light Division were not allowed to fight next to the Grenadier Guards, as the soldiers came from different social backgrounds[45]). And yet such arrogance – and the foolishness of not taking advantage of the Turkish troops' knowledge and experience of the terrain – did not go unnoticed by some observers in the British army, in particular the Irish officers. One officer complains of the arrogance of English cavalry officers in their attitude towards the Ottomans: 'although we always had a Turkish regiment brigaded with us, we had no experience and we omitted to take advantage of theirs'.[46] Another sympathetic source, again Irish, writes with disdain of how one infamous English officer, Lord (Earl) Cardigan, tried to cover his own incompetence by constantly blaming the Turkish troops:

Just returned from a Brigade field day, we had a quantity of Turks
out with us whom the Earl treats very badly, he gives them no orders
and then swears at them for not being in their proper places. Had
we been fighting Russians, we would have lost . . . his troop . . .[47]

Although it cannot be denied there was a poor level of relations
between the British and Ottoman troops, this should not distract us
from the friendships and positive contact which could spring up between
the two armies. One English captain from the 95th Rifles writes:

These Turkish soldiers fraternise immensely, a party of privates came
the other day into one of our tents where a party of us were sitting
talking and began admiring everything. They were particularly
delighted with an air bed and a revolver we showed them, the odd
thing is that they and apparently all troops but the English behave
quite like gentlemen, sitting down and talking perfectly at their ease
and lighting a pipe and sticking it between our lips with the most
courtly air in the world.[48]

This is not to attempt to gloss over the difficulties of the British-
Turkish relationship on the Crimean battlefield, but rather to show
that despite a general background of tension and mutual mistrust, a
number of British officers were able to strike up friendships with the
Ottoman troops.

Italian soldiers seemed to enjoy a better relationship with their
Turkish comrades. In early 1855, about six months into the conflict,
an army of around fifteen thousand Italians arrived from Sardinia to
assist the Allies (the British predictably nicknamed them 'Sardines').
Italian sources record that the Sardinian soldiers got on better with
the French than with the English; moreover, relations between the
Ottoman soldiers and the Italians were good primarily – we are told
by one observer – because 'it consoled us to see somebody worse off
than ourselves'.[49] If the British soldiers sometimes gave out gifts of
liquor and tobacco to the Italians, the Italians in turn would hand out
the salted meat they did not want to the Turks. Interestingly, in the
Italian accounts there are also reports of Catholic Masses held in the
Sardinian army which were attended by Turkish soldiers, as well as
by French and English officers and various Protestants.

The battle of Kürekdere (6 August 1854) – Russians, Azers, Armenians and Kurds

We could spend a whole book going through the close military operations that took place between Muslim and Christian soldiers in the Crimea: the Zouaves and Algerian Riflemen who came to the assistance of the British at the battle of Inkerman (and whose arrival was greeted with prolonged cheers by the weary soldiers); the combined effort of Ottoman and French troops which pushed the Russians and Cossacks back across the Tchernaya.[50] However, we shall close by concentrating our attention on another battle, one which took place on the other side of the Black Sea, deep into eastern Turkey, a good few months before the battle of Balaklava. It is a battle which, although by no means as important as the battle of Inkerman and the siege of Sevastopol, is of interest to us because of the remarkably interspersed array of Muslim and Christian soldiers on the Russian side.

Most histories of the Crimean war pay little attention to the war in the Caucasus, primarily because no European soldiers and only a small number of European officers were involved. The war consisted of a number of battles and a final siege which ran throughout the period of the Crimean conflict – from 1853 to the fall of the eastern Turkish city of Kars in 1855. The area in which it took place – the mountainous region of northeastern Turkey, Georgia and present-day Armenia – was historically a familiar area of conflict between Russian and Ottoman forces. The Ottomans already had over sixty thousand troops there in 1853, and the idea of diverting significant sections of the enormous Russian land army to the south Caucasus (and away from the Crimea) was an attractive proposal both for the Ottomans and the Allies. As events developed, however, it was the Russians who ended up bringing the offensive to the Turkish frontier, not vice versa.

Anyone who has ever travelled around the region of northeastern Turkey will have seen its formidable, sweeping terrain of mountains and steep valleys, not to mention the merciless winters which affect some of its highest cities (such as Erzurum and Kars). It was against this landscape of mountain slopes and narrow passes that the battles of Bashgedikler and Kürekdere took place. Thousands of troops marched with heavy pack, pulling carriages and heavy artillery behind them, through this terrain. The crucial ability of a land army to manoeuvre well in battle – to win vantage points overlooking the enemy, and not find itself trapped in gorges and low ravines – was what decided the battles fought here, in contrast to the relatively flatter fields of the Crimea.

Another interesting aspect of the wider region – and one we shall have to bear in mind, if we are to understand the multiple cultures within the Russian armies – is the astounding ethnic diversity of the area. It was through no coincidence that the Arab geographers called the Caucasus the *Jabal al-Alsine* or 'mountain of languages'. By the beginning of the nineteenth century, a city such as the Georgian capital, Tiflis (Tbilisi), offered an extraordinary cosmopolitan culture of Azerbaijan Turks, Armenians, Russians, Kurds, Assyrian Christians and ethnic Georgians. The Armenian poet of the Georgian king, Sayat Nova, would write over half his poems in Azeri Turkish, the remainder in Armenian and Georgian.[51] Popular Christian dance and song in the Caucasus, as well as high literary culture such as the sonnet, felt a strong Persian/Turkish influence, one which has never really been fully acknowledged. Although no one can deny the level of tensions and violence which have existed between Christians and Muslims among the Transcaucasian peoples, this should not distract us (I stress once again) from the lived, shared experience of the different cultures. During the Russo-Turkish war of 1828–9, the Russians had more success in Georgia recruiting Muslims for their cavalry than native (Christian) Georgians.[52] In order not to be surprised by the idea of a Russian commander sending over a thousand Azerbaijan Turks to protect a string of Armenian villages – or a Kurdish rebellion against the Ottoman authorities supported by local Greek and Nestorian Christians – we will have to bear in mind that in the inter-ethnic tapestries of the Caucasus, 'Christian' and 'Muslim' were not the only ways people had of talking about themselves.[53]

The battle of Kürekdere, today located almost exactly on the Armenian-Turkish border, was a minor disaster for the Ottomans, a battle in which the Turkish army was overcome by a Russian force half (some say a third) its size. A month earlier, the Russian army, advancing into Ottoman Turkey, had occupied the eastern Turkish town of Bayezid with a force of ten thousand – including over 1,200 Muslims (Azer Turks and Kurds) and 150 local Armenians.[54] The battle of Kürekdere was partly a consequence of this action: it sprang from an unexpected encounter between Russian troops and Ottoman forces along the Kuru river, when Russian soldiers suddenly 'bumped' into an Ottoman army they had thought to be retreating.

The general in charge of the Turkish army was an Irishman by the name of Richard Guyon/Hurşid Pasha (as Ottoman soldiers were reluctant to serve under Christian officers, all of the European and American staff officers had to use Ottoman names). A colourful, cosmopolitan figure, Guyon/Hurşid Pasha was a soldier of fortune who had fought in the Hungarian revolution and, prior to the outbreak of the Crimean War, had been living in the Syrian city of Damascus. Guyon was one of many European officers sent by the Allies to assist in the command of the Ottoman army; at the battle of Kürekdere, he was assisted by a Hungarian, General Kmety/Ismail Pasha. Relations were not always good; if we are to believe British reports (not necessarily the most reliable), Guyon was popular with the Ottoman troops because, upon arriving to take command, he discovered they had not been paid for over two years, and immediately demanded their remuneration – a gesture which did not go down well with his fellow Ottoman officers. The Irishman had a particularly abrasive relationship with one of the Turkish chief commanders there, a man by the name of Zarif Pasha. This may not necessarily have been cultural – Guyon had his share of quarrels with the Polish officers there, too. It should also be said that Zarif Pasha, although a bit of a bounder in many respects, was on very close terms with another Irish officer in the Ottoman service, a general called Coleman/Feyzi Bey. Coleman/Feyzi Bey was an Irishman who not only spoke excellent Turkish, but was one of the few Western officers who had converted to Islam. In any case, the poor relationship between Guyon and Zarif Pasha, not to mention their respective cronies, was certainly a factor in the defeat they suffered at the hands of a significantly smaller Russian army.

The Russians were led by a general called Bebutov. In the imperial army, working in surprisingly close collaboration with the Cossacks and Russian regiments, were a significant number of Muslim battalions – Karapapak (Azerbaijan Turkish) regiments of infantry, as well as Kurdish mercenaries or Bashibozouks (in Russian they were called *militsya*). The Kurds in the region were living under Ottoman rule and, like many Armenians, had hostile feelings towards Istanbul. The large number of Kurds in the Russian army were a result of Bebutov's own efforts to recruit from the local Kurdish villages, drawing on anti-Ottoman sympathy. The historian Badem records that by 1854, Kurdish chiefs were visiting the Russian officers every other day, promising them that if the Ottomans withdrew from the region, the Kurds would come over to the Russian side. Bebutov had even sent a Cossack regiment to some Kurdish villages to see how many Kurds could be recruited to fight the Ottomans; this exercise was repeated as Russian officers met the heads of various Armenian and Azer Turkish villages in the region.[55]

In other words, the battle of Kürekdere was a battle in which an Ottoman army, made up of Turkish and Syrian (Arab) soldiers and led by an Irishman and some Poles and Hungarians, fought a Russian army composed not just of (Christian) Georgians, Armenians and Russians, but also Muslim Azer Turks and Kurds. Moreover, this panoply of different cultures and identities at Kürekdere was typical of all of the battles fought on the Caucasian front of the Crimean War, from the opening battle of Bayindir (1853) to the Polish Cossacks who landed with the Ottoman contingent in Georgia in the very closing days of the conflict. Regardless of whatever propaganda was being issued from the direction of Moscow and Istanbul, a clash of civilisations it was not.

The battle itself took place on 6 August 1854. On the other side of the Black Sea, cholera was sweeping through the troops in Bulgaria and Istanbul. British, French and Ottoman forces in Varna were getting ready, in their thousands, to be transported across to the Crimea. Here in Kürekdere, on the very edge of eastern Turkey, it is curious to think of a small group of Irish, Polish and Hungarian officers preparing to lead an Ottoman army against the Russians.

The Ottoman attack on the Russians should have taken place on 4 August. Guyon had planned the assault around this date but Zarif Pasha, who was a superstitious soul, insisted the 4th and 5th were unlucky days – the moon being in the sign of the crab – and so the attack was deferred to the 6th.[56] Because of the Ottoman army's superior numbers, Guyon had prepared essentially a three-pronged attack, in which the third flank would envelop and close in on the smaller army. It was a well-thought-out plan, but one which unfortunately relied on an ability to manoeuvre on the field, which the Ottoman army did not have. One crucial condition of the plan was to attack very early in the morning; a quarrel between Guyon and Zarif Pasha, however, delayed the departure of the troops quite significantly ('*I* am the commander of this army', Zarif Pasha told the Irishman, '*I* know when to set out').[57] As a result, all three divisions of the army arrived later than expected.

Guyon had planned to fake what looked like a central attack on the Russians' main forces; another section (led by the Hungarian Kmety/Ismail Pasha) would move on a different flank, trying to distract Bebutov, while a third section quickly stole around the Russian flank and attacked them from behind with squadrons of Ottoman Kurdish cavalry. The plan was a good one, but unfortunately relied on the close co-operation and perfect timing of each of the sections. This was not to be.

The three-pronged attack began at dawn with an assault upon an observation post on a hill which was to prove central to the ensuing battle – Karayal Hill.[58] Strangely, General Bebutov, an otherwise highly competent commander, had omitted to check the position was sufficiently defended. A battalion of Istanbul riflemen quickly set themselves up on top of the hill, a major problem since the Ottoman troops (in contrast to the Russians) were equipped with the far more advanced Minié rifles. In response, Bebutov sent an infantry force to re-take the hill, supported by Cossacks, six squadrons of Nizhegorodski Dragoons and Muslim cavalry. The trick of Guyon's plan was that the Russians thought they were attacking the Ottomans' centre, whereas it was really only the far left flank of a much wider front.

Karayal Hill quickly became the site of a fierce battle between, on the one hand, Ottoman (Turkish, Syrian, Kurdish) soldiers and the Cossacks, Dragoons and Muslim irregulars trying to retake it. Towards seven o'clock, Bebutov gave up the idea of re-capturing the hill and instead concentrated on the Ottoman regiments around it. After some desperate Russian cavalry charges, the Ottoman lines broke and the Turkish army began to retreat on its left flank, with the Istanbul Riflemen now leaving the hill. Once this happened, many of the Bashibozouks and Kurdish mercenaries helping the Ottomans also began to disperse. Both Turkish and Western accounts blame the Ottoman officers for this rapid dissolution; whereas the soldiers themselves had apparently fought with great bravery and determination, the officers immediately abandoned their ranks as soon as the tide of the battle turned, and sent orders for their baggage to be transported away from the field of battle.

With one 'prong' of the attack already gone, the flanking movement intended on the other two sides became quite useless. The Russians were quickly able to re-focus their smaller forces (with great skill) on the other two fronts. When a large number of Ottoman Kurdish cavalry appeared on the Russian right flank, Bebutov replied by strengthening the section with a regiment of Cossacks and a brigade of Muslim horse.[59] A movement which had originally intended to be 'sneaking behind' the Russians was now the central front of battle. Heavy fighting commenced and by ten o'clock, the Anatolian infantry began to retreat, having learnt of how badly the fighting around Karayal Hill had already gone. The smaller Russian army, with its combination of Georgian infantry, Muslim cavalry, Russian Dragoons and Kurdish/Azer Turkish irregulars, had inflicted almost eight thousand dead and wounded upon the Ottoman foe. It was a defeat which led to the eventual fall of the eastern Turkish city of Kars, a Russian victory which in itself would become a crucial bargaining chip in the peace negotiations that ended the Crimean War.

As for our own study of Muslim-Christian alliances, ending with the Crimean conflict brings a mixed bag of reflections to our closing chapter. On the one hand, a very modern idea of the Muslim world as backward, inferior and primitive – in contrast with progressive, developed, technologically superior Europe – permeates many aspects of the Crimean War. In earlier periods of history, Muslim cultures and their armies were viewed with fear and awe; Muslim Spain, we will recall, looked on the Christian cities of the north largely as poor relatives, and hardly spoke of them at all. Similarly, the arrogance of the Ottoman sultans in the sixteenth century towards the 'infidel' was certainly a consequence of their own military and economic superiority. By the nineteenth century, the tables have very much turned – it is the West which now sees the Turks as 'half-savages' and British generals who, in the words of one Turkish source, 'treat the Ottoman officers like negroes'.[60] The overall disappointing relationship between French/British soldiers and their Ottoman colleagues in the Crimean War had more to do with this difference in military/economic power than in any perception of religion.

On the other hand, what remains fascinating is the undeniable level of co-operation between Muslim and Christian soldiers, of all creeds and colours, on the Crimean battlefield. The closeness with which the Russians employed cavalry and infantry of both faiths, for example, the intimate manoeuvring which took place as Kurds supported Cossacks or Azer Turks strengthened regiments of Georgians, does make us reflect on the Crimean War as a conflict in which Muslims and Christians were thoroughly interspersed. Equally fascinating is the way this Muslim involvement has been gradually diminished and faded out from our own Western recollection of events – for British readers, at least, in the most famous aspects of the Crimean War recalled today, it is hard to discern anything Muslim at all. The obvious images – the Charge of the Light Brigade, the 'Thin Red Line', the memory of Florence Nightingale – linger on, with any kind of Muslim involvement or background conveniently airbrushed out. This becomes even clearer when perusing the history books written about the war itself; although the Ottoman army was, after the French, the second-largest army in the Crimea, practically every index (even in an excellent and highly critical history such as Ponting's) will list the British/French/Italian/Russian army separately, but provide no equivalent heading for the Turkish. This may sound like a trivial point, but it says a great deal, even today, about the kind of events we want to remember, and the kind of alliances we would rather forget.

Sources

V.H. Aksan, 'The Ottoman Military and State Transformation in a Globalizing World', in *Comparative Studies of South Asia, Africa and the Middle East*, 27:2 (2007).

A.R. Alexiev and S. Enders Wimbush (eds), *Ethnic Minorities in the Red Army* (West View Press, 1988).

Candan Badem, 'The Ottomans and the Crimean War (1853–56)' (Unpublished PhD dissertation, Sabanci University, June 2007).

for Turkish speakers, further articles by Badem include:

—'Kırım Savaşi'nın Osmanlı Toplumsal Yasamına Etkileri', *Toplumsal Tarih* 133, Istanbul, January 2005, pp.64–71.

—'Rus ve Sovyet Tarih Yazımında Kırım Savası', *Toplumsal Tarih* 155, Istanbul, November 2006, pp.16–23.

—'Unutulmuş Bir Hikaye: Kırım Savası', news article, *Toplumsal Tarih* 156, Istanbul, December 2006, p.6.

Baron de Bazancourt, *L'Expedition de Crimée* (Paris, 1856).

Caucasian Battlefields: A History of the Wars on the Turco-Caucasian Border 1828–1921, W.E.D. Allen and P. Muratoff (Cambridge University Press, 1953).

Henry Clifford, VC, *His letters and sketches from the Crimea* (New York, 1956).

R. Crews, *For Prophet and Tsar: Islam and Empire in Russia and Central Asia* (Harvard University Press, 2006).

J.S. Curtiss, *The Russian Army Under Nicholas I* (Duke University Press, 1965).

R.B. Edgeton, *Death or Glory: The Legacy of the Crimean War* (Westview Press, 1999).

George Palmer Evelyn, *A Diary of the Crimea* (London, 1954).

Ian Fletcher and Natalia Ishchenko, *The Crimean War: A Clash of Empires* (Spellmount, 2004).

R.R. Florescu, *The Struggle Against Russia in the Romanian Principalities* (Iaşi, 1997).

A. Fisher, *Between Russians, Ottomans and Turks: Crimea and Crimean Tartars* (Isis Press, 1998).

T. Heinzelmann, *Heiliger Kampf oder Landesverteidigung? Die Diskussion um die Einführung der allegemeinen Militärpflicht im Osmanischen Reich 1826–56* (Peter Lang, 2004).

L. James, *Crimea 1854–56: The war with Russia from contemporary photographs* (Hayes Kennedy, 1981).

Austin Jersild and Neli Melkadze, 'The Dilemmas of Enlightenment in the Eastern Borderlands: The Theater and Library in Tbilisi', in *Kritika: Explorations in Russian and Eurasian History* 3(1): 27–49, Winter 2002.

Colonel Atwell Lake, *Narrative of the Defence of Kars Historical and Military* (London: Bentley, 1857).

A.D. Lambert, *The Crimean War: British Grand Strategy 1853–56* (Manchester University Press, 1990).

Letters from Headquarters: The Realities of War in the Crimea by an Officer on the Staff (London, 2nd edition: John Murray, 1857).

Löwe, Heinz-Dietrich, 'Poles, Jews and Tartars: Religion, Ethnicity and Social Structure in Tsarist Nationality Policies', in *Jewish Social Studies*, pp.52–96.

N.M. Houston, 'Reading the Victorian Souvenir: Sonnets and Photographs of the Crimean War', in *Yale Journal of Criticism*, 14:2 (2001), pp. 353–83.

Cristoforo Manfredi, *La Spedizione Sarda in Crimea del 1855–6* (Regionale in Roma, 1956).

Karl Marx, *The Eastern Question: A Reprint of Letters written 1853–6 dealing with the events of the Crimean War* (New York: Burt Franklin, 1968).

Lieutenant Edward Money, *Twelve Months with the Bashibozouks* (London: Chapman, 1857).

D. Murphy, *Ireland and the Crimean War* (Four Courts Press, 2002).

Le Vicomte de Noë, *Souvenirs d'Afrique: Les Bachi-Bozouks et les Chasseurs d'Afrique* (Paris, 1861).

Daniel Panzac, 'The Manning of the Ottoman Navy', in E.J. Zürcher, *Arming the State: Military Conscription in the Middle East and Central Asia* (I.B.Tauris, 1999).

Yohanan Petrovsky-Shtern, 'The "Jewish Policy" of the Late Imperial War Ministry: The Impact of the Russian Right', in *Kritika: Explorations in Russian and Eurasian History* 3(2): 217–54, Spring 2002.

Clive Ponting, *The Crimean War* (Chatto and Windus, 2004).

H. Ram, 'The Sonnet and the Mukhambazi: Genre Wars on the Edges of the Russian Empire', in *PMLA* 5:122 (October 2007).

Reminiscences of an Officer of Zouaves, translated from the French (New York: D. Appleton and Company, 1860).

I.L. Rudnytsky, *Essays in Modern Ukrainian History* (Edmonton, 1987).

W.H. Russell, *Russell's Despatch from the Crimea*, ed. N. Bentley (Panther, 1970).

Russia's Orient: Imperial Borderlands and Peoples 1700–1917, eds. D.R. Brower and E.J. Lazzerini (Indiana University Press, 1997).

A. Seaton, *The Crimean War: A Russian Chronicle* (St Martin's Press, 1977).

E.K. Wirtschafter, *From Serf to Russian Soldier* (Princeton University Press, 1990).

CONCLUSION

I spent six years in Turkey, teaching literature at a couple of universities in and outside Istanbul. For the first two years I worked in a fairly large provincial town in the middle of Turkey. It was a town where – at least up until the First World War – Greeks, Armenians and Turks had lived together for centuries. Although the buildings which gave witness to this fact were rapidly disappearing, the area around my old teacher's residence still had a number of old, crumbling Greek and Armenian houses, many of them dating back to the nineteenth century. On summer afternoons, partly out of curiosity, partly out of boredom, I would wander around the clusters of bricks and half-demolished houses, some inhabited, some abandoned, in any case their original residents long gone. One day I came across an inscription chiselled above the doorway of one house – a standard Muslim phrase, *Mashallah* or 'God bless you', often found above the doors of Muslim houses – but this time in Greek letters: ΜΑΣΑΛΛΑ. The doorway, in other words, of a Greek house, whose Christian owner had chosen to place a standard Arabic inscription above the entrance to his home for his Muslim neighbours.

The Greek phrase I saw that day – ΜΑΣΑΛΛΑ – is simply a word, a Muslim greeting written in Greek characters. It cannot be exaggerated, it should not be idealised, it is not a word which can magically make us forget the difficult history between Greeks, Armenians and Turks. It is not a word which can drown out certain screams, elide certain massacres, romanticise certain pasts. And yet it still lies there today, engraved in stone, testament to a time when Muslims and Christians ate the same food together, shared village gossip with one another, read the same newspapers and danced to the same tunes, with the same instruments, in the same coffee houses. It is a word which perfectly captures the spirit of what I have been trying, in this hasty history of Muslim-Christian alliances, to communicate: that the story of Europe, if we are to insist on the need to keep on telling it, is the story of *three* religions, not one. The point is not exclusive to Turkey: similar versions of the ΜΑΣΑΛΛΑ I glimpsed that afternoon could be found for the Muslims and Christians of Georgia, of Bosnia, of Greece, not to mention the long-departed Arabs of Sicily and Spain. To leave Muslims out of this story is to wipe the ΜΑΣΑΛΛΑ off the doorway of the Greek's house.

Although this book has been essentially a military history, the shared values and overlapping communities of Muslims and Christians throughout the centuries has been an unspoken background to my research. For there is certainly a kind of threshold, a level of need in all of us, which has to be reached before we decide to ally ourselves with another community, with people we perceive to be different from us. Various things raise or lower that threshold of necessity; the emergency of a situation, for one thing – we might not like our next-door neighbour enough to borrow a ladder from them, but we wouldn't refuse their help if our house was on fire. As we have seen, there have been many moments in which impending invasions or assaults brought together communities which otherwise felt little sympathy with one another.

Another related factor is the hatred of a common enemy. An antipathy towards a shared threat or foe appears to have brought different cultures closer to one another, and even prompted them to search for similarities. When the Protestant Elizabethans tried to persuade the North African emirates to create trouble for Catholic Spain (and thereby distract its Armada), one of their arguments was a common Muslim/Protestant hatred of 'papish' idolatry. Or when a Polish Ukrainian, in trying to persuade others in the Balkans to join the Ottomans in their anti-tsarist struggle, combs through the history books in an attempt to find dynastic links between Serb royalty and the lineage of the sultans, he is trying to justify a political necessity with a historical alibi. The act of resisting a common foe drives us, consciously or not, to look for similarities and connections with our new and unlikely allies (it was Nietzsche, after all, who said we should love our enemies, for our enemies tell us who we are).

The economic promise of material gain also reduces our unwillingness to ally ourselves with different communities; throughout this book, the endless stream of mercenaries and peasants who threw in their lot with armies of a different faith is testimony to this fact. Moreover, a kind of emotional investment has often seemed to follow this economic decision. The striking conviction with which some renegades fought for their new 'employers' – be it the Saracens of the Hohenstaufen or the Croat and Georgian converts of the Ottomans – suggests something more than a merely strategic decision. The fact that in the Crimean War, some European officers who worked with the Ottomans converted to Islam, while others simply adopted a Turkish name, does show how differently people respond to such close collaboration with 'other' cultures.

And then there are the peculiar, idiosyncratic reasons why, in certain moments, Muslims and Christians have come together – reasons which are not always clearly reducible to a set of economic, cultural or political circumstances, even though such circumstances have clearly helped to bring them about. Affections, marriages, curiosity, inexplicable attractions and fascinations; friendships such as those of Kantakouzenos and Umur, or attitudes such as those of Frederick II or Michal Czajkowski, seem to provide an impetus to inter-faith alliances which cannot be easily inserted into some all-explaining system of exchange. History is simply too messy, and too abundant, to be packed into such boxes; it spills everywhere, its anecdotes and marginalia and sidelines causing even the most confident historians to hesitate and falter.

Finally, and perhaps most significantly, it is the existence of a shared culture, a common language or set of values, which appears to bring down the threshold at which one religious group will fight on behalf of another. The Zaragozan Muslims whose knowledge of Spanish would have been fluent enough to sneak them into the Aragonese camp as spies; the Christian and Muslim Lucerans who would have defended the same walls of the same town against the French aggressors; the Balkan Christians, Serbs and Greeks who would have fought in the same companies as their Bosnian neighbours against the Habsburg foe – Ali fighting alongside Dimitri, Abdullah next to Tomas. A successful Muslim-Christian alliance took place when one or more of these factors – political need, a common enemy, similar values, the same language, fortuitous friendships or affinities between elites – were able to become significant enough to make a difference.

The sweep of history I have sketched here – from eleventh-century Spain to nineteenth-century Russia – is enormous by any standards. Certain paragraphs in this book have been the subject of entire sets of encyclopedias; certain sentences have skipped over whole centuries.

When dealing with a range of over eight hundred years, and a territory stretching from Barcelona to Bulgaria, it is difficult to provide even the most general conclusions. Perhaps the only meaningful point to be made is that, historically speaking, the terms 'Muslim' and 'Christian' simply cannot do all the things we expect them to – and those who claim they can almost always have a different, hidden agenda. The term 'Islam' reduces inconvenient complexities: as we have already seen, the Austrian Habsburgs used it as a constant excuse to 'protect' Hungary, just as certain Byzantine elites used the word 'Turk' to overlook their own corruption and self-centredness. The point is true even today, when an army of media experts uses Islam and jihad to 'explain' the violence in Palestine and Iraq – 'explanations' which are not only inadequate, but which free us in the West from any reflection on our own involvement in these situations. The current violence in Afghanistan may well be painted as a struggle between Islamism and democracy – but the fact that Afghanistan's president works for a Californian oil company does say a great deal about what kind of 'democracy' that is.

In many ways, this abuse of history and chronicle is one of the most strikingly regular phenomena of this study. The convenient deletion of Muslims from Christian armies – and vice versa – appears to have taken place in every epoch: Hungarian historians filtering Ottoman help out of victories over their rivals; the Ottoman poets who, when writing their historical epics, chose to leave out the Greek involvement in the founding century of the empire. This selective amnesia continues right up to the present day – the way many British historians have erased Turkish troops from any role in the Crimea, for example, or the manner in which Austrians, in celebrating the 'Tü rkenjahr' of 1683, make no mention of the fact that less than half of the army which threatened Vienna was actually Turkish.

An historian, in this sense, is a conscience with time to read. For myself, one of the most surprising results of writing this book has been to see how much history is lost, how easily it simply drops out of time. There are only so many narratives a society can offer itself to explain how it came into being; there are only so many books people can read, so many events a community can remember, so many titles which can fit onto the page of an internet search or a library query. The recollection of one thing involves, sooner or later, the obliteration of something else – and since society's mechanisms for understanding the past are always carried with it in the present, sources can be easily forgotten, like a passenger overboard, as the collective memory drifts off in a different direction. Before beginning this book, I confess, I had a somewhat naive view of history; I imagined that it was rather like climbing a hill, so that as you got higher and higher, you acquired an expanding view of an increasingly bigger terrain. The more books you read, the more you learnt about 'what really happened'. After two years of research, I now realise this analogy is hopelessly wrong; we don't learn more and more about ourselves, we simply modify our histories continually. The bibliography of a book (including this one) invariably refers to everything which has been written about the topic in the preceding forty years. As time moves on, we remain inside a kind of curve, our past and present forever informing one another. For the writing of history, a better metaphor than the hill would be that of a car, driving along a road in thick fog, with its headlights and rear-lights on so that it only sees ten metres in front of it and ten metres behind. The road the car drives along is constantly changing; the driver never sees any further ahead or behind.

I would like to end on a personal, and somewhat political, note. We live, we are told, in an age of increasing 'terror'. The word 'terrorist' – which has been used to describe everything from Islamic militants to Mexican immigrants, Kurdish separatists and trade union activists in the Philippines – has moved into public discourse in an unprecedented way, creating the atmosphere of a society which is effectively 'under threat'. With varying degrees of political sensitivity, this sense of terror – what one British newspaper recently referred to as 'the cosmic threat of terrorism' – has been extended not only to the question of foreign policy and immigration, but to the whole concept of Middle Eastern cultures in general. And, of course, to the religion of Islam in particular.

I am fully aware that there are a small number of fanatics who would seek to cause large-scale destruction, given half the chance. While travelling to work in Istanbul one morning in 2005, my own bus passed by the HSBC Bank an hour before it blew up, killing over thirty people: in no way do I wish to claim there is no such thing as a terrorist threat. What has to be repeated, however, is that the real danger is a tiny fraction of the threat being claimed. The security culture which is blossoming in Europe as a consequence of this obsession with 'terror' – from people being arrested for simply staring at corporate buildings to hecklers in public meetings being beaten and Tasered for their dissent – appears to be growing day by day, and has a number of deeply unpleasant agendas behind it. It is difficult to ignore the way a 'Muslim bogeyman' is used to distract public attention from the *real* threat to our society: that of the large-scale takeover of our public structures and resources by a small number of corporate and business elites. In a European Union which is increasingly becoming a synonym for privatisation and liberalisation, the constant, media-pumped anxiety concerning terror, immigrants and asylum-seekers can only offer a useful distraction from a series of much more urgent (and much less exotic) issues. For big business, leading news programmes with fresh stories of terror plots and images of leering imams with eye-patches and hooks is infinitely preferable to public debates concerning corporate ownership of the media or the influence of lobbies on government policy. Talking endlessly about 'the army of Islam', as both the Habsburg emperor and the Russian tsar knew all too well, certainly has its uses.

NOTES

Chapter One

1 J.F. O'Callaghan, *A History of Medieval Spain* (Cornell University Press, 1975), pp.129–30. For more on the advanced Arab state of siege machinery, with respect to its eleventh-century Christian counterparts, see Paul E. Chevedden, 'The Artillery of King James I the Conqueror' in P.E. Chevedden, D.J. Kagay and P.G. Padilla (eds) *Iberia and the Mediterranean World of the Middle Ages* (Leiden, 1996), vol. II, pp.57–63.

2 This treatment of both Ibn Habib's *Kitab al-Ta'rij* and the anonymous tenth-century *Akhbar Majmu'a* can be found in J.M. Safran's 'Landscapes in the Conquest of al-Andalus' in J. Howe and M. Wolfe (eds), *Inventing Medieval Landscapes: Senses of Place in Western Europe* (University Press of Florida, 2002), pp.136–49. For a valuable in-depth study of the Muslim conquest, see 'Abdulwahid Dhanun Taha, *The Muslim Conquest and Settlement of North Africa and Spain* (Routledge, 1989), pp.84–110.

3 Norman Roth, *Jews, Visigoths and Muslims in Medieval Spain: Cooperation and Conflict* (Leiden, 1994), pp.46–7.

4 Makki, p.44, in S.K. Jayyusi (ed.), *The Legacy of Muslim Spain* (Leiden, 1992).

5 For the relative silence of Maghrib writers in general on Christians, see Aziz al-Azmeh, 'Mortal Enemies, Invisible Neighbours: Northerners in Andalusi Eyes' in Jayyusi (ed.), pp.260–5.

6 O'Callaghan, p.188.

7 Brian A. Catlos, *The Victors and the Vanquished: Christians and Muslims of Catalonia and Aragon 1050–1300* (Cambridge University Press, 2004), pp.29–31.

8 Azmeh, p.264; Roth, p.46.

9 Richard Fletcher, *The Quest for El Cid* (London: Hutchinson, 1989), p.141.

10 Hugh Kennedy, *Muslim Spain and Portugal* (London: Longman, 1996), pp.130–2.

11 Simon Barton, 'Traitors to the Faith? Christian Mercenaries in al-Andalus and the Maghrib c.1100– 1300' in R. Collins and A. Goodman (eds), *Medieval Spain: Culture, Conflict and Coexistence in Honour of Angus MacKay* (London: Palgrave, 2002), p.26.

12 O'Callaghan, p.127.

13 Barton, p.25.
14 Catlos, p.265. For an interesting later example of a Muslim mercenary, see Catlos' essay. 'Mahomet Abenadalill: A Muslim Mercenary in the service of the Kings of Aragon (1290–1)' in H.J. Hames (ed.), *Jews, Muslims and Christians in and around the Crown of Aragon* (Leiden, 2004), pp.257–302.
15 Ibid, p.74-5.
16 B.F. Reilly, *The Kingdom of Leon-Castilla under King Alfonso VI* (Princeton: Princeton University Press, 1988), p.240; Arabic source for the Muslim ruler of Huesca's exile found in Catlos, p.75.
17 Ross Brann, *Power in the Portrayal: Representations of Jews and Muslims in Eleventh and Twelfth Century Islamic Spain* (Princeton University Press, 2002), p.3.
18 M. Fierro, 'Christian Success and Muslim Fear in Andalusi Writings' in *Israel Oriental Studies* XVII, p.157.
19 From *Indiculus Luminosus*, cit. in O'Callaghan, p.188.
20 Cit. in Fletcher, p.52.
21 Roth, pp.54–5.
22 Brann, pp.95–7.
23 Catlos, p.37.
24 Catlos, p.73; the reference to Christians helping the Muslims keep hold of Huesca can be found in Antonio Duran Gudiol, 'Francos, Pamploneses y Mozarabes en la Marca Superior de al-Andalus' in P. Sénac (ed.), *La Marche Supérieure d'Al-Andalus et l'Occident Chrétien* (Madrid, 1991), p.146.
25 O'Callaghan, p.196.
26 Roth, p.93.
27 O'Callaghan, p.201.
28 This is reported in the *Latin Chronicles of the Kings of Castile*, ed. J.F. O'Callaghan (Arizona, 2002), p.4.
29 Reilly, p.83.
30 Reilly, p.163.
31 Reilly, pp.169–73.
32 See B.F. Reilly's follow-up volume to his work on Alfonso VI, *The Kingdom of Leon-Castile under King Alfonso VII 1126–1157* (University of Pennsylvania Press, 1998), for twelfth-century developments in the aftermath of Zallaqah.
33 Pierre Guichard, *Les Musulmans de Valence et la Reconquête (xi-xiii siècles)* (Damas: Paris, 1990), pp.65–9.
34 Catlos, p.84.
35 Elena Lourie, 'A Society Organized for War' in *Past and Present* 35 (1966), pp.54–76.

Chapter Two

1 J. Göbbels, *Das Militärwesen im Königreich Siziliens zur Zeit Karls I von Anjou* (Hiersemann: Stuttgart, 1984), p.19.
2 S. Runciman, *The Sicilian Vespers* (Cambridge University Press, 1958), p.60.
3 David Abulafia, *The Western Mediterranean Kingdoms* (London: Longman, 1997), p.23; F. Gabrieli, *Arab Histories of the Crusades*, trans. E.J. Costello (London: Routledge, 1969), p.280.

4   Aziz Ahmad, *A History of Islamic Sicily* (Edinburgh University Press, 1975), p.6.
5   Julie Taylor, *Muslims in Medieval Italy: The Colony at Lucera* (Lexington University Press, 2003), pp.1–2.
6   Giovanni Amatuccio, 'Saracen Archers in Southern Italy', E-HAWK June 1997. www.idir.net.
7   David Abulafia, 'The End of Muslim Sicily', in J.M. Powell (ed.), *Muslims Under Latin Rule 1100–1300* (Princeton University Press, 1990), p.121.
8   J.P. Lomax, 'Frederick II, His Saracens and the Papacy', in John V. Toran (ed.), *Medieval Christian Perceptions of Islam* (London: Routledge, 1996), p.177.
9   Runciman, *Vespers*, p.10.
10 Abulafia, 'End of Muslim Sicily', p.109.
11 Eberhard Horst, *Der Sultan von Lucera* (Freiburg: Herder Verlag, 1997), p.10.
12 See section 60 of Nietzsche's *The Antichrist*.
13 J.L. Baird, G. Baglivi, J.R. Kane (eds), *The Chronicle of Salimbene de Adam* (Binghamton, NY, 1986), pp.356, 353.
14 Ibid, pp.352, 355.
15 David Abulafia, *Medieval Encounters, Economic, Religious, Political 1100–1350* (Ashgate, 2000), p.219.
16 Ahmad, *Islamic Sicily*, pp.89–91.
17 See F. Gabrieli, 'Friedrich II und die Kultur des Islam', in G. Wolf (ed.), *Stupor Mundi: Zur Geschichte Friedrichs II von Hohenstaufen* (Darmstadt, 1982) pp.88–9.
18 Kurt Victor Selge, 'Die Ketzerpolitik Friedrichs II', in G. Wolf, *Stupor Mundi*, p.451.
19 Taylor, *Muslims in Medieval Italy*, p.7.
20 For more on Damietta, see Douglas Sterling, 'The Siege of Damietta,' in D.J. Kagay and L.J.A. Villalon (eds), *Crusaders, Condottieri and Cannon: Medieval Warfare in Societies Around the Mediterranean* (Brill: Leiden, 2003), pp.101–32.
21 Taylor, *Muslims in Medieval Italy*, pp.8–10, Ahmad, *Islamic Sicily*, p.83.
22 Abulafia, *Medieval Encounters*, p.217.
23 Taylor, *Muslims in Medieval Italy*, p.47.
24 Ibid, pp.83–4.
25 Ibid, p.70.
26 Ibid, p.55.
27 Ibid, p.115.
28 J.P. Lomax, 'Frederick II', p.185.
29 Peter Thorau, *The Lion of Egypt: Sultan Baybars I and the Near East in the Thirteenth Century* (New York: Longman, 1987), p.8.
30 Amin Maalouf, *The Crusades Through Arab Eyes*, trans. J. Rothschild (Zed Books, 1984), p.226.
31 David Abulafia, *Frederick II: A Medieval Emperor* (Penguin, 1988) p.166.
32 Ibid, p.167.
33 Taken from Ibn Wasil's chronicle in Gabrieli, *Arab historians*, pp.279–80.
34 H.L. Gottschalk, *Al-Malik al-Kamil von Egypten und seine Zeit* (Wiesbaden, 1958), p.151.
35 Ibid, p.154.
36 Ibid.
37 Gabrieli, *Arab Histories*, p.275 (taken from the chronicle of Sibt ibn al-Jauzi).

38 Maalouf, *The Crusades*, p.229.
39 Abulafia, *Frederick II*, pp.189–90.
40 Taylor, *Muslims in Medieval Italy*, pp.103–4.
41 J.F. Verbruggen, *The Art of Warfare in Western Europe*, trans. C.S. Willard and R.W. Southern (Woodbridge: Boydell Press, 1997), p.7.
42 Amatuccio, 'Saracen Archers'; Abulafia, *Frederick II*, p.199.
43 Abulafia, *Frederick II*, p.201.
44 J.P. Lomax, 'Frederick II', pp.183–5.
45 *Salimbene de Adam*, p.74.
46 Abulafia, *Frederick II*, p.270.
47 Ibid, p.308.
48 Piero Pieri, 'I Saraceni di Lucera nella storia militare medievale', *Archivo Storico Pugliese* 6 (1953) p.96.
49 Pieri, 'I Saraceni', p.98.
50 Abulafia, *Frederick II*, p.327.
51 *Salimbene de Adam*, p.164.
52 See Amatuccio, 'Saracen Archers' and Taylor, *Muslims in Medieval Italy*, pp.104–11; also Göbbels, *Das Militärwesen*, pp.22–3.
53 Ahmad, *Islamic Sicily*, p.92; Enrico Pispisa, *Il Regno di Manfredi* (Sicania: Messina, 1991), p.301.
54 Gabrieli, *Arab Histories*, p.279.
55 Runciman, *Vespers*, pp.32–3.
56 Amatuccio, 'Saracen Archers'.
57 Runciman, *Vespers*, p.57.
58 Ibid, p.70.
59 Abulafia, *Frederick II*, p.415.
60 Runciman, *Vespers*, p.85.
61 Ibid, pp.92–4.
62 Ibid, p.96.
63 Pietro Egidi, *La Colonnia dei Saraceni e la sua distruzione* (Naples, 1915) vol. 1, p.45; Taylor, *Muslims in Medieval Italy*, pp.140–2.
64 Taylor, *Muslims in Medieval Italy*, p.145.
65 Ibid.
66 Göbbels, *Das Militärwesen*, p.119.
67 Amatuccio, 'Saracen Archers'.
68 Taylor, *Muslims in Medieval Italy*, p.105.
69 Ibid, p.174.
70 Ibid, p.183.

Chapter Three

1 S. Vryonis, Jr, *Byzantium and Europe* (London, 1967).
2 See Michael Balivet's essay in *Byzantinische Forschungen* XVI (Amsterdam, 1991), p.322.
3 S. Runciman, *The Fall of Constantinople* (Cambridge University Press, 1965), p.21.
4 A.A. Vasiliev, *History of the Byzantine Empire* (University of Wisconsin Press, 1952), vol. II, p.607.

5 M.C. Bartusis, *The Late Byzantine Army: Arms and Society 1204–1453* (University of Pennsylvania Press, 1992), p.70.

6 E.A. Zachariadou, *Romania and the Turks 1300–1500* (London: Variorum, 1985), vol. III, p.338.

7 See Chapter 5 of A. Eastmond, *Art and Identity in Thirteenth-century Byzantium* (London: Ashgate, 2004).

8 Bartusis, p.330.

9 See Keith Hopwood, 'Mudara', in A. Singer, A. Cohen (eds), *Aspects of Ottoman History* (Jerusalem: The Magras Press, 1994), p.158. The reference to Eskisehir can be found in R.P. Lindner, *Nomads and Ottomans in Medieval Anatolia* (Bloomington, Indiana, 1983), p.25.

10 D.M. Nicol, *The Reluctant Emperor* (Cambridge University Press, 1996), pp.62–3; G.T. Dennis, ManII letters, p.86.

11 Bartusis, p.78; A.E. Laiou, *Constantinople and the Latins: The Foreign Policy of Andronikos II 1282–1328* (Harvard, 1972), pp.191–2.

12 G.T. Dennis SJ, *The Reign of Manuel II Palaeologus in Thessalonica 1382–1387* (Rome, 1960), p.89.

13 See Pal Fodor, *In Quest of the Golden Apple* (Isis Press: Istanbul, 2000), pp.13–21.

14 Lindner, p.33.

15 Taken from the *Tevarih* of Ashikpashazade, cit. in Heath W. Lowry, *The Nature of the Early Ottoman State* (SUNY Press, 2003), p.56.

16 Dimitri Kitsikis, *Turk-Yunan Imparatorlugu: Arabolge Gercegi Isiginda Osmanli Tarihine Bakis* (Istanbul, 1996).

17 V. Dimitriades, 'Byzantine and Ottoman Thessaloniki', in A.M. Hakkert and W.E. Kaegi Jr (eds) *Byzantinische Forschungen* XVI:268 (1991).

18 Lowry, p.52.

19 See Balivet, pp.314–22; C. Kafadar, *Between Two Worlds: The Construction of the Ottoman State* (University of California Press, 1995), p.74.

20 J. Raby and Z. Tanindi, *Turkish Bookbinding in the Fifteenth Century* (London: Azimuth, 1993), pp.3, 20, 34.

21 See Aptullah Kuran, *The Mosque in Early Ottoman Architecture* (Chicago, 1968), pp.114–19.

22 Vasiliev, p.583.

23 Bartusis, pp.68–9.

24 Pachymeres II:308, cit. in Laiou, p.90. For more on Alans, see Istvan Vasary, *Cumans and Tatars: Oriental Military in the Pre-Ottoman Balkans 1185–1365* (Cambridge University Press, 2005), pp.108–11.

25 Bartusis, pp.60–2, 244.

26 Laiou, p.141.

27 Bartusis, pp.78–9.

28 Pachymeres II:451–2, cit. in Laiou, p.137.

29 Bartusis, p.77.

30 *The Chronicle of Muntaner*, trans. Lady Goodenough (London: Hakluyt Society, 1920), vol. 2, pp.543–4.

31 Bartusis, p.80.

32 Bartusis, p.82.

33 Zachariadou, *Romania and the Turks*, vol. V, p.831.

34 Halil Inalcik, *Studies in Ottoman Social and Economic History* (London, 1985), p.72; Lindner, p.14–15.

35 Laiou, pp.84, 292.
36 Gregoras, I:649, cit. in Nicol, Kanta, p.35.
37 Bartusis, p.97.
38 P. Lemerle, *L'Emirat d'Aydin* (Paris, 1957), p.9.
39 The Turkish chronicler is the poet Enveri, author of the *Duşturname*, trans. Irene Melikoff-Sayar, in *Le Destan d'Umur Pacha* (Paris, 1954), pp.84–5. Kantakouzenos' memoirs are found in *Johannes Kantakuzenos: Geschichte II*, trans. G. Fatouros and T. Krischer (Stuttgart: Hiersemann, 1986).
40 Lowry, p.67.
41 Bartusis, p.94.
42 Nicol, Kanta, p.35.
43 H.A.R. Gibb, *The Travels of Ibn Battuta* (Cambridge University Press, 1962), vol. II, p.443.
44 Nicol, Kanta, p.37.
45 Bartusis, p.256.
46 Ibid, pp.323–31.
47 Nicol, Kanta, p.48; Lemerle, pp.141–2.
48 Bartusis, pp.94–6.
49 Lemerle, pp.215–17; Nicol, Kanta, pp.68–73.
50 C. Kafadar, p.70; *Duşturname,* pp.106–7.
51 *Duşturname,* p.108.
52 See for example Lemerle, p.175.
53 A. Bryer, 'The Case of the first Byzantine-Ottoman marriage', in R.H.C. Davis and J.M. Wallace-Hadrill (eds), *The Writing of History in the Middle Ages* (Clarendon Press, 1981), pp.478–80.
54 Cit. in Bryer, p.481.
55 Ibid, p.480. Demetrius, the brother of the last emperor Constantine, gave Mehmet II his sister in marriage and so obtained his support. See Aryeh Shmowelevitz, 'Ottoman History and Society', in *Analecta Isisiana* XXXVIII (1999), p.43.
56 The historian is the Ottoman Greek Kritovoulos, cit. in Kafadar, p.9.
57 Bryer, p.473.
58 Bryer, p.487.
59 Bartusis, p.100.
60 Klaus Peter Matschke, *Die Schlacht bei Ankara und das Schicksal von Byzanz* (Weimar, 1981), p.52.
61 See his wonderful prose poem in C. Dendrinos, J. Harris, E. Harvalia Crook and J. Herrin (eds), *Porphryogenita: Essays on the History and Literature of the Byzantine and Latin East* (Ashgate, 2003), pp.413–20, translated by J. Davis.
62 See Zachariadou, vol. IV, pp.471–2, 478. Also Lowry, p.28.
63 David Nicolle, *The Mongol Warlords* (Firebird Books, 1990), p.166.
64 Rene Grousset, *L'Empire des Steppes* (Paris, 1960), p.528.
65 Doukas, *Decline and Fall of Byzantium to the Ottoman Turks,* trans. H.J. Magoulias (Detroit, 1975), p.90.
66 John W. Barker, *Manuel II Palaeologus* (Rutgers University Press, 1969), p.119.
67 M. Braun, *Lebensbeschreibung des Despoten Stefan Lazarevic* (Göttingen, 1956), p.11.
68 M.M. Alexandrescu-Dersca, *Le Campagne de Timur en Anatolie* (London: Variorum, 1977), p.73. What follows is largely based on the Romanian scholar's detailed twelve-page account of the battle.

69 Ibid, pp.68–79.
70 Runciman, p.93; Doukas, p.233.
71 Runciman, p.82 – the commentator is Phrantzes, who is citing 'a Polish Janissary'; Runciman, pp.134–5.
72 Runciman, p.78.
73 Lowry, pp.115–16.

Chapter Four

1 See J. and W. Grimm, *Deutsches Wörterbuch* (Munich: DTV, 1984), 22: 1852. For more on Leibniz, see my own 'Leibniz, Historicism and the Plague of Islam', *Eighteenth Century Studies* 39:4 (2006).
2 P. Fodor, *In Quest of the Golden Apple: Imperial Ideology, Politics and Military Administration of the Ottoman Empire* (Isis Press, 2000), p.71.
3 Ibid, pp.84–5. For more on background of Hungarians, see Nora Berend, *At the Gate of Christendom: Jews, Muslims and Pagans in Medieval Hungary 1000–1300* (Cambridge University Press, 2001), pp.19–30.
4 F. Szakály, *Lodovico Gritti in Hungary 1529–1534* (Budapest, 1995), p.8.
5 Berend, *Jews, Muslims and Pagans*, pp.66, 110.
6 Ibid, pp.239–40.
7 A. Várkonyi, 'Rákóczi's War of Independence', in J.M. Bak and B.K. Király (eds), *From Hunyadi to Rákóczi: War and Society in Late Medieval and Early Modern Hungary* (Brooklyn College Press, 1982), p.370.
8 L. Benczédi, 'The Warrior Estate', in *From Hunyadi to Rákóczi*, p.358.
9 T.M. Barker, *Double Eagle and Crescent: Vienna's Second Turkish Siege and its Historical Setting* (SUNY, 1967), p.214.
10 Miklós Molnár, *A Concise History of Hungary* (trans. A. Magyar – Cambridge University Press, 2001), pp.97–9.
11 Cit. in Pál Fodor, *Quest of the Golden Apple*, p.88.
12 Ibid, p.87.
13 P. Fodor, 'Volunteers in the 16th century Ottoman Army', in Géza David and Pál Fodor (eds), *Ottomans, Hungarians and Habsburgs in Central Europe* (Leiden, 2000), p.240.
14 The writer is Miklós Esterházy, cit. in F. Szakály, 'Das Bauerntum und die Kämpfe gegen die Türken', in G. Heckenast (ed.), *Aus der Geschichte der Ostmitteleuropaischen Bauernbewegungen im 16te und 17te Jahrhunderten* (Budapest, 1977), p.259.
15 Ibid, p.261.
16 Ibid, p.256.
17 A. Várkonyi, 'The Principatus Transylvaniae', in *Etudes Historiques Hongroises* (1985) vol. 2, p.601.
18 Fodor, *Quest of the Golden Apple*, p.88. Halil Inalcik makes some similar observations for Anatolian Turkey – how many Ottoman writers were unhappy about the arming of landless Anatolian peasants and saw it as a development which could bring no good. See H. Inalcik, *Studies in Ottoman Social and Economic History* (Variorum, 1985), pp.294–8.
19 F. Szakály, 'Das Bauerntum', p.261.
20 L.M. Alföldi, 'The Battle of Mohács' in Bak and Király (eds), *From Hunyadi*

to *Rákóczi*, pp.194–6; A. Várkonyi, *Europica Varietas – Hungarica Varietas 1526–1762* (Budapest, 2000), p.13.

21 Molnár, *A Concise History of Hungary*, p.87.

22 L. Fekete, *Buda and Pest under Turkish Rule* (Budapest, 1976), pp.19, 86.

23 J. Strauss, 'Ottoman Rule Experienced and Remembered', in F. Adanir and S. Farooqhi (eds), *The Ottomans and the Balkans: A Discussion of Historiography* (Leiden, 2002), pp.198–9.

24 Ibid, pp.204, 206–7.

25 A. Velkov and E. Radushev, *Ottoman Garrisons on the Middle Danube* (Budapest, 1995), with an introduction by S. Dimitrov, pp.19–21, 447.

26 Ibid, p.25. Out of the 116 immigrant places listed as the provenance of the soldiers concerned, only seven were Anatolian Turkish towns – Kayseri, Ankara, Nigde and Erzincan among them. The overwhelming majority of places are listed as Bosnian, Albanian and Bulgarian.

27 K. Hegyi, V. Zimányi (eds), *Muslime und Christen: Das Osmanische Reich im Europa* (Corvina: Budapest, 1988), p.71.

28 G. Ágoston, *Guns for the Sultan: Military Power and the Weapons Industry in the Ottoman Empire*, (Cambridge University Press, 2005), p.46.

29 Ibid, p.48.

30 F. Szakály, *Lodovico Gritti*, pp.16–17.

31 Ibid, p.80.

32 Ibid, p.18.

33 Cit. in Szakály, *Lodovico Gritti*, p.38.

34 Ibid, p.20.

35 Ibid, pp.25–6.

36 Ibid, p.27.

37 Ibid, p.31.

38 Ibid, p.33.

39 Ibid.

40 F. Szakály, 'Türkenherrschaft und Reformation im Ungarn um die Mitte des 16te Jahrhunderts', in *Etudes Historiques Hongroises* II:1985, p.438.

41 Ibid, p.445.

42 Ibid, p.452.

43 Ibid, p.451.

44 Cit. in M. Bucsay, *Der Protestantismus im Ungarn 1521–1978* (Bohlau, 1977) I:127. The writer is Flacius from Magdeburg.

45 *A Short Memorial of the Most Grievous Sufferings* – cit. in B. Köpeczi, *Staatsräson und Christliche Solidarität: Die Ungarischen Aufstände und Europa in der zweiten Hälfte des 17. Jahrhunderts* (Vienna, 1983), p.135.

46 F. Szakály, 'Türkenherrschaft', p.453.

47 Bucsay, *Der Protestantismus*, p.85.

48 Bucsay, p.86; Szakály, 'Türkenherrschaft', p.450.

49 Cit. in Szakály, 'Türkenherrschaft', p.446.

50 Bucsay, p.128.

51 Ibid, p.184.

52 Géza David and Pál Fodor, 'Hungarian Studies in Ottoman History', in Adanir and Farooqhi (eds), *The Ottomans and the Balkans*, pp.315, 321–3.

53 For the profusion of synagogues, mosques and churches in Bosnia, see Amir Pašić, 'Islamic Art and Architecture of Bosnia and Herzegovina', in R.M.Z. Keilani and S. Todorova (eds), *Proceedings of the International Symposium on*

Islamic Civilisation in the Balkans (Istanbul, 2002), p.85; the story of a Macedonian merchant who successfully imitates an imam can be found in B. McGowan, 'Matija Mažuranic's *Look at Bosnia*', in *Journal of Turkish Studies* 8:1984, p.179.

54 Fekete, *Buda and Pest under Turkish Rule* pp.49, 50.
55 Ibid, p.53.
56 Ibid, p.43.
57 Molnár, *A Concise History of Hungary*, p.104.
58 Géza David and Pál Fodor, 'Hungarian Studies', pp.342–3.
59 Fodor, *Quest of the Golden Apple*, pp.102–3.
60 C. Finkel, *The Administration of Warfare: the Ottoman Military Campaigns in Hungary, 1593–1606* (Vienna, 1988), p.9.
61 Ibid, pp.107–9.
62 Ibid, p.109.
63 Fodor, 'Volunteers in the Sixteenth Century Ottoman Army', in David and Fodor (eds), *Ottomans, Hungarians and Habsburgs in Central Europe*, pp.256–9.
64 L. Makkai, 'Bocksai's insurrectionary army', in *From Hunyadi to Rákóczi*, pp.282–3.
65 Ibid, p.277.
66 Ibid p.288 – the poet is Szappanyos.
67 Molnár, *A Concise History of Hungary*, p.118.
68 The poet is Alexander Tyler, cit. in Köpeczi, *Staatsräson und Christliche Solidarität*, p.350.
69 Bela Köpeczi's *Staatsräson und Christliche Solidarität* is a work practically devoted to this subject – see, in particular, the collection of photoplates at the very end of the book (pp.408 f). See also B. Köpeczi, 'The Hungarian Wars of Independence', in *From Hunyadi to Rákóczi*, pp.451–2.
70 Barker, *Double Eagle and Crescent*, pp.27–8.
71 Bela Köpeczi, *Hongrois et Français: De Louis XIV à la Revolution Française* (Corvina Kiadó, 1983), p.106.
72 Molnár, *A Concise History of Hungary*, p.129.
73 Cit. in Köpeczi, *Staatsräson und Christliche Solidarität*, pp.147, 196.
74 Ibid, p.16.
75 D.M.Vaughan, *Europe and the Turk: A Pattern of Alliances 1350–1700* (Liverpool, 1954), p.253.
76 Köpeczi, *Hongrois et Français*, p.91.
77 D. Kolodziejczyk, *Ottoman-Polish Diplomatic Relations (15th–18th centuries)* (Leiden, 2000), p.xvi.
78 K.Wawrzyniak, *Ottoman-Polish Relations in the Sixteenth Century* (unpublished MA thesis, Bilgi University, 2003), p.6.
79 See F. Posch, *Flammende Grenzen: Die Steiermark in den Kuruzzstürmen* (Verlag Styria, 1986), p.13.
80 L. Benczédi, 'The Warrior Estate', pp.359–61.
81 Köpeczi, *Staatsräson und Christliche Solidarität*, p.19.
82 Miklos, *Concise History of Hungary*, p.130.
83 Jean Leclerc, *Histoire d'Emeric Comte de Tekeli, ou memoirs pour servir à sa vie* (Cologne, 1693 – copy located in Staatsbibliothek Berlin Unter den Linden), pp.121–4; see also the Ottoman Greek chief interpreter's account (Alexandros Mavrocordatos) in R.F. Kreutel and K. Teply (eds), *Kara Mustafa Vor Wien: 1683 aus der Sicht türkischer Quellen* (Verlag Styria, 1982), pp.74–6.

84 See Ahmet Tesrifatizade's account in Kreutel and Teply, *Kara Mustafa Vor Wien*, pp.139, 174.

85 Barker, *Double Eagle and Crescent*, p.203.

86 Ibid, p.410, −12.

87 Rhoades Murphey, *Ottoman Warfare 1500–1700* (Rutgers University Press, 1999), p.98.

88 Barker, pp.217–18; Leopold's flight is found in J. Goodwin, *Lords of the Horizons* (Chatto, 1998), pp.227–8.

89 Barker, pp.241–4.

90 Ibid, p.283.

91 Kreutel and Teply, *Kara Mustafa Vor Wien*, pp.224–6.

92 For Ottoman Turkish responses to the fall of Buda, an event which elicited a great deal of lamentation and mourning, see M. Köbach, 'Der Literarische Widerhall des Verlustes von Ofen 1686', in B Köpeczi and A. Tarnai (eds), *Laurus Austriaca-Hungarica: Literarische Gattungen und Politik in der 2te Halfte des 17. Jahrhunderts* (Budapest, 1988), pp.225–48.

Chapter Five

1 Ian Fletcher and Natalia Ishchenko, *The Crimean War: A Clash of Empires* (Spellmount, 2004), p.10.

2 Clive Ponting, *The Crimean War* (Chatto and Windus, 2004), pp.12, 8.

3 *The Observer*, 3 July 1853; *Daily News*, 4 July, 1853 – cit. in Candan Badem, 'The Ottomans and the Crimean War (1853–56)' (Unpublished PhD dissertation, Sabanci University, June 2007), p.84.

4 Lord Beaumont to Lord Stuart (dated 9 October 1853) – printed in *The Times*, cit. in Badem, 'The Ottomans and the Crimean War', p.87.

5 Ponting, *The Crimean War*, pp.11, 59; A.D. Lambert, *The Crimean War: British Grand Strategy 1853–56* (Manchester University Press, 1990), p.3.

6 R.R. Florescu, *The Struggle Against Russia in the Romanian Principalities* (Iaşi, 1997), p.307.

7 R.B. Edgeton, *Death or Glory: The Legacy of the Crimean War* (Westview Press, 1999), p.179.

8 *Reminiscences of an Officer of Zouaves, translated from the French* (D. Appleton and Company: New York, 1860), p.150.

9 Lieutenant Edward Money, *Twelve Months with the Bashibozouks* (Chapman: London, 1857), pp.23, 102; Colonel Atwell Lake, *Narrative of the Defence of Kars Historical and Military* (London: Bentley, 1857), p.85.

10 Money, *Twelve Months*, pp.44, 104.

11 Edgeton, *Death or Glory*, p.56; Baron de Bazancourt, *L'Expedition de Crimée* (Paris, 1856), p.II:85.

12 Fletcher and Ishchenko, *The Crimean War*, p.181.

13 Le Vicomte de Noë, *Souvenirs d'Afrique: Les Bachi-Bozouks et les Chasseurs d'Afrique* (Paris, 1861), p.116.

14 W.H. Russell, *Russell's Despatch from the Crimea*, ed. N. Bentley (Panther, 1970), pp.135, 190.

15 *Reminiscences of an Officer of Zouaves*, pp.132, 143.

16 *Reminiscences of an Officer of Zouaves*, p.240.

17 Fletcher and Ishchenko, *The Crimean War*, p.253; *Reminiscences of an Officer of Zouaves*, p.4.

18 A.R. Alexiev and S. Enders Wimbush (eds), *Ethnic Minorities in the Red Army* (West View Press, 1988), p.16.

19 R. Crews, *For Prophet and Tsar: Islam and Empire in Russia and Central Asia* (Harvard University Press, 2006), p.17.

20 Alexiev, *Ethnic Minorities*, pp.13–16; see Goethe's letter to Trebra in *Goethes Werke*, ed. Erich Trunz, 14 vols, (Hamburg, 1948–64), III:251.

21 A. Seaton, *The Crimean War: A Russian Chronicle* (St Martin's Press, 1977), pp.138, 82.

22 See Mark von Hoyen's essay, 'The Limits of Reform', in B.W. Menning, *Reforming the Tsar's Army*, p.36.

23 Crews, *For Prophet and Tsar*, p.92.

24 J.S. Curtiss, *The Russian Army Under Nicholas I* (Duke University Press, 1965), p.180; E.K. Wirtschafter, *From Serf to Russian Soldier* (Princeton University Press, 1990), p.140.

25 The writer concerned is Krestovskii – see Yohanan Petrovsky-Shtern, 'The 'Jewish Policy' of the Late Imperial War Ministry: The Impact of the Russian Right', in *Kritika: Explorations in Russian and Eurasian History* 3(2): 217–54, Spring 2002 (p.225); Marshall Paskevich to Tsar Nicholas I, 23 September 1853 – cit. in Badem, 'The Ottomans and the Crimean War', p.99.

26 Daniel Panzac,'The Manning of the Ottoman Navy', in E.J. Zürcher, *Arming the State: Military Conscription in the Middle East and Central Asia* (I.B.Tauris, 1999), p.54.

27 T. Heinzelmann, *Heiliger Kampf oder Landesverteidigung? Die Diskussion um die Einführung der allegemeinen Militärpflicht im Osmanischen Reich 1826–56* (Peter Lang, 2004), p.270.

28 Heinzelmann, *Heiliger Kampf*, p.281.

29 Heinzelmann, *Heiliger Kampf*, p.269; taken from the Basbakanlık Osmanlı Arsivi, (hereafter BOA) HR. SYS. 1346/52, 10 January 1854, OBKS, pp. 104–6 – cit. in Badem, 'The Ottomans and the Crimean War', p.52.

30 Heinzelmann, *Heiliger Kampf*, p.291; cit. in *The Times*, 17 June, 1853 and found in Karl Marx, *The Eastern Question: A Reprint of Letters written 1853–6 dealing with the events of the Crimean War* (New York: Burt Franklin, 1968), p.41.

31 Florescu, *Romanian Principalities*, p.307; Heinzelmann, *Heiliger Kampf*, p.274; V.H. Aksan, 'The Ottoman Military and State Transformation in a Globalizing World', in *Comparative Studies of South Asia, Africa and the Middle East* 27:2 (2007), p.264.

32 Edgeton, *Death or Glory*, pp.48, 165.

33 For more, see I.L. Rudnytsky, *Essays in Modern Ukrainian History* (Edmonton, 1987), pp.173–86.

34 Badem, 'The Ottomans and the Crimean War', pp.135, 141.

35 Ponting, *The Crimean War*, p.300.

36 Ibid, p.283.

37 Badem, 'The Ottomans and the Crimean War', 197.

38 Fletcher and Ishchenko, *The Crimean War*, p.44; Ponting, *The Crimean War*, pp.53, 182.

39 Edgeton, *Death or Glory*, p.168.

40 Ponting, *The Crimean War*, p.126.

41 Fletcher and Ishchenko, *The Crimean War*, p.179.
42 Ponting, *The Crimean War*, p.132.
43 Ponting, *The Crimean War*, p.135; Fletcher and Ishchenko, *The Crimean War*, p.181.
44 Fletcher and Ishchenko, *The Crimean War*, p.184.
45 Ponting, *The Crimean War*, pp 259, 103.
46 D. Murphy, *Ireland and the Crimean War* (Four Courts Press, 2002), p.39.
47 Captain Godfrey T. Williams' account – found in Murphy, *Ireland and the Crimean War*, p.39.
48 L. James, *Crimea 1854–56: The war with Russia from contemporary photographs* (Hayes Kennedy, 1981), p.134.
49 Cristoforo Manfredi, *La Spedizione Sarda in Crimea del 1855–6* (Regionale in Roma, 1956), p.95.
50 *Letters from Headquarters: The Realities of War in the Crimea by an Officer on the Staff* (London, 2nd edition: John Murray, 1857), vol. I:362; Russell, *Despatch from the Crimea*, p.187.
51 See H. Ram, 'The Sonnet and the Mukhambazi: Genre Wars on the Edges of the Russian Empire', in *PMLA* 5:122 (October 2007), p.1551; see also Austin Jersild and Neli Melkadze, 'The Dilemmas of Enlightenment in the Eastern Borderlands: The Theater and Library in Tbilisi', in *Kritika: Explorations in Russian and Eurasian History* 3(1): 27–49, Winter 2002, p.35.
52 W.E.D. Allen and P. Muratoff, *Caucasian Battlefields: A History of the Wars on the Turco-Caucasian Border 1828–1921* (Cambridge University Press, 1953), p.67.
53 P.I. Averyanov, *Kurdy v voinakh Rossii s Persiey i Turtsiey v techenie XIX stoletiya* (Tiflis, 1900), p.149 – cit. in Badem, 'The Ottomans and the Crimean War', pp.143, 323.
54 Badem, 'The Ottomans and the Crimean War', p.190.
55 Taken from a letter of General Muravyov to Prince Dolgorukov, dated 21 Mart (2 April) 1855 – cit. in Badem, 'The Ottomans and the Crimean War', p.321.
56 Badem, 'The Ottomans and the Crimean War', p.197.
57 Taken from the trial records of Zarif Pasha and Guyon, 11 April 1855, in BOA. Ġ. MMS. 5/170 lef 2. – cit. in Badem, 'The Ottomans and the Crimean War', p.194.
58 Following scheme of battle comes from Allen and Muratoff, *Caucasian Battlefields*, pp.76–8.
59 Ibid, p.78.
60 Badem, 'The Ottomans and the Crimean War', p.210.

BIBLIOGRAPHY

'Abdulwahid Dhanun Taha, *The Muslim Conquest and Settlement of North Africa and Spain* (Routledge, 1989).

David Abulafia, *Frederick II: A Medieval Emperor* (Penguin, 1988).

—*The Western Mediterranean Kingdoms* (London: Longman, 1997).

—*Medieval Encounters, Economic, Religious, Political 1100–1350* (Ashgate, 2000).

—'The End of Muslim Sicily', in J.M. Powell (ed.), *Muslims Under Latin Rule 1100–1300* (Princeton University Press, 1990).

G. Ágoston, *Guns for the Sultan: Military Power and the Weapons Industry in the Ottoman Empire*, (Cambridge University Press, 2005).

Aziz Ahmad, *A History of Islamic Sicily* (Edinburgh University Press, 1975).

V.H. Aksan, 'The Ottoman Military and State Transformation in a Globalizing World', in *Comparative Studies of South Asia, Africa and the Middle East* 27:2 (2007).

M.M. Alexandrescu-Dersca, *Le Campagne de Timur en Anatolie* (London: Variorum, 1977).

A.R. Alexiev and S. Enders Wimbush (eds), *Ethnic Minorities in the Red Army* (West View Press, 1988).

L.M. Alföldi, 'The Battle of Mohács', in Bak and Király (eds), *From Hunyadi to Rákóczi*.

W.E.D. Allen and P. Muratoff *Caucasian Battlefields: A History of the Wars on the Turco-Caucasian Border 1828–1921* (Cambridge University Press, 1953).

Ian Almond, 'Leibniz, Historicism and the Plague of Islam', *Eighteenth Century Studies* 39:4 (2006).

Aziz al-Azmeh, 'Mortal Enemies, Invisible Neighbours: Northerners in Andalusi Eyes', in Jayyusi (ed.), pp.260–5.

Giovanni Amatuccio, 'Saracen Archers in Southern Italy' E-HAWK June 1997. www.idir.net.

Candan Badem, 'The Ottomans and the Crimean War (1853–56)' (Unpublished PhD dissertation, Sabanci University, June 2007).

For Turkish speakers, further articles by Badem include:

—'Kırım Savaşi'nın Osmanlı Toplumsal Yaşamına Etkileri', *Toplumsal Tarih* 133, Istanbul, January 2005, pp.64–71.

—'Rus ve Sovyet Tarih Yazımında Kırım Savaşı', *Toplumsal Tarih* 155, Istanbul, November 2006, pp.16–23.

—'Unutulmuş Bir Hikaye: Kırım Savaşı', news article, *Toplumsal Tarih* 156, Istanbul, December 2006, p.6.

J.M. Bak and B.K. Kerály (eds), *From Hunyadi to Rákóczi: War and Society in Late Medieval and Early Modern Hungary* (Brooklyn College Press, 1982).

Michel Balivet, 'The long-lived relations between Christians and Moslems in Central Anatolia: dervishes, papadhes and country folk', in *Byzantinische Forschungen* XVI (Amsterdam, 1991), pp.313–22.

John W. Barker, *Manuel II Palaeologus* (Rutgers University Press, 1969).

T.M. Barker, *Double Eagle and Crescent: Vienna's Second Turkish Siege and its Historical Setting* (SUNY, 1967).

Simon Barton, 'Traitors to the Faith? Christian Mercenaries in al-Andalus and the Maghrib c.1100–1300', in R. Collins and A. Goodman (eds), *Medieval Spain: Culture, Conflict and Coexistence in Honour of Angus MacKay* (London: Palgrave, 2002).

M.C. Bartusis, *The Late Byzantine Army: Arms and Society 1204–1453* (University of Pennsylvania Press, 1992).

Baron de Bazancourt, *L'Expedition de Crimée* (Paris, 1856).

L. Benczédi, 'The Warrior Estate', in J.M. Bak and B.K. Király (eds), *From Hunyadi to Rákóczi: War and Society in Late Medieval and Early Modern Hungary* (Brooklyn College Press, 1982).

Nora Berend, *At the Gate of Christendom: Jews, Muslims and Pagans in Medieval Hungary 1000–1300* (Cambridge University Press, 2001).

Ross Brann, *Power in the Portrayal: Representations of Jews and Muslims in Eleventh and Twelfth Century Islamic Spain* (Princeton University Press, 2002).

M. Braun, *Lebensbeschreibung des Despoten Stefan Lazarevic* (Göttingen, 1956).

A. Bryer, 'The Case of the first Byzantine-Ottoman marriage', in R.H.C. Davis and J.M. Wallace-Hadrill (eds), *The Writing of History in the Middle Ages* (Clarendon Press, 1981).

M. Bucsay, *Der Protestantismus im Ungarn 1521–1978* (Bohlau, 1977).

Brian A. Catlos, *The Victors and the Vanquished: Christians and Muslims of Catalonia and Aragon 1050–1300* (Cambridge University Press, 2004).

—'Mahomet Abenadalill: A Muslim Mercenary in the service of the Kings of Aragon (1290–1)', in H.J. Hames (ed.), *Jews, Muslims and Christians in and around the Crown of Aragon* (Leiden, 2004), pp.257–302.

Paul E. Chevedden, 'The Artillery of King James I the Conqueror', in P.E. Chevedden, D.J. Kagay and P.G. Padilla (eds), *Iberia and the Mediterranean World of the Middle Ages* (Leiden, 1996), vol. II, pp.57–63.

The Chronicle of Muntaner, trans. Lady Goodenough (London: Hakluyt Society, 1920).

The Chronicle of Salimbene de Adam, J.L. Baird, G. Baglivi and J.R. Kane (eds) (Binghamton, NY, 1986).

Henry Clifford, VC, *His letters and sketches from the Crimea* (New York, 1956).

R. Crews, *For Prophet and Tsar: Islam and Empire in Russia and Central Asia* (Harvard University Press, 2006).

J.S. Curtiss, *The Russian Army Under Nicholas I* (Duke University Press, 1965).

G.T. Dennis SJ, *The Reign of Manuel II Palaeologus in Thessalonica 1382–1387* (Rome, 1960).

V. Dimitriades, 'Byzantine and Ottoman Thessaloniki', in A.M. Hakkert and W.E. Kaegi Jr (eds), *Byzantinische Forschungen* XVI:268 (1991), pp.265–74.

Doukas, *Decline and Fall of Byzantium to the Ottoman Turks*, trans. H.J. Magoulias (Detroit, 1975).

A. Eastmond, *Art and Identity in Thirteenth century Byzantium* (London: Ashgate, 2004).

R.B. Edgeton, *Death or Glory: The Legacy of the Crimean War* (Westview Press, 1999).

Pietro Egidi, *La Colonnia dei Saraceni e la sua distruzione* (Naples, 1915).

Enveri, author of the *Duşturname*, trans. Irene Melikoff-Sayar, in *Le Destan d'Umur Pacha* (Paris, 1954).

George Palmer Evelyn, *A Diary of the Crimea* (London, 1954).

L. Fekete, *Buda and Pest under Turkish Rule* (Budapest, 1976).

M. Fierro, 'Christian Success and Muslim Fear in Andalusi Writings', in *Israel Oriental Studies* XVII.

C. Finkel, *The Administration of Warfare: the Ottoman Military Campaigns in Hungary, 1593–1606* (Vienna, 1988).

Ian Fletcher and Natalia Ishchenko, *The Crimean War: A Clash of Empires* (Spellmount, 2004).

Richard Fletcher, *The Quest for El Cid* (London: Hutchinson, 1989).

R.R. Florescu, *The Struggle Against Russia in the Romanian Principalities* (Iaşi, 1997).

A. Fisher, *Between Russians, Ottomans and Turks: Crimea and Crimean Tartars* (Isis Press, 1998).

P. Fodor, *In Quest of the Golden Apple: Imperial Ideology, Politics and Military Administration of the Ottoman Empire* (Isis Press, 2000).

—'Volunteers in the 16th century Ottoman Army', in Géza David and Pál Fodor (eds), *Ottomans, Hungarians and Habsburgs in Central Europe* (Leiden, 2000).

Géza David and Pál Fodor, 'Hungarian Studies in Ottoman History', in Adanir and Farooqhi (eds), *The Ottomans and the Balkans*.

F. Gabrieli, *Arab Histories of the Crusades*, trans. E.J. Costello (London: Routledge, 1969).

—'Friedrich II und die Kultur des Islam', in G. Wolf (ed.), *Stupor Mundi: Zur Geschichte Friedrichs II von Hohenstaufen* (Darmstadt, 1982).

H.A.R. Gibb, *The Travels of Ibn Battuta* (Cambridge University Press, 1962).

H.L. Gottschalk, *Al-Malik al-Kamil von Egypten und seine Zeit* (Wiesbaden, 1958).

J. Göbbels, *Das Militärwesen im Königreich Siziliens zur Zeit Karls I von Anjou* (Hiersemann: Stuttgart, 1984).

Rene Grousset, *L'Empire des Steppes* (Paris, 1960).

Antonio Duran Gudiol, 'Francos, Pamploneses y Mozarabes en la Marca Superior de al-Andalus', in P. Sénac (ed.), *La Marche Supérieure d'Al-Andalus et l'Occident Chrétien* (Madrid, 1991).

Pierre Guichard, *Les Musulmans de Valence et la Reconquête (xi-xiii siècles)* (Paris: Damas, 1990).

T. Heinzelmann, *Heiliger Kampf oder Landesverteidigung? Die Diskussion um die Einführung der allegemeinen Militärpflicht im Osmanischen Reich 1826–56* (Peter Lang, 2004).

Keith Hopwood, 'Mudara', in A. Singer and A. Cohen (eds), *Aspects of Ottoman History* (Jerusalem: The Magras Press, 1994).

Eberhard Horst, *Der Sultan von Lucera* (Freiburg: Herder Verlag, 1997).

H. Inalcik, *Studies in Ottoman Social and Economic History* (Variorum, 1985).

L. James, *Crimea 1854–56: The war with Russia from contemporary photographs* (Hayes Kennedy, 1981).

S.K. Jayyusi (ed.), *The Legacy of Muslim Spain* (Leiden, 1992).

Austin Jersild and Neli Melkadze, 'The Dilemmas of Enlightenment in the Eastern Borderlands: The Theater and Library in Tbilisi', in *Kritika: Explorations in Russian and Eurasian History* 3(1), pp.27–49, Winter 2002.

C. Kafadar, *Between Two Worlds: The Construction of the Ottoman State* (University of California Press, 1995).

Johannes Kantakuzenos: Geschichte II, trans. G. Fatouros and T. Krischer (Stuttgart: Hiersemann, 1986).

Hugh Kennedy, *Muslim Spain and Portugal* (London: Longman, 1996).

Dimitri Kitsikis, *Turk-Yunan Imparatorlugu: Arabolge Gercegi Isiginda Osmanli Tarihine Bakis* (Istanbul, 1996).

M. Köbach, 'Der Literarische Widerhall des Verlustes von Ofen 1686', in B. Köpeczi and A. Tarnai (eds), *Laurus Austriaca-Hungarica: Literarische Gattungen und Politik in der 2te Halfte des 17. Jahrhunderts* (Budapest, 1988), pp.225–48.

D. Kolodziejczyk, *Ottoman-Polish Diplomatic Relations (15th–18th centuries)* (Leiden, 2000).

B. Köpeczi, *Staatsräson und Christliche Solidarität: Die Ungarischen Aufstände und Europa in der zweiten Hälfte des 17. Jahrhunderts* (Vienna, 1983).

—*Hongrois et Français: De Louis XIV à la Revolution Française* (Corvina Kiadó, 1983).

—'The Hungarian Wars of Independence', in Bak and Király (eds), *From Hunyadi to Rákóczi,*.

R.F. Kreutel and K. Teply (eds), *Kara Mustafa Vor Wien: 1683 aus der Sicht türkischer Quellen* (Verlag Styria, 1982).

Aptullah Kuran, *The Mosque in Early Ottoman Architecture* (Chicago, 1968).

A.E. Laiou, *Constantinople and the Latins: The Foreign Policy of Andronikos II 1282–1328* (Harvard, 1972).

Colonel Atwell Lake, *Narrative of the Defence of Kars Historical and Military* (London: Bentley, 1857).

A.D. Lambert, *The Crimean War: British Grand Strategy 1853–56* (Manchester University Press, 1990).

Latin Chronicles of the Kings of Castile, ed. J.F. O'Callaghan (Arizona, 2002).

Jean Leclerc, *Histoire d'Emeric Comte de Tekeli, ou memoirs pour servir à sa vie* (Cologne, 1693 – copy located in Staatsbibliothek Berlin Unter den Linden).

P. Lemerle, *L'Emirat d'Aydin* (Paris, 1957).

Letters from Headquarters: The Realities of War in the Crimea by an Officer on the Staff (London, 2nd edition: John Murray, 1857).

R.P. Lindner, *Nomads and Ottomans in Medieval Anatolia* (Bloomington, Indiana, 1983).

J.P. Lomax, 'Frederick II, His Saracens and the Papacy', in John V. Toran (ed.), *Medieval Christian Perceptions of Islam* (London: Routledge, 1996).

Elena Lourie, 'A Society Organized for War', *Past and Present* 35 (1966), pp.54–76.

Heinz-Dietrich Löwe, 'Poles, Jews and Tartars: Religion, Ethnicity and Social Structure in Tsarist Nationality Policies' *Jewish Social Studies* pp.52–96.

Heath W. Lowry, *The Nature of the Early Ottoman State* (SUNY Press, 2003).

Amin Maalouf, *The Crusades Through Arab Eyes*, trans. J. Rothschild (Zed Books, 1984).

L. Makkai, 'Bocksai's insurrectionary army' in Bak and Király (eds), *From Hunyadi to Rákóczi*.

Cristoforo Manfredi, *La Spedizione Sarda in Crimea del 1855–6* (Regionale in Roma, 1956).

Karl Marx, *The Eastern Question: A Reprint of Letters written 1853–6 dealing with the events of the Crimean War* (New York: Burt Franklin, 1968).

Klaus Peter Matschke, *Die Schlacht bei Ankara und das Schicksal von Byzanz* (Weimar, 1981).

B. McGowan, 'Matija Mažuranic's *Look at Bosnia*', in *Journal of Turkish Studies*, 8:1984.

Miklós Molnár, *A Concise History of Hungary*, trans. A. Magyar (Cambridge University Press, 2001).

Lieutenant Edward Money, *Twelve Months with the Bashibozouks* (Chapman: London, 1857).

Rhoades Murphey, *Ottoman Warfare 1500–1700* (Rutgers University Press, 1999).

D. Murphy, *Ireland and the Crimean War* (Four Courts Press, 2002).

Muslime und Christen: Das Osmanische Reich im Europa, K. Hegyi and V. Zimányi (eds) (Corvina: Budapest, 1988).

Le Vicomte de Noë, *Souvenirs d'Afrique: Les Bachi-Bozouks et les Chasseurs d'Afrique* (Paris, 1861).

D.M. Nicol, *The Reluctant Emperor* (Cambridge University Press, 1996).

David Nicolle, *The Mongol Warlords* (Firebird Books, 1990).

J.F. O'Callaghan, *A History of Medieval Spain* (Cornell University Press, 1975).

Ottoman Garrisons on the Middle Danube, A. Velkov and E. Radushev (Budapest, 1995) with an introduction by S. Dimitrov.

Daniel Panzac, 'The Manning of the Ottoman Navy', in E.J. Zürcher, *Arming the State: Military Conscription in the Middle East and Central Asia* (I.B.Tauris, 1999).

Amir Pašić, 'Islamic Art and Architecture of Bosnia and Herzegovina', in R.M.Z. Keilani and S. Todorova (eds), *Proceedings of the International Symposium on Islamic Civilisation in the Balkans* (Istanbul, 2002).

Yohanan Petrovsky-Shtern, 'The "Jewish Policy" of the Late Imperial War Ministry:

The Impact of the Russian Right', in *Kritika: Explorations in Russian and Eurasian History* 3(2), pp.217–54, Spring 2002.

Piero Pieri, 'I Saraceni di Lucera nella storia militare medievale' *Archivo Storico Pugliese* 6 (1953).

Enrico Pispisa, *Il Regno di Manfredi* (Sicania: Messina, 1991).

Clive Ponting, *The Crimean War* (Chatto and Windus, 2004).

Porphryogenita: Essays on the History and Literature of the Byzantine and Latin East , C. Dendrinos, J. Harris, E. Harvalia Crook and J. Herrin (eds)(Ashgate, 2003).

F. Posch, *Flammende Grenzen: Die Steiermark in den Kuruzzstürmen* (Verlag Styria, 1986).

H. Ram, 'The Sonnet and the Mukhambazi: Genre Wars on the Edges of the Russian Empire', in *PMLA* 5:122 (October 2007).

B.F. Reilly, *The Kingdom of Leon-Castilla under King Alfonso VI* (Princeton University Press, 1988).

—*The Kingdom of Leon-Castile under King Alfonso VII 1126–1157* (University of Pennsylvania Press, 1998).

Reminiscences of an Officer of Zouaves, translated from the French (New York: D. Appleton and Company, 1860).

Norman Roth, *Jews, Visigoths and Muslims in Medieval Spain: Cooperation and Conflict* (Leiden, 1994).

I.L. Rudnytsky, *Essays in Modern Ukrainian History* (Edmonton, 1987).

S. Runciman, *The Sicilian Vespers* (Cambridge University Press, 1958).

—*The Fall of Constantinople*, (Cambridge University Press, 1965).

W.H. Russell, *Russell's Despatch from the Crimea*, ed. N. Bentley (Panther, 1970).

Russia's Orient: Imperial Borderlands and Peoples 1700–1917, eds D.R. Brower and E.J. Lazzerini (Indiana University Press, 1997).

J.M. Safran, 'Landscapes in the Conquest of al-Andalus', in J. Howe and M. Wolfe (eds), *Inventing Medieval Landscapes: Senses of Place in Western Europe* (University Press of Florida, 2002), pp.136–49.

A. Seaton, *The Crimean War: A Russian Chronicle* (St Martin's Press, 1977).

Kurt Victor Selge, 'Die Ketzerpolitik Friedrichs II', in G. Wolf (ed.), *Stupor Mundi*.

Aryeh Shmowelevitz, 'Ottoman History and Society', in *Analecta Isisiana* XXXVIII:43 (1999).

Turkish Bookbinding in the Fifteenth Century, J. Raby and Z. Tanindi (eds), (London: Azimuth, 1993).

Douglas Sterling, 'The Siege of Damietta', in D.J. Kagay and L.J.A. Villalon (eds), *Crusaders, Condottieri and Cannon: Medieval Warfare in Societies Around the Mediterranean* (Brill: Leiden, 2003), pp.101–32.

J. Strauss, 'Ottoman Rule Experienced and Remembered', in F. Adanir and S. Farooqhi (eds), *The Ottomans and the Balkans: A Discussion of Historiography* (Leiden, 2002).

F. Szakály, *Lodovico Gritti in Hungary 1529–1534* (Budapest, 1995).

—'Das Bauerntum und die Kämpfe gegen die Türken', in G. Heckenast (ed.), *Aus der Geschichte der Ostmitteleuropaischen Bauernbewegungen im 16te und 17te Jahrhunderten* (Budapest, 1977).

—'Türkenherrschaft und Reformation im Ungarn um die Mitte des 16te Jahrhunderts', in *Etudes Historique Hongroises*, II:1985.

Julie Taylor, *Muslims in Medieval Italy: The Colony at Lucera* (Lexington University Press, 2003).

Peter Thorau, *The Lion of Egypt: Sultan Baybars I and the Near East in the Thirteenth Century* (New York: Longman, 1987).

Istvan Vasary, *Cumans and Tatars : Oriental Military in the Pre-Ottoman Balkans 1185–1365* (Cambridge University Press, 2005).

A.A. Vasiliev, *History of the Byzantine Empire* (University of Wisconsin Press, 1952).

A. Várkonyi, 'Rákóczi's War of Independence', in J.M. Bak and B.K. Király (eds), *From Hunyadi to Rákóczi*.

—'The Principatus Transylvaniae', in *Etudes Historiques Hongroises* (1985), vol. 2.

—*Europica Varietas – Hungarica Varietas 1526–1762* (Budapest, 2000).

D.M. Vaughan, *Europe and the Turk: A Pattern of Alliances 1350–1700* (Liverpool, 1954).

J.F. Verbruggen, *The Art of Warfare in Western Europe*, trans. C.S. Willard and R.W. Southern (Woodbridge: Boydell Press, 1997).

S. Vryonis, Jr, *Byzantium and Europe* (London, 1967).

K. Wawrzyniak, *Ottoman-Polish Relations in the Sixteenth Century* (Unpublished MA thesis, Bilgi University, 2003).

E.K. Wirtschafter, *From Serf to Russian Soldier* (Princeton University Press, 1990).

G. Wolf (ed.), *Stupor Mundi: Zur Geschichte Friedrichs II von Hohenstaufen* (Darmstadt, 1982).

E.A. Zachariadou, *Romania and the Turks 1300–1500* (London: Variorum, 1985).

INDEX